GREAT POWER COMPETITION
AND OVERSEAS BASES

GREAT POWER COMPETITION AND OVERSEAS BASES

CHINESE, RUSSIAN, AND AMERICAN FORCE POSTURE IN THE TWENTY-FIRST CENTURY

ANDREW YEO AND ISAAC KARDON

BROOKINGS INSTITUTION PRESS
Washington, D.C.

Published by Brookings Institution Press
1775 Massachusetts Avenue, NW
Washington, DC 20036
www.brookings.edu/bipress

Co-published by Rowman & Littlefield
An imprint of The Rowman & Littlefield Publishing Group, Inc.
4501 Forbes Boulevard, Suite 200, Lanham, Maryland 20706
www.rowman.com

86-90 Paul Street, London EC2A 4NE

Copyright © 2024 by The Brookings Institution

All rights reserved. No part of this book may be reproduced in any form or by any electronic or mechanical means, including information storage and retrieval systems, without written permission from the publisher, except by a reviewer who may quote passages in a review.

The Brookings Institution is a nonprofit organization devoted to research, education, and publication on important issues of domestic and foreign policy. Its principal purpose is to bring the highest quality independent research and analysis to bear on current and emerging policy problems.

British Library Cataloguing in Publication Information Available

Library of Congress Cataloging-in-Publication Data
Names: Yeo, Andrew, 1978– editor. | Kardon, Isaac B., editor.
Title: Great power competition and overseas bases : Chinese, Russian, and
   American force posture in the twenty-first century / edited by Andrew Yeo and
   Isaac Kardon.
Other titles: Chinese, Russian, and American force posture in the twenty-first
   century
Description: Washington, D.C. : Brookings Institution Press, [2024] |
   Includes bibliographical references and index.
Identifiers: LCCN 2024005884 (print) | LCCN 2024005885 (ebook) | ISBN
   9780815740698 (cloth) | ISBN 9780815740704 (paperback) | ISBN
   9780815740711 (ebook)
Subjects: LCSH: Military bases, American—Foreign countries—History—21st century. |
   Military bases, Russian—Foreign countries—History—21st century. | Military bases,
   Chinese—Foreign countries—History—21st century. | United States—Military relations. |
   Russia (Federation)—Military relations. | China—Military relations. | Strategy. | Great
   powers.
Classification: LCC UA26.A2 G74 2024 (print) | LCC UA26.A2 (ebook) | DDC
   355.7—dc23/eng/20240506
LC record available at https://lccn.loc.gov/2024005884
LC ebook record available at https://lccn.loc.gov/2024005885

CONTENTS

Preface and Acknowledgments   vii

1 Great Power Competition and Overseas Bases: U.S., Chinese, and Russian Force Posture in the Twenty-First Century   1
ANDREW YEO | ISAAC KARDON

2 Temperatures Rising: Great Powers, Regional Players, and the Struggle for Bases and Access in the Pacific Islands   19
BRUCE JONES

3 Geostrategic Competition and U.S., Chinese, and Russian Basing in East Asia   35
ANDREW YEO | MICHAEL E. O'HANLON

4 Military Basing and Access in the Indian Ocean Region: Strategic Asymmetries among the Major Powers   51
ISAAC KARDON

5 Overseas Basing Logistics at a Crossroads in the Middle East, Sub-Saharan Africa, and the Western Indian Ocean: Strategic Asymmetries among the Major Powers   67
JASON B. WOLFF

6 Strategic Competition for Overseas Basing in Sub-Saharan Africa   83
DAWN C. MURPHY

7 International Ordering and Great Power Competition: Lessons from Central Asia's Post–Cold War Basing Relations   103
ALEXANDER COOLEY

8 Great Power Competition and Overseas Basing in the Arctic   121
JEREMY GREENWOOD

9 European Maritime Security and Strategic Access in an Age of Great Power Competition   137
GEOFFREY F. GRESH

10 Strategic Competition and Basing in Central and Eastern Europe   157
EMILY HOLLAND

11 Competing for Consent: Public Support and the Foundations of U.S. Overseas Basing in Europe   171
MICHAEL ALLEN | MICHAEL E. FLYNN | CARLA MARTÍNEZ MACHAIN

12 The Future of Geostrategic Competition and Overseas Bases: Lessons for U.S. Strategic Planners   195
MICHAEL E. O'HANLON | MELANIE W. SISSON | ANDREW YEO

Index   209

About the Authors   223

PREFACE AND ACKNOWLEDGMENTS

This book project began as a collaborative effort beginning in 2019 when we met during the sidelines of a conference in Washington, D.C., to discuss the possibility of developing a paper comparing U.S., Chinese, and Russian basing strategies. Our meeting led to several conversations and e-mail exchanges throughout the year between us and a few other scholars, including Alex Cooley, who recognized the potential for greater comparative work in light of growing Chinese and renewed Russian interests in overseas bases and base access. Our plan was to assemble a group of regional and functional experts to examine the underexplored topic of comparative base strategy, especially Chinese and Russian bases.

Neither a global pandemic nor the tyranny of distant time zones following Andrew's move to the Philippines in January 2020 for the next two years could stifle our intellectual curiosity. Although we initially planned to host an in-person conference among a group of base scholars at the U.S. Naval War College in Newport, Rhode Island, where Isaac was then based, we ultimately decided to pursue a virtual conference, "Comparative Basing and Great Power Competition," hosted by the Center for Study of Statesmanship at The Catholic University of America in December 2020. The conference led to several fruitful conversations comparing Chinese and Russian to American military basing objectives. We remain grateful to all participants and discussants who joined us for the full-day virtual workshop from Europe, the People's Republic of China, and the U.S. academic and think-tank communities.

Although our project was initially conceived as a special issue for an academic journal—and indeed a couple of papers initially developed out of the virtual conference were accepted for publication in the journal *Security Studies*—the strong policy bent of many of the papers allowed us to take the project in a somewhat different direction. Andrew's return to Washington, D.C., and his new appointment at the Brookings Institution in January 2022 offered new opportunities for engagement with the policy community on issues related to geostrategic competition and overseas bases. We are especially indebted to Michael O'Hanlon, director of the Strobe Talbott Center for Security, Strategy, and Technology (Talbott Center) at the Brookings Institution, who took a keen interest on the topic of overseas bases and generously offered to provide funding for the project with support from Brookings Trustee Phil Knight. The grant allowed us to host an in-person workshop at Brookings in November 2022, bringing together scholars across different centers housed within the Brookings Foreign Policy program as well as experts from other universities and think tanks. The workshop resulted in a series of policy reports published by Brookings in January 2023. Our contributors (and a few authors recruited afterward) later expanded the depth and scope of their analysis, allowing us to put together a full volume on geostrategic competition and Chinese, Russian, and U.S. bases.

Given the number of people directly and indirectly involved in this project over the past four years, there is a long list of friends and colleagues we need to thank. We are most of all grateful to all the contributors to this volume who responded to our many requests for revisions and meeting deadlines over the past year despite their busy schedules. We also extend our thanks to those who participated in the November 2022 Brookings workshop. This includes Joshua White and Jason Wolff, who served as discussants, and also Sebastian Schmidt, Steve Watts, and Darshana Baruah for their input and participation. We (especially Isaac) would like to thank the National Bureau of Asian Research and National Defense University's National Asian Research Program fellowship for providing the platform for initial research on Chinese basing that resulted in Andrew reaching out to discuss comparative directions for future research.

We thank Ron Krebs and Sheena Greitens as well as two anonymous reviewers for the journal *Security Studies* who gave us valuable feedback in earlier iterations of the project. We also want to acknowledge participants who joined our virtual conference at Catholic University during an earlier stage of this project as either a presenter or a discussant. This group includes Andrew Scobell, Hu Bo, Jeff Becker, Dmitry Gorenburg, Maria Shagina, Brian Blankenship, Renanah Miles Joyce, Andrew Stravers, Drew Winner, Carla Martinez Machain, Michael Flynn, Michael Allen, Charlie Edel, Sebastian Schmidt, John Caverley, Paul MacDonald, and Alex Cooley. Alex helped spark the idea of studying overseas bases comparatively during our panel session at the 2019 International Studies Association annual convention in Toronto. We hope to one day take up his other suggestion to organize a study tour to Djibouti to understand foreign bases! Finally, Valerie De Koeijer graciously took notes for us, and Matthew Cantirino provided logistical support.

We would like to thank several people at the Brookings Institution who provided extensive support and encouragement toward the completion of this project. This includes Suzanne Maloney, vice president of the Foreign Policy program, and Mike O'Hanlon (again) for allowing us (specifically Andrew) to run with the project. Andrew thanks Mike for agreeing to coauthor not one but two chapters in this volume. We also benefited from conversations with several Brookings federal executive fellows serving in different branches of the military, including Colonel Jason Wolff, U.S. Air Force; Colonel Marcos Melendez, U.S. Marine Corps; Captain Brad McNally, U.S. Coast Guard; and Jeremy Greenwood, U.S. Coast Guard. Alex Dimsdale, Lori Merritt, and Rachel Slattery helped refine initial arguments with their editing and layout of the earlier policy reports. Jennifer Mason helped manage our grant and offered her sage logistical advice and support. At Brookings Institution Press, we are very grateful to Yelba Quinn, who remained supportive of our project from the moment we first pitched our book idea to her. With wisdom and patience, Yelba helped us navigate our proposal with Rowman & Littlefield, led by Jon Sisk and his editorial and production team, including Mary Wheelehan. Finally, we could not have pushed this edited book past the goalpost without the able assistance of Hanna Foreman. Hanna played a hand in almost every aspect of this project from the first day she joined the Brookings Institution as a research assistant in October 2022. We (especially Andrew) very much appreciate her support, good humor, and baked goods.

1

Great Power Competition and Overseas Bases

U.S., Chinese, and Russian Force Posture in the Twenty-First Century

ANDREW YEO
ISAAC KARDON

Chinese and Russian strategic ambitions on land and sea and in aerospace and cyberspace are transforming the contemporary international security environment. The 2017 U.S. National Security Strategy (NSS) characterized these trends as the return of "great power competition";[1] the 2022 NSS continued in this vein, expressing U.S. intent to "out-compete" China and "constrain" Russia in order to "maintain a competitive edge."[2] This competitive characterization of world affairs also holds sway in Moscow and Beijing, where, in word and in deed, overt great power strategic competition is also the prevailing mindset.

The global military posture of the United States is arguably one of its remaining competitive edges in a challenging international system. The United States stands alone in fielding a genuinely global military force, with power projection capabilities deployed forward in Europe, Asia, and the Middle East since World War II. The basing and access arrangements afforded by a robust network of allies and partners are fundamental to the presence and high-end capability of U.S. forces in all major world regions. Since the collapse of the Soviet Union and the consolidation of U.S. basing posture over the course of wars in the Balkans and the Middle East, there has been little competition on this account.

However, the apparently unique advantage of overseas bases that the United States holds is not unassailable. Russia's invasion of Ukraine and China's saber-rattling around Taiwan and the western Pacific present acute, near-term threats as well as long-term, strategic challenges. This onset of direct, great power military competition is testing the geostrategic value proposition of America's global force posture. American forces are operating forward from foreign basing infrastructure as its great power rivals engage in actual (Russia) and potential (China) regional conflicts. These are profound tests of both deterrent and war-fighting roles for American forces based in eastern Europe and East Asia.

In parallel, these resurgent authoritarian nations have reestablished military footholds in East Asia, the Middle East, and Africa—and are pursuing further access and basing in other theaters. The People's Republic of China (PRC) established its first overseas military base in 2017 at Djibouti and further signaled that the People's Liberation Army (PLA) will continue to expand its foreign military operations.[3] Russia increasingly utilizes elements of the former Soviet basing network in Europe, Central Asia, and the Middle East. Russian forces staged part of the 2022 invasion of Ukraine from positions in Belarus.[4] The United States, meanwhile, is seeking to counter the expansion of rival basing positions while rebalancing its global posture toward the primary strategic challenge of China.[5]

This volume takes stock of the emerging dynamics of great power competition for overseas military bases and base access. The chapters that follow demonstrate that overseas military bases play crucial but distinct roles in each great power's global strategy in select world regions. In general, bases are a means to project power and influence abroad, meet logistics requirements, secure economic access and trade flows, forge and maintain alliances and partnerships, and deter adversaries. They are also ends, signaling prestige and strength in distant theaters. Their actual, practical functions are far from obvious, however, and there has been no systematic effort to date that stacks up U.S., Chinese, and Russian basing postures and ambitions in an effort to understand their competitive dynamics.

Our comparative analysis of great power military bases is the first of its kind. By exploring the security, political economic, and domestic political dynamics of specific regions, we offer structured comparisons that reveal varied great power motivations for overseas bases and access. This regional approach yields greater leverage in understanding the political-military stakes and geographic positions for which great powers are competing. From this perspective, we find that great power competition and the dynamics of basing progresses unevenly in different parts of the world. The particulars of each region, explored in this volume's chapters, give us a valuable window into the nature and scope of the competition under way in the contemporary "great power competition."

GEOSTRATEGIC COMPETITION FOR BASING

The Existing Basing Literature

Scholarship on base politics and overseas basing has grown significantly over the past few decades. Whereas early studies tended to present either macro-historical accounts of U.S. overseas basing strategy and force posture[6] or in-depth case studies of U.S. basing in specific countries,[7] a new generation of scholars in the 2000s delved deeper into the underlying mechanisms driving base politics. These later studies touch on issues of regional security and strategy but lay greater emphasis on the roles of host governments and local politics and their effects on measurable basing outcomes. Domestic variables, such as political institutions,[8] regime type,[9] and anti-base protests,[10] factored significantly in this mode of analysis. Other researchers demonstrated how contentious politics challenged U.S. force presence, thereby creating vulnerabilities in great power basing strategy.[11] Scholars have explained this shift from large, permanent bases toward a smaller and lighter footprint over time in reference to a combination of strategic, technological, and domestic political factors.[12]

The existing research on overseas bases has focused almost entirely on the experience of the United States.[13] Such a concentration stands to reason given that the vast majority of foreign bases around the world today are U.S. bases (some 544 by the Department of Defense's last public inventory in 2021).[14] The other countries that maintain overseas bases—France, the United Kingdom, Italy, Japan, Turkey, and a few others—are largely U.S. allies and also host U.S. bases on their own territory. These may reasonably be deemed lesser-included cases or a peripheral subset of the larger phenomenon of a U.S.-led basing network. Yet they are also part of a more interesting and underappreciated story of the United States and its allies facing new competitive pressures from powerful new (or, in the case of Russia, returning) entrants to overseas basing in the twenty-first century with growing appetites for friction and confrontation.

A Comparative Tack

The case for "apples to apples" comparisons between Chinese, Russian, and U.S. bases will remain quite weak. There is no alternative (i.e., authoritarian) network of allies with mutual defense commitments and status-of-forces agreements and complex, long-term basing relationships. However, this difference also offers a productive analytical point of entry. China and Russia are starting from very different baselines and have varied motivations and opportunities for overseas basing. Similar to the United States, they are pursuing quite distinct strategic objectives in the different regions, but unlike Washington, neither has the capacity or existing commitments to field a high-end combat force anywhere but their respective near abroad. Both China and Russia aim to keep the United States from massing its military capability and strategic attention against them and seek external positions that advance somewhat narrower national goals than U.S. ambitions for global order.

Even the limited analysis that does exist on Chinese and Russian bases has tended to adopt a U.S.-centered perspective.[15] For understandable reasons, policy researchers tend to investigate Chinese and Russian basing in reference to the challenges they might pose to U.S. grand strategy. Key documents, such as the 2022 NSS, state that China "is the only competitor with both the intent to reshape the international order and increasingly, the economic, diplomatic, military, and technological power to do it."[16] Meanwhile, Russia "seeks to restore its great power status and establish spheres of influence near its borders."[17] With such prompts, researchers (especially in the policy world) have been primed to evaluate Chinese and Russian bases through the exclusive lens of geopolitical competition with the United States. The relative newness of Chinese and Russian forays into overseas bases also explains some of the lack of sustained analysis on non-U.S. basing strategy.[18] However, this provides all the more reason to build a viable research program comparing the overseas basing strategy of all three major powers across different regions.

REGIONAL DYNAMICS TO THE FORE

China, Russia, and the United States pursue varied strategic objectives through military basing and access in different world regions. Among them, only the United States has a truly global military base network and strategy to employ it at scale in different theaters. The United States also faces the starkest trade-offs in allocating assets and attention across its forward military postures given its reach into multiple regions. Despite announcing a "pivot" away from the Middle East and toward Asia since the late 2000s, Washington has struggled in practice to recalibrate its global force posture. Successive administrations have made an effort to rebalance to Asia only to face urgent and acute pressures from other theaters that have diverted these efforts. In the 2010s, it was ongoing conflict in Afghanistan and Iraq that continued to lure U.S. forces back into the region And since the buildup to the Russia-Ukraine War in late 2021, the U.S. military has kept a close eye on and channeled significant resources to Ukraine and its NATO allies in eastern Europe.[19]

By attending to these regional dynamics, we are able to draw out several underappreciated facets of geostrategic competition among these great powers. Whereas the United States aims to draw down legacy positions and redistribute assets between regions to better meet contemporary threats, China is for the first time seeking foreign military basing and making progress in certain places despite significant geopolitical headwinds.[20] Russia, for its part, is aggressively employing its severely constrained basing assets and resources for military operations and influence beyond the Ukraine theater.[21]

The contributions to this volume are also attuned to commonalities in great power basing but in general find significant national and regional variation in the purposes and possibilities for overseas military bases and access. In other words, there is no one-size-fits-all model for great power basing. In consequence, the interactions between great powers and relevant regional actors—such as rivals, allies, and other potential states hosting or offering military base access—will also vary along with the distinct great power interests and strategic purposes in particular regional theaters. As such, each of the chapters points to key factors and strategic demands driving Chinese, Russian, and U.S. basing across widely different geographies in places like sub-Saharan Africa, the Indian Ocean, the Baltic and Black seas, the Pacific Islands, and the Arctic Circle. In addition to providing important historical and political insights behind the overseas bases and military access potential of great powers, each chapter addresses several important questions that carry long-term implications for regional and global order.

For example, to what degree has Russian military presence in its near abroad, such as Belarus, Georgia, and Armenia, been a factor in sustaining or supporting Russia's invasion of Ukraine? Would additional U.S. presence in eastern Europe further aggravate Russian president Vladimir Putin's security dilemma? Why have overseas bases become a major narrative in U.S.–China competition in far-flung places such as the Pacific Islands? Will reinforcing U.S. presence in Oceania drive an arms race or risk overmilitarizing the region? Where or how should the U.S. prioritize its basing posture in light of present, acute threats in places like Ukraine and eastern Europe but also address force posture needs suited for long-term strategic competition in other regions, such as the Korean Peninsula?

A MISSING LINK: THE ECONOMIC BASIS FOR BASING DEMAND

One particular strength of this comparative and regional approach is that it sheds light on economic interests that are inseparable from basing and access decisions. These tend to be siloed in the U.S. conversation on global force posture, but this analysis draws our attention to strong linkages between commercial interests and base expansion. In certain respects, China's quest for port access and, by extension, potential basing access rights mirrors the experience of British and U.S. maritime expansion in the nineteenth century. China is unlikely to harbor territorial ambitions given the vastly different normative environment today regarding sovereignty. However, British and American merchants and their government backers identified the importance of securing new and existing markets in the wake of rising geopolitical competition. Writing about imperial Britain, J. A. Hobson noted that German and U.S. encroachment on British trade and manufacturing made it urgent for the British to secure new markets. Hobson states, "The diplomacy and the arms of Great Britain had to be used in order to compel the owners of the new markets to deal with us, and experience showed that the safest means of security and developing such markets is by establishing 'protectorates.'"[22]

While favoring ports over protectorates today, the PLA Navy (PLAN) is also called on to "protect overseas interests." Its maritime access is among the key elements of national policy employed to mitigate China's growing vulnerability across intertwined economic and security phenomena. According to the official white paper that canonized the concept of "China's overseas interests," they consist of "overseas energy and resources, strategic sea lines of communication (SLOCs), and Chinese nationals and legal persons overseas."²³ China's domestic economy relies heavily on foreign suppliers for an ever-increasing proportion of its massive domestic energy consumption. Geographically, these resources must pass through vulnerable choke points and traverse congested commercial sea-lanes to reach China's coast. Protection of the SLOCs that supply critical resources to Chinese markets (and Chinese-manufactured exports to foreign markets) is fundamental to China's economic health.²⁴ Chinese maritime strategists thus identify SLOCs among China's "core maritime interests" and consider their control necessary.²⁵ The PLAN is now charged with "open seas protection,"²⁶ a major expansion of its traditional near-seas role, and has been actively and urgently developing capability and doctrine to carry out this mission. As one prominent Chinese scholar argued, the consequence of these proliferating "overseas interests" is that the "requirement to build overseas military bases is unavoidable."²⁷

From a comparative standpoint, perhaps the most notable aspect of this national policy process is the commercial character of China's military footprint and influence in multiple regions—a point raised in several chapters in this volume, including chapters 4, 9, and 11. Chinese firms, banks, infrastructure, products, entrepreneurs, workers, and diplomats are establishing the "beachhead" for a somewhat belated military presence. The lag between the demand for security and the supply of military power projection is notable. That "the flag" follows trade is a reversal of the old chestnut²⁸ and a key explanation for why the PLA's presence abroad has relied on PRC-owned and -operated commercial facilities.

As with Chinese overseas basing, Russian economic and security interests are closely intertwined. For example, in 2014, Russian defense minister Sergei Shoigu advocated establishing a global network of air and naval bases, particularly near the equator, for refueling purposes.²⁹ While the main military priority is homeland defense, Russia's basing strategy supports its overall strategic aims, which include facilitating trade and Russia's economic investments abroad. Russia's 2017 Naval Doctrine supports this claim; it states that the main objectives of the State Policy on Naval Operations include "ensuring favorable conditions for the development and sustainable use of natural resources of the world ocean in the interests of the country's socio-economic development and to expand the use of state-private partnership resources to meet the strategic goals of economic development and establishment of basic transport, energy, information and military infrastructure at naval installations on the world ocean."³⁰ Russia's naval base at Tartus offers a good example of this strategy. Moscow's base in Syria solidifies its position as a central player in the eastern Mediterranean and enables the Russian state to defend its numerous investments in the region.

To what extent expanding commercial interests and the need to protect overseas investments and resources drives great power basing is an empirical question that will need to be examined in light of contemporary Chinese and Russian basing efforts. If overseas bases closely follow commerce, as the experience of British and U.S. basing in the nineteenth century suggests, we should anticipate a steady rise in the number of Chinese (and perhaps Russian) basing agreements in the next decade. However, the trajectory of great power basing may differ from the past. Not only do great and aspiring powers face a different structural and normative environment, as noted in chapter 7, but late base developers need not follow the precise pattern of past imperial basing. Whereas the United States maintains large force presence and "permanent bases" designed for a previous era of battle, Russian and Chinese bases will look much more similar to post-9/11 "forward operating sites" and "cooperative security locations" with a relatively light military footprint. Great powers may avoid establishing a network of formal bases altogether, instead relying on quasi bases and civilian–military dual-use ports established in friendly states or leaning on private military contractors to provide security with less national accountability.

PRIORITIZATION AS THE PRIMARY POLICY CHALLENGE

Strategic prioritization is the main policy challenge for U.S. competitiveness in different regions. The "Indo-Pacific" priority is defined and appropriate to U.S. national security interests, but it is not specific enough or adequately scoped to changing regional demands. Determining the relative importance of Chinese or Russian access to particular locations or types of military basing and logistics facilities requires clear articulation of which Chinese and Russian objectives must be denied, which can be leveraged toward U.S. interests, and which must be accepted as the cost of doing business. Given different short- and long-term strategic interests and motivations marked by varying levels of current geopolitical tension across regions (e.g., high in eastern Europe and East Asia and low in the Arctic), the United States need not be compelled to push back against China and Russia in every space where Beijing and Moscow gain a basing foothold, especially given the limited (and overstretched) capacity of the U.S. military.

As Colonel Jason B. Wolff argues in chapter 5, "As the United States evaluates its resources and force posture in response to military and geoeconomic challenges from China and Russia, it is at a crossroads; Washington cannot place a base in every partner nation to keep pace with or deter its competitors."[31] Wolff's suggestion is to instead strengthen ties with allies and partners and to think about bases beyond their military function and consider leveraging other agencies and the U.S. defense and commercial industry to gain access and footholds in places like sub-Saharan Africa and the western Indian Ocean. And in other regions where competition may be less acute, such as the Arctic, the United States may look to avenues for cooperation in regions where China and Russia might still play a constructive role toward regional governance. For example, in chapter 8, Jeremy Greenwood finds that Russia may still find the application of the rules-based international order favorable to their interests. Greenwood states, "Whether it is the UN Charter, the UN Convention on the Law of the Sea (UNCLOS), or customary international law, the current order grants Russia wide swaths of territory, sovereign rights and interests, and influence."[32] Russia's efforts to preserve its chairmanship of the Arctic Council after its invasion of Ukraine and the possibility of limited cooperation between Russia and other members given the consensus-based approach to the Arctic Council indicate the possibility of taming great power competition in some regions if not others.

THE ROAD AHEAD

In the chapters that follow, each of the authors was asked to reflect on several questions, including (1) the current status and likely future trajectory of U.S., Chinese, and Russian basing in regions of strategic competition; (2) how the military postures of great powers in these regions interact and with what consequences for international security; and (3) whether we are witnessing the emergence of exclusive spheres of influence across distinct regions or whether there is greater overlap and competition for regional political-military predominance in certain regions. Most of the authors assess geostrategic competition and bases with an eye toward U.S. strategy in the wake of conflict with Russia and China. However, there is some variance in the degree to which authors see the degree of threat emanating from Beijing and Moscow in a given region and how fast and hard the United States should respond to Chinese and Russian military presence. The remaining chapters are presented beginning with the Indo-Pacific region and generally move westward toward the Indian Ocean region and Africa to the Arctic and finally Europe. Latin America and the Caribbean is the only major region not addressed in our volume, although there too, suspicion exists that China and Russia may be paving the way for greater military presence in the Western Hemisphere, including in places such as Cuba and Venezuela.[33]

Following this introduction, in chapter 2, Bruce Jones takes us to the Pacific Islands, which in recent years have been transformed into a microcosm for geopolitical competition. The United States has retained an arc of territories and bases across the northern reaches of Oceania. More recently, however, China has taken advantage of U.S. neglect in the area by advancing its economic resources and diplomatic interests in the region. Not all Chinese advances have been successful, but China is making inroads across the southern reaches of the region through several tactics, including PLA presence, economic investments, and elite ties to acquire diplomatic relationships and logistics access. While the United States, Australia, and Japan are undertaking robust (albeit belated) soft power efforts to dull China's expanding influence, questions around employing hard power loom.

Shifting toward the Chinese mainland and central hub of U.S. presence in East Asia, in chapter 3, Andrew Yeo and Michael E. O'Hanlon explore whether and to what degree geostrategic competition between the United States and China and the expanded focus from East Asia to a broader Indo-Pacific region impacts U.S. and Chinese (and to a lesser extent Russian) thinking on overseas basing and force posture. Washington's obligation to defend allied territory in Northeast Asia with ground forces means that the needs and dynamics of U.S. basing in that region will differ from the maritime theaters of the South Pacific and Indian oceans. At the same time, Beijing and Moscow have little incentive to challenge U.S. presence directly in Japan or South Korea. However, China may seek to strengthen its claims over Taiwan and the South China Sea while expanding its own military presence toward the second island chain, where U.S. force posture remains relatively sparse.

In chapter 4, Isaac Kardon analyzes competitive dynamics among the major powers competing for military bases and access points in the Indian Ocean region. Kardon makes the case that the region's geography, especially its maritime layout, structures the basic security environment. From there, he examines each major power's distinct interests in the theater—including India, Australia, and France—before focusing on the competitive dynamics among these powers, especially the United States and China. The asymmetry between U.S. and Chinese military capabilities highlights the distinct postures of the two armed forces, the mix of military and commercial facilities they employ, and the different economic and defense relationships that each state has cultivated across the region.

In chapter 5, Jason B. Wolff takes the conversation from the western Indian Ocean to the Middle East and sub-Saharan Africa. Wolff argues that the U.S. military sits at a crossroads in the region as it responds to strategic developments pursued by China and Russia in the region. Wolff addresses the important but often neglected issue of logistics, demonstrating how a more robust logistics network will help the United States keep pace with China and deter Russia.

In chapter 6, Dawn C. Murphy focuses more explicitly on Chinese, Russian, and U.S. basing interests in sub-Saharan Africa, noting differences in their basing strategy and outlook. Beijing's interests in the region are about securing and maintaining access to resources and markets and safeguarding its citizens and businesses abroad. Russia, with more limited economic and political stakes in the region, is more opportunistic. Moscow tends to pursue its security interests in an ad hoc fashion, often through undertaking profit-seeking and destabilizing activities with the support of the Wagner Group. Murphy remains concerned about the potential development of Chinese bases on Africa's west coast, which gives the PLAN access to the Atlantic, and also bases in East Africa that could significantly impact SLOCs and provide China with greater power projection capability in the Indian Ocean. Other areas for potential Chinese bases in sub-Saharan Africa should be of less concern to the United States, especially where shared security interests between the United States and China might exist in support of economic and political stability.

In chapter 7, Alexander Cooley puts a spotlight on Central Asia by illustrating how the rise of China and Russia as influential revisionist powers complicates and challenges U.S. leadership, including U.S. access to bases in Central Asia. A clear example includes several Central Asian republics denying the United States basing rights to facilitate its withdrawal from Afghanistan in 2021—a move that Cooley contends may have been influenced by China's and Russia's growing regional influence. More broadly, Cooley discusses how negotiations over base access and rights between sending and host states reflect broader dynamics related to international order.

Jeremy Greenwood takes readers farther north to the Arctic region in chapter 8. With rising global temperatures increasing the accessibility of the

Arctic Ocean, the United States, Russia, and China all recognize the need for guaranteed freedom of access, protection of sovereign rights and interests, and the potential to exploit new sources of natural resources. In light of climate change, Greenwood argues that the basing requirements of the great powers in the Arctic, including the United States, will require building strategic partnerships that offer access rights and agreements to bases, particularly those of a dual-use civil–military nature. Subsequently, the Arctic may be one of the few areas where productive conversations related to bases may be possible among the United States, China, and Russia, along with other stakeholders in the region.

The next three chapters shed light on overseas bases and geostrategic competition in Europe. Russia's invasion of Ukraine, both in 2014 and in 2022, has put Russian geostrategic interests and U.S. and NATO bases into sharper focus. In chapter 9, Geoffrey F. Gresh argues that China and Russia have transformed Europe's maritime security seascape through their military basing access and port investments across maritime Europe from the Baltic and Black seas to the Mediterranean. In the past several years, Europe has faced a range of maritime security challenges, including the sabotage of the Nord Stream pipelines, the mysterious rupture of submarine fiber-optic cables near France and the United Kingdom, Russian aggression toward NATO ships, a Russian naval blockade in the Black Sea around Ukraine, and significant Chinese investments at various European shipping hubs. Increasing attention must therefore be given to base access and rights in the maritime domain.

In chapter 10, Emily Holland argues that the Russia-Ukraine War has "recentered Europe as a focal point of strategic competition."[34] Even after the war, Russia will continue to pose a threat to peace and stability. In light of this reality, Holland articulates the challenge that the United States confronts in balancing its European commitments to force posture with high-priority commitments to address the pacing threat of China in the Indo-Pacific. Nevertheless, Holland contends that defending Europe and maintaining transatlantic unity are critical tasks for Washington that may require greater sustained troop presence in eastern and Central Europe.

In chapter 11, Michael Allen, Michael E. Flynn, and Carla Martínez Machain examine overseas bases from a domestic angle by evaluating public support for U.S. military presence in Europe. The authors note that China's rise and expansion offer an alternative model to the U.S.-led order, while Russia's invasion of Ukraine attempts to create a hard line against further NATO expansion and influence in eastern Europe and Central Asia. For now, surveys indicate that support for U.S. military presence in Europe remains high, especially in light of the Russia-Ukraine War. However, this support remains contingent on engaging with domestic audiences in host nations. As the authors argue, the future of U.S. military presence and influence in Europe is not based purely on external challenges from rival states but is contingent in "win[ning] the support of domestic audiences to maintain its overseas security arrangements."[35]

In the final chapter, Michael E. O'Hanlon, Melanie W. Sisson, and Andrew Yeo reflect on the future of geostrategic competition and U.S., Chinese, and Russian overseas bases. Drawing on insights from the preceding chapters, the authors provide a forward-looking assessment on force posture amid U.S.–China rivalry and the Russia-Ukraine War and their longer-term impact. Particular attention is given to the Indo-Pacific, Europe, and the Middle East regions, where geostrategic competition among great powers appears most salient.

NOTES

1. "China seeks to displace the United States in the Indo-Pacific region, expand the reaches of its state-driven economic model, and reorder the region in its favor. Russia seeks to restore its great power status and establish spheres of influence near its borders." "National Security Strategy of the United States," White House, December 2017, https://trumpwhitehouse.archives.gov/wp-content/uploads/2017/12/NSS-Final-12-18-2017-0905.pdf, 25.

2. "National Security Strategy," White House, October 22, 2023, https://www.whitehouse.gov/wp-content/uploads/2022/10/Biden-Harris-Administrations-National-Security-Strategy-10.2022.pdf.

3. Zhao Lei, "PLA Establishes Base in Horn of Africa," *China Daily*, July 12, 2017, http://usa.chinadaily.com.cn/china/2017-07/12/content_30081657.htm; Peter Dutton, Isaac Kardon, and Conor Kennedy: "Djibouti: China's First Overseas Strategic Strongpoint," *CMSI Maritime Report*, no. 6 (April 2020), https://digital-commons.usnwc.edu/cmsi-maritime-reports/6.

4. Emily Holland, "Strategic Competition and Basing in Central and Eastern Europe," *Brookings Institution Policy Brief* (February 2023), https://www.brookings.edu/wp-content/uploads/2023/02/FP_20230207_europe_basing_holland.pdf.

5. U.S. Department of Defense, "Global Posture Review," Office of the Secretary of Defense, November 2021, https://www.defense.gov/News/Releases/Release/Article/2855801/dod-concludes-2021-global-posture-review; U.S. National Security Council, "National Security Strategy," October 2022, https://www.whitehouse.gov/wp-content/uploads/2022/10/Biden-Harris-Administrations-National-Security-Strategy-10.2022.pdf.

6. See James R. Blaker, *United States Overseas Basing: An Anatomy of the Dilemma* (New York: Praeger, 1990); C. T. Sandars, *America's Overseas Garrisons the Leasehold Empire* (Oxford: Oxford University Press, 2000); Melvyn Leffler, "The American Conception of National Security and the Beginnings of the Cold War, 1945–48," *American Historical Review* 89, no. 2 (April 1984): 346–81; and Paul M. Kennedy, *The Rise and Fall of British Naval Mastery* (London: A. Lane, 1976).

7. John W. McDonald Jr. and Diane Bendahmane, eds., *U.S. Bases Overseas: Negotiations with Spain, Greece, and the Philippines* (Boulder, CO: Westview Press, 1990).

8. Kent E. Calder, *Embattled Garrisons: Comparative Base Politics and American Globalism* (Princeton, NJ: Princeton University Press, 2007).

9. Alexander Cooley, *Base Politics: Democratic Change and the U.S. Military Overseas* (Ithaca, NY: Cornell University Press, 2008).

10. Andrew Yeo, *Activists, Alliances, and Anti-U.S. Base Protests* (New York: Cambridge University Press, 2011); Amy Austin Holmes, *Social Unrest and American Military Bases in Turkey and Germany since 1945* (New York: Cambridge University Press, 2014); Yuko Kawato, *Protests against U.S. Military Base Policy in Asia: Persuasion and Its Limits* (Redwood City, CA: Stanford University Press, 2015); Claudia J. Kim, "War over Framing: Base Politics in South Korea," *Pacific Review* 30, no. 3 (2017): 309–27.

11. Yeo, *Activists, Alliances, and Anti-U.S. Base Protests*; Michael A. Allen, Michael E. Flynn, Carla Martínez Machain, and Andrew Stravers, *Beyond the Wire: US Military Deployments and Host Country Public Opinion* (Oxford: Oxford University Press, 2023); Maria Höhn and Seungsook Moon, *Over There: Living with the U.S. Military Empire from World War Two to the Present* (Durham, NC: Duke University Press, 2010); Michael O'Hanlon, *Unfinished Business: U.S. Overseas Military Presence in the 21st Century* (Washington, D.C.: Center for a New American Security, 2008); Sheila A. Smith, "Shifting Terrain: The Domestic Politics of U.S. Military Presence in Asia," East-West Center, March 1, 2006, https://www.eastwestcenter.org/publications/shifting-terrain-the-domestic-politics-the-us-military-presence-in-asia.

12. Kurt Campbell and Celeste Johnson Ward, "New Battle Stations?," *Foreign Affairs* 82, no. 5 (September/October 2003): 95–103.

13. For notable exceptions that offer a more sustained treatment of U.S. basing alongside other cases of great power basing, see Barry M. Blechman and Robert G. Weinland, "Why Coaling Stations Are Necessary in the Nuclear Age," *International Security* 2, no. 1 (1977): 88–99; Robert E. Harkavy, *Great Power Competition for Overseas Bases: The Geopolitics of Access Diplomacy* (London: Pergamon, 1982); Robert E. Harkavy, *Bases Abroad: The Global Foreign Military Presence* (New York: Oxford University Press, 1989); and Robert E. Harkavy, *Strategic Basing and the Great Powers, 1200–2000* (Abingdon: Routledge, 2007). Although Harkavy may have been one of the first scholars to examine overseas basing through the lens of international relations theory and great power (i.e., U.S.–Soviet) competition, the base politics research program did not really develop until the post–Cold War

period. With the end of bipolarity, attention focused almost exclusively on U.S. bases and/or the domestic politics of host governments in relation to U.S. overseas basing. The return of great power politics, however, will likely bring renewed attention to the issue of foreign basing and thus a need for greater comparative work. For recent work on great power competition, see Stacie E. Goddard, *When Right Makes Might: Rising Powers and World Order* (Ithaca, NY: Cornell University Press, 2018); David M. Edelstein, *Over the Horizon: Time, Uncertainty, and the Rise of Great Powers* (Ithaca, NY: Cornell University Press, 2017); Joshua Shifrinson, *Rising Titans, Falling Giants: How Great Powers Exploit Power Shifts* (Ithaca, NY: Cornell University Press, 2019); and Matthew Kroenig, *The Return of Great Power Rivalry: Democracy versus Autocracy from the Ancient World to the U.S. and China* (New York: Oxford University Press, 2020).

14. See U.S. Department of Defense, "Base Structure Report" for fiscal year 2022, which lists the number of overseas U.S. bases at 544 sites. The report is found only in Excel form made available from the Office of the Assistant Secretary of Defense for Energy, Installations, and Environment. See https://www.acq.osd.mil/eie/Downloads/BSI/Base%20Structure%20Report%20FY22.xlsx. In another study from the Quincy Institute, scholar David Vine sites around 750 overseas military bases. See David Vine, Patterson Deppen, and Leah Bolger, "Drawdown: Improving U.S. and Global Security through Military Base Closures Abroad," Quincy Institute, September 20, 2021. https://quincyinst.org/report/drawdown-improving-u-s-and-global-security-through-military-base-closures-abroad.

15. See, for example, Evan Ellis, "Chinese Security Engagement in Latin America," Center for Strategic and International Studies, November 2020, https://www.csis.org/analysis/chinese-security-engagement-latin-america; Michael Mazarr et al., "Understanding Influence in the Strategic Competition with China," RAND Corporation, Report RRA290-1, 2021, https://www.rand.org/pubs/research_reports/RRA290-1.html; and Christopher Yung et al., "'Not an Idea We Have to Shun': Chinese Overseas Basing Requirements in the 21st Century," *China Strategic Perspectives*, no. 7 (2014), https://apps.dtic.mil/sti/pdfs/ADA610424.pdf (in this case using U.S. benchmarks and operational analysis to assess Chinese basing objectives and potential).

16. "National Security Strategy."

17. "National Security Strategy of the United States," 25.

18. But on China, see Cristina L. Garafola, Stephen Watts, and Kristin Leuschner, *China's Global Basing Ambitions: Defense Implications for the United States* (Santa Monica, CA: RAND Corporation, 2022), and Issac B. Kardon, "China's Global Maritime Access: Alternatives to Overseas Military Bases in the Twenty-First Century," *Security Studies* 31, no. 5 (2022): 885–916.

19. From January 2022 until May 2023, the United States had provided close to $50 billion in military and security assistance to Ukraine, not to mention additional logistical and military support to NATO allies in eastern Europe. See Jonathan Masters and Will Merrow, "How Much Aid Has the U.S. Sent Ukraine? Here Are Six Charts," Council on Foreign Relations, July 10, 2023, https://www.cfr.org

/article/how-much-aid-has-us-sent-ukraine-here-are-six-charts#:~:text=Since%20the%20war%20began%2C%20the,Economy%2C%20a%20German%20research%20institute.

20. See Kardon, "China's Global Maritime Access."

21. "Putin Signs Law Allowing Expansion of Russian Naval Facility in Syria," Radio Free Europe/Radio Liberty, December 19, 2017, https://www.rferl.org/a/putin-signs-law-syria-tartus-naval-facility/28946167.html; Samy Magdy, "Sudan Military Finishes Review of Russian Red Sea Base Deal," Associated Press, February 11, 2023, https://apnews.com/article/politics-sudan-government-moscow-803738fba4d8f91455f0121067c118dd; Dan De Luce, "U.S. Accuses Russia's Wagner Group Mercenaries of Fueling War in Sudan," NBC News, May 26, 2023, https://www.nbcnews.com/news/world/us-accuses-russias-wagner-group-mercenaries-fueling-war-sudan-rcna86492.

22. J. A. Hobson, *Imperialism: A Study* (Ann Arbor: University of Michigan Press, 1983), 71.

23. "The Diversified Employment of China's Armed Forces, 2013," Information Office of the State Council, April 2013, http://eng.mod.gov.cn/TopNews/2013-04/16/content_4442750.html.

24. See, for example, this monograph by a leading PLA scholar: Liang Fang [梁芳], *Theory of Maritime Strategic Channels* [海上战略通道论] (Beijing: Current Affairs Press, 2011).

25. Hu Bo [胡波], "On China's Important Maritime Interests [论中国的重要海洋利益]," *Asia-Pacific Security and Maritime Affairs* [亚太安全与海洋研究], no. 3 (2015): 14–28.

26. PRC State Council Information Office, "China's Military Strategy," May 2015.

27. PRC State Council Information Office, "China's Military Strategy," 3.

28. Andrew Scobell and Nathan Beauchamp-Mustafaga, "The Flag Lags but Follows: The PLA and China's Great Leap Outward," in *Chairman Xi Remakes the PLA: Assessing China's Military Reforms*, ed. Phillip C. Saunders et al. (Washington, D.C.: National Defense University Press, 2019), 171–202.

29. Bruce Jones, "Russia Searches for Strategic Airbase Partner," *Jane's Defence Weekly*, March 4, 2014, http://www.janes.com/article/34916/russia-searches-for-strategic-airbase-partner.

30. Decree of the President of the Russian Federation, "Fundamentals of the State Policy of the Russian Federation in the Field of Naval Operations for the Period until 2030," translated by Anna Davis, 2017, https://dnnlgwick.blob.core.windows.net/portals/0/NWCDepartments/Russia%20Maritime%20Studies%20Institute/RMSI_RusNavyFundamentalsENG_FINAL%20(1).pdf?sr=b&si=DNNFileManagerPolicy&sig=fjFDEgWhpd1ING%2FnmGQXqaH5%2FDEujDU76EnksAB%2B1A0%3D.

31. Wolff, chapter 5 in this volume.

32. Greenwood, chapter 8 in this volume.

33. Aamer Madhani, "US Confirms China Has Had a Spy Base in Cuba since at Least 2019," Associated Press, June 11, 2023, https://apnews.com/article/china-cuba-spy-base-us-intelligence-0f655b577ae4141bdbeabc35d628b18f; Rafael Bernal, "Russia Suggests Military Deployments to Cuba, Venezuela an Option," *The Hill*, January 13, 2022, https://thehill.com/policy/defense/589595-russia-suggests-military-deployments-to-cuba-venezuela-an-option.

34. Holland, chapter 10 in this volume.

35. Allen, Flynn, and Machain, chapter 11 in this volume.

2

Temperatures Rising

Great Powers, Regional Players, and the Struggle for Bases and Access in the Pacific Islands

BRUCE JONES[1]

The sheer vast scale of the Pacific Ocean can be hard to convey by any but the most clichéd observation. Just ponder this one fact: taken as a whole, the Pacific encompasses a larger surface area than *all* the continents combined. Its populated concentration, though, is in Oceania, which runs from the Hawaiian Islands to the east coast of the Philippines and from Australia's eastern coast to Easter Island, straddling the equator. Even this subsection of the Pacific encompasses almost 9 million square kilometers of water and more than 10,000 islands, atolls, and other land features. Transposed to a surface map of the world, it would stretch from the north of Scotland to central Africa along its western edge and from Murmansk to Nepal along its eastern boundary. Spread across this domain are a mere 45 million people, fully 60 percent of whom live in Australia alone, with New Zealand and Papua New Guinea (PNG) hosting the other major concentrations of people. Across the rest of this watery domain, population is thinly spread.

The Pacific Islands are roughly divided by history and culture into four zones. These are Australasia, which encompasses primarily the continental island of Australia itself; Melanesia off the northeastern coast of Australia and encompassing PNG, the Solomon Islands, Vanuatu, and Fiji; Micronesia, encompassing the Northern Mariana Islands, the Federated States of Micronesia, Guam, Palau, the Marshall Islands, and Kiribati; and Polynesia, which stretches from Tonga to Cook Islands to French Polynesia and eventually Easter Island. Polynesia technically encompasses Hawaii—though by American politics and governance perhaps more than by culture, Hawaii has closer ties to Micronesia. Each of these regions has a distinct history, culture, and set of international relations, as do the major island nations within them. But they share a common geographical and geopolitical fate—for they lie in the increasingly contested waters that separate the world's two largest economies and military powers, a contest for influence, for resources, for economic ties, for presence—and, increasingly, for bases.

In the voluminous commentary and growing scholarship about the U.S.–China rivalry, much of the focus is on those waters that lap up against China's eastern shores. It was the East China Sea that first drew Western strategic attention when China and Japan tussled over the Senkaku/Diaoyu islands. It was in the South China Sea that Beijing, having made a massive claim for rights under the UN Convention on the Law of the Sea, began to build out its military presence. And of late, the Taiwan Strait has been the focus of concerted attention as the tensest flash point in U.S.–China relations. But our strategic gaze should look to the farther reaches of the Pacific as well, for these waters are primus inter pares of the "Far Seas" that drive China's strategic ambition.

Over the past several decades, the United States has had an enviable position here, with a string of states, possessions, federated territories, and legal associations that give it a defensible "sea line of communication" across the northern reaches of the Pacific. These connect rear bases in San Diego, California, and in the Puget Sound to Pearl Harbor and onward to Guam, the Marianas, and eventually the vital forward U.S. bases in Japan. This uncontested string of assets has been an essential part of how the U.S. Navy has maintained dominance in the blue waters of the Pacific and projected power into Asia and the Indian Ocean. Now, though, China is contesting that dominance and maneuvering for position in these waters. In addition to extensive economic, diplomatic, and political ties, built up over the past twenty years while the United States was otherwise preoccupied, Beijing has turned its ambition to bases, logistics, and security relationships in the Pacific Islands. And thus the Pacific Islands are once again thrust onto history's stage, the only territorial elements in the vast maritime space that separates the world's two most powerful countries.

A BRIEF HISTORY OF CONTESTATION IN THE REGION

The Pacific Islands are the terrestrial elements of a maritime region whose history has long been shaped by the ambitions of foreign powers. In the imperial nineteenth century, British, French, Spanish, and Russian explorers found their way to these islands, and the experience was often violent, disease-ridden, and exploitative. Americans found their way there too. The famous U.S. Exploring Expedition, the first entrance by the United States into the nineteenth-century great power game of oceanographic missions, started by charting Antarctic waters but ended by exploring Fiji and other islands in the central Pacific—a process accompanied by episodes of brutal violence, notably including the Malolo massacre on Fiji in July 1842.[2]

The region was spared the worst of the brutality of World War I, but in World War II, it found itself again caught in the extra-regional affairs of the world's major military powers. For Japan, these territories were essential to its eastern strategy, of which the attack on Pearl Harbor was a signature part. In 1942, the United States fought back, and Oceania became the site of some of the largest naval battles in history (in the Coral Sea and at Midway) but also of ferocious land combat as the United States and its allies sought to dislodge Japanese forces from strongholds across the central reaches of the Pacific. This history has left a legacy or residue in the form of substantial external influence and presence.

Ironically, given their long dominance and network of coaling stations across these waters, Britain retains little of its former presence in Oceania, limited to its overseas possession of Pitcairn Island (population: all of forty-seven souls). But London retains an important set of military assets in Australia and New Zealand as well as its naval base at Sembawang, Singapore, which anchors the first island chain (though it is rarely referred to in those terms).

In Polynesia and the eastern reaches of Melanesia, the more important external actor is France. Overseas possessions in this region contribute to France having the second-largest exclusive economic zone in the world, with 6.8 million square kilometers of waters surrounding its Pacific Island possessions in Clipperton Island, French Polynesia, Wallis and Futuna, and New Caledonia. These host the largest European military presence in the

Pacific, with 2,800 French armed forces personnel permanently based in the region between its theater headquarters in Papeete, French Polynesia, and regional commands in La Reunion and New Caledonia. The last of these also hosts a French naval base that supports a surface fleet of ten ships.[3]

More important than all of this are the U.S. possessions and relationships across the northern reaches of Oceania. These encompass several different forms of legal or governance relationships, ranging from Hawaii, which became a U.S. state in 1959; to Guam, which is a federated state, meaning that its residents are U.S. citizens but without full voting rights; to Wake Island, an unincorporated territory under the jurisdiction of the Department of the Interior; to what are known as the Freely Associated States (the Marshall Islands, the Federated States of Micronesia, and Palau), independent nations that have signed Compacts of Association with the United States, establishing wide-ranging diplomatic, economic, and strategic relations between these three independent entities and the United States.[4] All this gives the United States extensive basing rights in those islands and access/defense rights in their exclusive economic zones—which, collectively, cover more territory than the continental United States.

The most extensive U.S. basing (beyond Hawaii) is in Guam, which sits 3,500 kilometers west of Hawaii and 1,500 kilometers east of the Philippines and south of Japan and is home to the commander of Joint Region Marianas. That commander oversees U.S. Naval Base Guam and Andersen Air Force Base as well as subsidiary (but essential) facilities, such as a maritime expeditionary group, submarine tenders, a combat helicopter squadron, a munitions depot, and Naval Computing and Telecommunications Station Guam—a vital link in the chain of Naval Information Forces facilities that string together U.S. military awareness and operational intelligence from Hawaii to Japan. Five U.S. submarines are home-ported in Guam, whose port is also deep enough to host a visiting U.S. aircraft carrier. The U.S. Coast Guard also has a base of operations in Guam—and, since October 2020, so does the U.S. Marine Corps.[5]

Geopolitical questions may frame the new perspective of the United States on Oceania, but from the vantage point of the islands themselves, geopolitical questions are subordinate to a global and transnational question about the health of the ocean that surrounds them. These are the issues of climate change (both mitigation and adaption), illegal fishing, and deep-sea mining—closely related topics.

Many of the countries in the region have fishing as their largest source of national income, central to their development, to their livelihoods, and to their culture. Episodically through their history, which has been threatened by outsiders' fleets, the Spanish, the British, the French, the Americans, the Russians, and the Japanese have all fished these waters extensively, often not in compliance with the Pacific Islanders' own sense of boundaries and limits.

Their situation was measurably improved by the passing into force of the UN Convention of the Law of the Sea and the establishment of exclusive economic zones around their land borders that limit the legal right of foreign fishing fleets to draw from their waters. But even as their *legal* position improved, two developments began to erode their *actual* position: (1) climate change, manifest in increasing average ocean temperatures, with a deleterious impact on the health of fishing stocks, and in increasingly frequent storm surges that have caused continuous damage to many low-lying states, and (2) overfishing, especially by the newest entrant to the commercial, diplomatic, and strategic life of Oceania: China.

ENTER THE CHINESE

An essential driver of contemporary Chinese grand strategy is its geographical and commercial position: heavily dependent on sea-based commerce but constrained by limited and contested access to the seas.[6] The drive to defend itself from sea-mounted foreign invasion shaped Chinese naval strategy in the 1960s and 1970s, focused on coastal defense. As China turned to outside markets in the 1980s, its interest and naval capacity grew into a near-seas defense strategy.[7] But so too did its dependence on sea-based imports of raw materials and exports of manufactured and intermediate goods, and thus so did its naval ambition. As it struggled with its "Malacca Dilemma" (the vulnerable choke point through which its critical flows of energy and trade flow), Chinese leaders sought to develop the capability to deter blockades and protect its interests in the sea-lanes of communication that run through its "near seas"—all of this while keeping a sharp eye on Taiwan and the possibility of eventual reincorporation of that territory into the Chinese state. By the mid-2010s, frank American assessment of the new capacity and presence of the People's Liberation Army Navy (PLAN) in the Yellow Sea, East China Sea, and South China Sea was that Beijing had succeeded in dulling American dominance. While China does not "own" those seas, it does have enough capacity and sufficiently threatening weapons systems (both on land formations in those waters and on the Chinese mainland) to limit American options and control escalation dynamics. That "near-seas" capacity is essential for Chinese self-defense, to limit America's options of a near blockade, and to have the option of a military move against Taiwan.[8]

But having built up a defensive and offensive suite of capabilities in the first set of waters around its shores, China began to secure those new capacities themselves. And at the same time, China sought to reach farther than its "near seas" both for trade and for commercial reasons and to be able to secure its interests in those farther waters. It began to participate in both regional and global counter-piracy operations and to develop a network of what have been best described as "strategic strong points"—clusters of port, infrastructure, and diplomatic relationships at useful locations alongside key waterways, from Djibouti on the Red Sea to Haifa on the Mediterranean. All this was done under the rubric of a "Far Seas" strategy designed to make China a competitive power in the Arctic, in the Indian Ocean—and, above all, in the wider reaches of the Pacific.[9]

Here China has myriad interests. There are vital fishing stocks in these waters, for which the Chinese population, large parts of which have become used to the protein-rich diet of the middle classes, are increasingly hungry. And there are minerals and metals in the subsea terrain here. Estimates range, but for metals like manganese and cobalt, estimated reserves on the seabed exceed all known reserves on land and may have a value in the order of $5 trillion.[10] For both industrial and military-industrial purposes, access to rare earth metals is vital for China (and the West), and the Pacific seabed appears to host the world's greatest quantity of them.[11] And then there is the issue of diplomatic relations with Taiwan. Of the dwindling number of countries that recognize Taiwan as an independent country, three are Pacific Island nations: Palau, the Marshall Islands, and Kiribati.[12]

For all these reasons and more, China increasingly seeks closer diplomatic ties and an improved strategic position in the western Pacific. In addition, China remains vulnerable to a "distant blockade" of its vital seaborne trade, as it does to a U.S. effort to surge naval forces in through the Luzon Strait to reinforce its own or allied/partner positions inside the first island chain.[13] If the United States sought to impose a blockade on China—for any one of a number of possible reasons—the PLAN would have to try to defeat them in the Indian Ocean and the Philippine Sea. Should China decide to exercise a military option against Taiwan—either a blockade or full-blown military intervention—its concept is to have the PLAN to prevent the United States (and its allies) from coming to Taiwan's aid by blocking U.S. reinforcements *outside* the first island chain.[14]

All this makes the Philippine Sea and the farther reaches of Oceania essential to Chinese strategy. And the Philippine Sea is ringed on its eastern edge by Palau, Guam and the Northern Mariana Islands—collectively the "second island chain" or, as it might better be referred to, the "second island cloud," as seen in figure 2.1.[15]

Figure 2.1. Second Island Cloud.

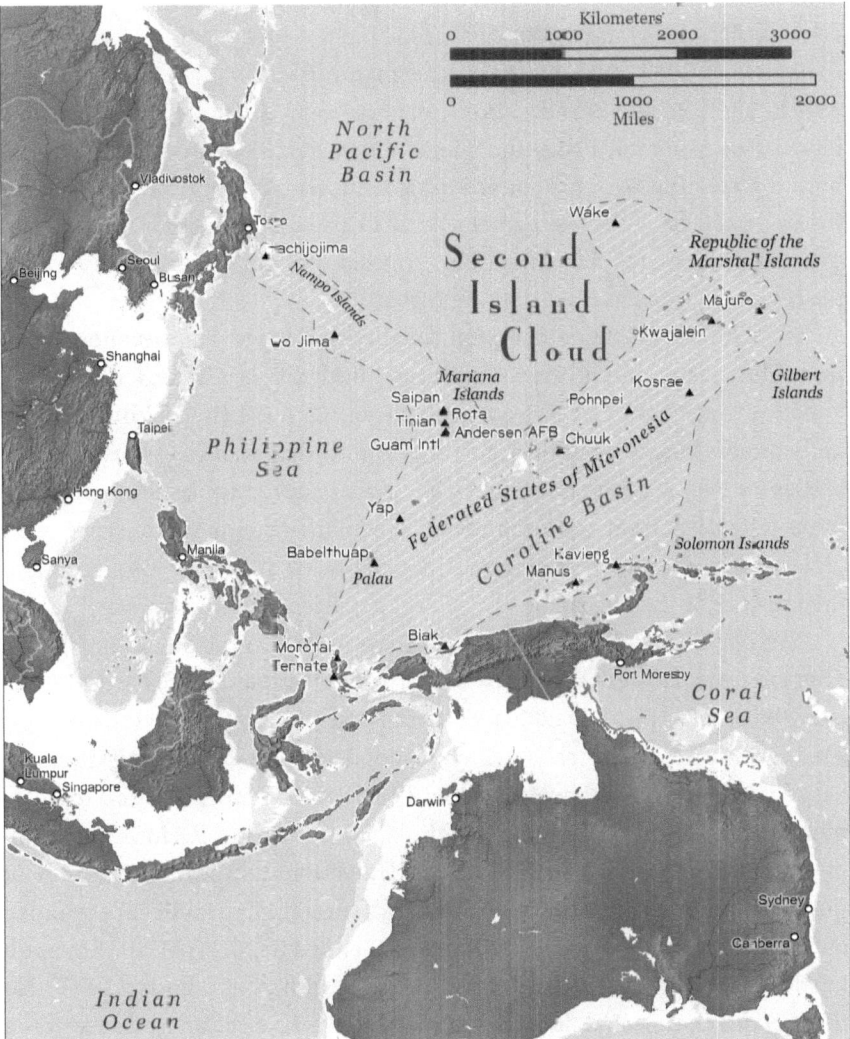

Map created by Andrew Rhodes, 2022.

Just east are the Federated States of Micronesia, and just south is Manus Island of PNG. In a full-blown confrontation between the United States and China, Beijing would seek to make these islands the first line of contestation.[16] Although China does not yet have the net surface or submarine capacity to realize this objective, it is building fast toward it—very fast.[17]

And that in turn is creating a new dynamic of competition and contestation over the Pacific Islands—for maritime access (for fishing and mining), maritime awareness, diplomatic relations, port ownership, and ultimately naval basing or chasing capabilities.

Chinese Efforts and Results

In late May 2022, then Chinese foreign minister Wang Yi undertook a visit to eight Pacific Island nations: the Solomon Islands, Kiribati, Samoa, Fiji, Tonga, Vanuatu, PNG, and Timor-Leste. Partway through the trip, he hosted a meeting with his counterparts from ten countries across Oceania where he sought collective agreement to a new set of regional trade and security arrangements. He failed; his proposal was not endorsed. But across the region, China has been making inroads.[18]

The Chinese playbook has been roughly as follows: build economic ties through investment and debt financing; build elite ties through both diplomatic engagement and "sweeteners"; engage Chinese émigré communities and overseas business families; posture Chinese diplomatic support in global bodies for Pacific Island interests on key global questions like climate change (especially adaptation and loss and damage financing); pursue deeper, formal diplomatic ties and, where relevant, a reversal of Taiwan recognition; and then seek either basing rights or rights of persistent PLAN presence.[19]

This blend of tools has had most success to date in the Solomon Islands. This took American observers by surprise, but it should not have. From the late 1990s until the early 2000s, Solomons was wracked by civil conflict. It sued for help from Australia, which responded by a UN Security Council–backed "regional assistance" mission: *Regional Assistance Mission* to Solomon Islands (RAMSI). Leaving diplomatic niceties aside, RAMSI was for all intents and purposes an Australian-run transitional authority arrangement for the Solomon Islands in which Honiara's sovereignty was de jure retained but de facto shared with Canberra. RAMSI ended in 2013, and the Solomon Islands signed a security and defense treaty with Australia in 2017.[20] But throughout that period, local resentment of the Australian presence was a constant factor, playing into domestic politics and elections. Current president Manasseh Sogavare was long hostile to the Australian presence and oversaw the end of the RAMSI arrangements. When he returned to power in 2019, one of his first moves was to shift away from Canberra toward Beijing. He withdrew Solomon's recognition of Taiwan in 2019. What followed in March 2022 was a memorandum of understanding with Beijing that allowed for Chinese deployments of police and security assistance personnel at Solomon's request to deal with internal unrest (essentially replacing the Australians) as well an ongoing Chinese military and naval presence. Sogavare has publicly stated that this does not entail a permanent Chinese naval base, but it does appear to allow for what amounts to rotational basing.[21] American and Australian efforts to get Sogavare to reverse course have met with decidedly limited success.[22] Sogavare also skipped a September 2023 summit meeting of the Pacific Islands Forum in Washington, D.C., hosted by President Joe Biden.

The Australian press has reported that China has made similar overtures to Vanuatu, though so far, much less is known about the status of Vanuatu–China ties. Certainly, no formal agreement has been announced, but China continues to press its claim there. Chinese financing and construction of a major wharf at Luganville in the southeast corner of Espiritu Santo (the largest island in Vanuatu) led to discussion about its being converted into a "dual-use" facility for the PLAN.[23] Australian and U.S. pressures have fended off that development so far, but the wharf remains under Chinese ownership.[24] Australian scholars have argued that it is in effect a "trojan horse" facility—a commercial facility formally but far larger and deeper than needed for commercial vessels.[25]

China has also had success in Kiribati, long a British colony, independent since 1979. Kiribati is, among other things, host to a spaceport owned by Japan's National Space Development Agency (a civilian, not a military, agency). It is also the country most likely to be the first to be compelled to evacuate *all* its citizens due to climate change–induced sea-level rise—an issue the West has given little more than lip service.[26] In 2019, Kiribati dropped its recognition of Taiwan, reportedly in exchange for loans, funding to refurbish aircraft, and ferries (though these details are unconfirmed).[27] Then in 2021, it announced that it had accepted Chinese financing for a project to upgrade a 6,000-plus-foot airstrip (officially for civilian use only) on the island of Canton.[28]

If built, the airstrip would give China access to a facility farther east into the Pacific than any other in its current tool kit. It should also be presumed that this facility, as well as facilities to be established in the Solomon Islands, will eventually give the Chinese additional options in undersea detection and overall increased maritime awareness in the central reaches of Oceania—a significant fact in potentially deterring American forces along the southern shipping lanes.

Not all such Chinese efforts have been successful. Tuvalu has rejected Chinese efforts to reverse its recognition of Taiwan, for example.[29] But China's most important failure to date—indeed, an example of overreach—came in Manus Island, PNG. There, Beijing sought PNG backing to finance the renovation of an important port facility that could also serve dual use for PLAN basing or presence. Instead, PNG offered Australia and the United States a joint arrangement for the facility.[30] In October 2021, the U.S. Navy's Naval Mobile Construction Battalion 5 began refurbishment of the old World War II–era Lombrum Naval Base on the island.[31] Eventually, this will allow for Australian frigates to dock there, providing Australia with its first Pacific Island base and the United States with a strategically relevant hub on the southern shipping route—and just outside of the 3,000-kilometer range of China's longest-range missiles.[32]

Better Late Than Never: American and Allied Responses, Options, and Issues

China's political, economic, and military reach in the Pacific Islands leads to an essential question: where should the United States concentrate its Pacific basing, and how can it secure its existing position in the Pacific Islands?

On September 28–29, 2022, President Biden hosted the leaders of fourteen Pacific Island nations for the first-ever U.S.–Pacific Island Country Summit. It was but one of a flurry of diplomatic initiatives: the White House released the first-ever U.S. Pacific Islands strategy, announced the creation of the post of envoy to the Pacific Islands Forum, and announced three new embassies across the region and the return of a U.S. Agency for International Development office to Fiji. The strategy highlighted the major issues of concern to the region: the status of legal negotiations over updated "compacts" with the Freely Associated States, illegal and extra-jurisdictional fishing, climate change and sea-level rise, marine conservation, and economic development. It invoked partnerships with the Quad, the Blue Pacific grouping (Australia, New Zealand, Canada, and the United Kingdom), the Association of Southeast Asian Nations, and the Pacific Islands Forum and pledged greater diplomatic presence as well as greater presence from the Department of Defense, the U.S. Coast Guard, and the National Oceanic and Atmospheric Administration (the major civilian hub for the ocean sciences and climate change research).[33] If fully funded and realized—both big ifs—this would represent a significant upgrade in the quantity and quality of attention paid by the United States to the region after two decades of perceived neglect.

The U.S. and allied effort to bolster their ties to and presence among the Pacific Islands nations has five core elements:

- Reinforcing the legal basis of U.S. claims and presence with the Freely Associated States and, where possible, expanding physical presence throughout the region—for example, in a new agreement for basing facilities in the Federated States of Micronesia.[34]
- Use of the U.S. Coast Guard, remote sensing technologies, and legal relations to aid the Pacific Islands in combating illegal and extra-jurisdictional fishing—all under the rubric of the Indo-Pacific Maritime Domain Awareness initiative of the Quad.
- A rhetorical shift toward greater sympathy for the issue of climate adaptation, sea-level rise, and storm surges that threaten the livelihoods—and in some cases the very existence—of Pacific Island nations and an increase in access to climate adaptation financing, facilitated by greater U.S. and Australian credibility on climate mitigation (for now).[35]
- Increased support for development and infrastructure, both from the United States and through joint efforts by Japan and Australia, the other two major financial and development partners of the Pacific Island states.
- Efforts by major U.S. allies and partners to increase their presence and base access options. Key developments here include reciprocal base access arrangements between France and India, covering both French possessions in the Pacific and Indian oceans, and a similar agreement between the United Kingdom and Japan. While none of these countries has been able to—or really aspires to—establish new bases in the region per se, these arrangements certainly allow for more flexible passage through these waters and enable them potentially to contribute more readily to military operations or blockading operations in the South China Sea/Taiwan Strait.

This is a lot, but it is late. As early as 2014, a senior Australian politician told me, "Every few months, one of our ministers travels to one of the Pacific Islands, carrying a promise of 15–20 million new aid dollars, with several conditions. Two weeks later, a Chinese minister follows, carrying an offer of 150–200 million new aid dollars, with no conditions—and several 'sweeteners.'" Nearly a decade later, the United States is playing catch-up. China's overreach not just in this region but elsewhere is helping the United States regain some lost ground. But a region long dominated by the U.S. Navy is now once again genuinely contested—in diplomatic terms and, at the present rate of developments, soon in naval terms.[36] It also puts the Pacific Islands in a strong position to leverage Washington's and Beijing's competing interests, giving them if not leverage per se, then certainly bargaining chips in the geopolitical contest.

The issue has become more acute as China has continuously strengthened its PLAN, PLAN Air Force, and Rocket Force posture inside the first island chain—and to a lesser degree beyond.[37] Should the United States reinforce its posture inside the first island chain to deter Chinese aggression more convincingly, as the commandant of the U.S. Marine Corps has argued? Or does that leave too much U.S. hardware within reach of Chinese missile attack? Is it better, then, to reinforce the U.S. presence along the second island chain? This position, including Guam, is within range of the longest-range Chinese missiles, but that distance probably increases American capacity to use its cutting-edge naval information warfaring capacities to fool Chinese targeting sensors, divert Chinese missiles, and survive a first barrage. There are merits and demerits to this argument, but the option goes away if the United States loses diplomatic ground in Micronesia—as it has begun to do in Melanesia.

Which leaves Australasia—that is to say, the option of increasing the U.S. military presence or co-basing arrangements in Australia itself. This is the likely outcome of the Australia–U.K.–U.S. submarine, missile, and technology agreement of 2021; of the joint basing arrangement with PNG in Manus Island; and of the logic of distance and resilience.

CONCLUSION: COME HELL OR HIGH WATER

The Pacific Islands face an unenviable near future. Rising sea levels, increasingly frequent storm surges, and declining fishing stocks portend decreased livelihoods and growing strains—in some cases threatening their very survival as inhabited nations. Increasing Chinese interest in these waters for commercial, mineral, and strategic purposes is a potential source of revenue and has triggered renewed American attention—another source of revenue and support. But the cost of this is likely to be that these islands become increasingly squeezed between Washington and Beijing. There are positives there in the possibility of greater leverage as the two giants vie for attention and access, but they are likely to be outweighed by the costs and consequences of rivalry.

Seen from the vantage point of China and the United States and their respective regional and global partners and allies, the Pacific Islands will only grow in importance. As China rapidly increases its military capabilities inside the first island chain, the area out to the second island chain and beyond will become a central zone of competition and contestation. Basing rights, or "persistent access" along both the northern and the southern sea-lanes of communication across Oceania, look set to be a source of persistent *tension*. Further Chinese successes in deepening its diplomatic relationships and logistical access across the southern arc of Oceania will complicate but not materially degrade American access. But if the United States reverts to a pattern of neglect or otherwise loses ground across the southern stretches of the Pacific Islands, its strategic position in the western Pacific—and thus Asia as a whole—will be measurably weakened.

NOTES

1. Thanks to Sophia Hart for research assistance on this chapter.
2. Nathaniel Philbrick, *Sea of Glory: America's Voyage of Discovery, The U.S. Exploring Expedition, 1838–1842* (New York: Penguin Books, 2003).
3. Thomas Flichy de la Neuville and Eleonore de Gentile, "France in the Pacific: History of a Discreet Presence," *Zeitschrift für Außen- und Sicherheitspolitik* 15, no. 1 (March 2022): 69–82, https://doi.org/10.1007/s12399-022-00893-w.
4. "Statehood Process and Political Status of U.S. Territories: Brief Policy Background," Congressional Research Service, July 29, 2022, https://crsreports.congress.gov/product/pdf/IF/IF11792.
5. Oriana Skylar Mastro, "Defense, Deterrence, and the Role of Guam," in *Defending Guam*, ed. Rebeccah Heinrichs (Stanford, CA: Freeman Spogli Institute for International Studies, 2022), 44–45, https://fsi.stanford.edu/publication/defending-guam.
6. Michael J. Green, *By More Than Providence: Grand Strategy and American Power in the Asia Pacific since 1783* (New York: Columbia University Press, 2019); James R. Holmes and Toshi Yoshihara, *Red Star over the Pacific: China's Rise and*

the Challenge to U.S. Maritime Strategy (Annapolis, MD: Naval Institute Press, 2013); Bruce Jones, *To Rule the Waves: How Control of the World's Oceans Shapes the Fate of the Superpowers* (New York: Scribner, 2021).

7. Jennifer Rice and Erik Robb, "China Maritime Report No. 13: The Origins of 'Near Seas Defense and Far Seas Protection,'" U.S. Naval War College, 2021, https://digital-commons.usnwc.edu/cmsi-maritime-reports/13.

8. Andrew S. Erickson, Ryan D. Martinson, and Peter A. Dutton, *China Near Seas Combat Capabilities* (Newport, RI: China Maritime Studies Institute, U.S. Naval War College, 2014).

9. Rice and Robb, "China Maritime Report No. 13."

10. Daina Paulikas, Steven Katona, Erika Ilves, and Saleem H. Ali, "Life Cycle Climate Change Impacts of Producing Battery Metals from Land Ores versus Deep-Sea Polymetallic Nodules," *Journal of Cleaner Production* 275 (December 2020), https://www.sciencedirect.com/science/article/pii/S0959652620338671?via%3Dihub.

11. Wycliff Tupiti, "Rare Metal Resources in Polymetallic Nodules from the Eastern Equatorial Pacific Ocean," PhD diss., University of Plymouth, 2021, https://pearl.plymouth.ac.uk/handle/10026.1/16922.

12. USIP China-Freely Associated States Senior Study Group, "China's Influence on the Freely Associated States of the Northern Pacific," United States Institute of Peace, September 5, 2022, https://www.usip.org/publications/2022/09/chinas-influence-freely-associated-states-northern-pacific.

13. Fiona S. Cunningham, "The Maritime Rung on the Escalation Ladder: Naval Blockades in a US-China Conflict," *Security Studies* 29, no. 4 (October 2020): 730–68, https://www.tandfonline.com/doi/abs/10.1080/09636412.2020.1811462.

14. Cunningham, "The Maritime Rung on the Escalation Ladder."

15. Andrew Rhodes, "The Second Island Cloud: A Deeper and Broader Concept for American Presence in the Pacific Islands," *Joint Force Quarterly* 95 (Fourth Quarter 2019): 46–53, https://ndupress.ndu.edu/JFQ/Joint-Force-Quarterly-95.aspx.

16. A point that underscores the shortsightedness of the post–Cold War decision to let go of the vast American naval base at Subic Bay, the Philippines, over a funding dispute. The requested amount in question, $500 million per year for seven years, adjusted for 2022 dollars, represents roughly half the cost of one aircraft carrier and one two-thousandth of the Department of Defense budget allocation. In 2023, the United States regained a more limited set of basing capacities in the Philippines: Jim Gomez, "US Seeks Expansion of Military Presence in Philippines," *AP News*, November 21, 2022, https://apnews.com/article/china-united-states-kamala-harris-beijing-philippines-cc5aa1fbad47cdc95443d480eb8bca03.

17. "China Naval Modernization: Implications for U.S. Navy Capabilities—Background and Issues for Congress," Congressional Research Service, November 10, 2022, https://crsreports.congress.gov/product/pdf/RL/RL33153/263.

18. Asanga Abeyagoonasekera, "China in Sri Lanka and Solomon Islands: Role of Littorals in the Geopolitical Competition," Institute for Security and Development Policy, July 6, 2022, https://isdp.eu/publication/china-in-sri-lanka-and-solomon-islands-role-of-littorals-in-the-geopolitical-competition.

19. Oriana Skylar Mastro, "The PLA's Evolving Role in China's South China Sea Strategy," *China Leadership Monitor* 66 (December 1, 2020), https://aparc.fsi.stanford.edu/publication/pla%E2%80%99s-evolving-role-china%E2%80%99s-south-china-sea-strategy.

20. "Regional Assistance Mission to Soloman Islands (RAMSI)," Nautilus Institute for Security and Sustainability, June 9, 2009, https://nautilus.org/publications/books/australian-forces-abroad/solomon-islands/regional-assistance-mission-to-solomon-islands-ramsi.

21. Patricia M. Kim, "Does the China-Solomon Islands Security Pact Portend a More Interventionist Beijing?," Brookings Institution, May 6, 2022, https://www.brookings.edu/blog/order-from-chaos/2022/05/06/does-the-china-solomon-islands-security-pact-portend-a-more-interventionist-beijing.

22. Nick Perry, "Solomon Islands Leader Hits Back at Criticism of Deepening Security Ties with China," Associated Press, July 17, 2023, https://apnews.com/article/solomon-islands-china-united-states-48993476d33d40c816dd895e80868e3e.

23. "U.S. to Open Vanuatu Embassy in Latest Move to Counter China in Pacific," Reuters, March 31, 2023, https://www.reuters.com/world/us-plans-open-embassy-south-pacific-island-nation-vanuatu-2023-03-31.

24. Xinhua News Agency, "China to Further Elevate Comprehensive Strategic Partnership with Vanuatu Spokesperson," *Macau Business*, January 31, 2023, https://www.macaubusiness.com/china-to-further-elevate-comprehensive-strategic-partnership-with-vanuatu-spokesperson.

25. David Wroe, "The Great Wharf from China, Raising Eyebrows across the Pacific," *Sydney Morning Herald*, April 11, 2013, https://www.smh.com.au/politics/federal/the-great-wharf-from-china-raising-eyebrows-across-the-pacific-20180411-p4z8yu.html.

26. Rana Balesh, "Submerging Islands: Tuvalu and Kiribati as Case Studies Illustrating the Need for a Climate Refugee Treaty," *Environmental and Earth Law Journal* 5, no. 1 (2015): 78, https://commons.law.famu.edu/studentworks/8.

27. Kate Lyons, "Taiwan Loses Second Ally in a Week as Kiribati Switches to China," *The Guardian*, September 20, 2019, https://www.theguardian.com/world/2019/sep/20/taiwan-loses-second-ally-in-a-week-as-kiribati-switches-to-china.

28. Jonathan Barrett, 'Kiribati Says China-Backed Pacific Airstrip Project for Civilian Use," Reuters, May 13, 2021, https://www.reuters.com/world/asia-pacific/kiribati-says-china-backed-pacific-airstrip-project-civilian-use-2021-05-13.

29. Yimou Lee, "Tuvalu Rejects China Offer to Build Islands and Retains Ties with Taiwan," Reuters, November 21, 2019, https://www.reuters.com/article/us-taiwan-diplomacy-tuvalu/tuvalu-rejects-china-offer-to-build-islands-and-retains-ties-with-taiwan-idUSKBN1XV0H8.

30. Brian Harding and Camilla Pohle, "China's Search for a Permanent Military Presence in the Pacific Islands," United States Institute of Peace, July 21, 2022, https://www.usip.org/publications/2022/07/chinas-search-permanent-military-presence-pacific-islands.

31. Stephane Belcher, "U.S. Navy Seabees Construct Dental Facility," USINDOPACOM, December 28, 2021, https://www.pacom.mil/Media/News/News-Article-View/Article/2884747/us-navy-seabees-construct-dental-facility.

32. Tim Fish, "Australia, U.S. Set to Expand Papua New Guinea Naval Base," *OSNI News*, November 23, 2018, https://news.usni.org/2018/11/23/australia-u-s-set-expand-papa-new-guinea-naval-base.

33. "U.S.-Pacific Island Country Summit," U.S. Department of State, https://www.state.gov/u-s-pacific-islands-country-summit.

34. USIP China-Freely Associated States Senior Study Group, "China's Influence on the Freely Associated States of the Northern Pacific."

35. It remains unlikely that the United States will give ground on the fraught issue of loss-and-damage claims for countries adversely affected by climate change—as the largest historical contributor to climate change, this would open the United States up to untold financial liability. As countries like Pakistan reel under the human and financial costs of major climate-related disasters, diplomatic pressure on the West will grow, to the advantage of non-Western nations like China—which, while currently a major emitter, is not viewed in the Global South as having caused the problem of climate change; from their vantage point, that remains the responsibility primarily of the industrial West.

36. Mastro, "Defense, Deterrence, and the Role of Guam," 44–45.

37. "China Naval Modernization."

3

Geostrategic Competition and U.S., Chinese, and Russian Basing in East Asia

ANDREW YEO
MICHAEL E. O'HANLON[1]

East Asia is one of the few geographic regions in the world where Chinese, Russian, and U.S. military powers have all intersected. In the late nineteenth and early twentieth centuries, China and Russia jockeyed for political influence in Northeast Asia along with Japan. Half a century later, the Soviet Union declared war on Japan toward the end of World War II and dispatched the Red Army from Manchuria toward the Korean Peninsula. During the Korean War, Chinese forces engaged in direct combat against the U.S. military.

Fast-forwarding to the present, the Department of Defense (DOD) now enfolds East Asia within the broader regional framework of the Indo-Pacific. However, significant U.S. forward presence and the likely U.S. obligation to defend allied territory in Northeast Asia with ground forces in some combat scenarios means that the needs and dynamics of great power basing in that region will differ from the maritime theaters of the South Pacific and Indian oceans, where the Chinese People's Liberation Army (PLA) has recently established inroads to overseas basing access.

In this chapter, we address how questions related to basing and force posture remain central to our understanding of geostrategic competition in East Asia. We pay particular attention to U.S. basing requirements in light of intensified U.S.–China competition since the late 2010s and, to a lesser extent, Russian basing interested in its Far East. Recent analysis on U.S. basing calls for strengthening force posture in the Indo-Pacific in response to China's military growth and U.S. vulnerability to Chinese attacks. Although the DOD is aware of this need as evidenced in the 2023 Pacific Deterrence Initiative, some analysts have argued that a significant "say-do gap" exists between strategy and posture;[2] these critics assert that the changes in force posture that the Pentagon recommended in the 2021 Global Posture Review do not fulfill the strategic needs outlined by the most recent Indo-Pacific Strategy as well as the National Security Strategy and the National Defense Strategy.[3] As one expert argues, institutional inertia, bureaucratic politics, budgeting priorities, and a lack of will at the top levels of leadership have prevented the United States from making significant changes to its force posture over the past decade.[4] The fact that the Global Posture Review was completed and released before the other strategies may have contributed to the problem as well since the former could not fully benefit from the guidance or vision of the broader strategic reviews of the Biden administration.

Broadly speaking, the U.S. force posture in the Pacific looks very much like it did in the mid-1990s, with the preponderance of the 100,000-strong U.S. troop presence there concentrated in Japan and South Korea. Since that time, the only major changes involving thousands of forces have been the reduction in the U.S. Army presence in South Korea by about 10,000 in the early 2000s and the more recent gradual shift of about half of the 18,000 U.S. marines on Okinawa to Guam.[5] Decisions to make these changes predated former president Barack Obama's announcement that the administration would "rebalance" or "pivot" its focus to Asia around 2011—a shift in strategy that the Donald Trump and Joe Biden presidencies then reinforced at least in spirit. Put differently, since the rebalance, there has been no major change in U.S. thinking about basing in East Asia except for some modest increases in presence and access in the Philippines, Guam, and Australia.

Long-term geostrategic competition with China may require a rethink in U.S. military posture—that is, its "bases, places, and agreements"—in the broader Indo-Pacific.[6] In East Asia, renewed tensions over the Taiwan Strait and the Korean Peninsula, as well as ongoing concerns about Chinese claims in the South China Sea, have called attention to whether the United States has the adequate capabilities and means to defend its interests and those of its allies. The combination of old Cold War rivalries and new threats within the first island chain thus favors maintaining a substantial U.S. presence in East Asia. However, U.S. bases and capabilities should evolve according to ongoing strategic developments in the region and the broader Indo-Pacific. Fortunately, given the sound foundation of forward presence with which the United States entered this era of great power competition, evolution, not revolution, is what is required.

U.S., CHINESE, AND RUSSIAN BASES IN EAST ASIA

The U.S. Footprint in East Asia

In East Asia, a system of U.S. bilateral alliances underpinned by the constant presence of U.S. bases and troops has helped sustain American power—and deterrence—in the region since the 1950s. Whereas U.S. force presence in Europe experienced a rapid decline in force numbers at the end of the Cold War, troop levels in Asia for much of the 1990s stayed nearly constant. Even during the 2000s at the height of the U.S. troop surge in the Middle East and amid the DOD's global base consolidation and realignment efforts, East Asia experienced only a small, gradual decline in force numbers.[7] The persistence of Cold War–era threats, including heightened conflict on the Korean Peninsula and in the Taiwan Strait, justified sustaining a robust U.S. military presence. Rising concerns regarding China's rapid military growth and its increasing assertiveness in the Indo-Pacific region over the past decade have also provided a strong rationale for sustaining a significant force presence in East Asia.

The heaviest U.S. overseas footprint is concentrated in East Asia with approximately 28,500 troops on the Korean Peninsula,[8] 50,000 on Japan (including Okinawa),[9] and 12,000 on Guam.[10] There is also typically a naval presence in the region with several thousand sailors, sometimes sourced out of the U.S. presence in Japan and sometimes involving additional vessels from Hawaii or the continental United States. The United States has also been gradually growing its rotational presence in the Philippines since the closure of major U.S. bases there in 1992. This included around 600 U.S. military advisers and troops in the southern Philippines to help the Armed Forces of the Philippines combat Islamic extremist groups for much of the

2000s. More recently, through the U.S.-Philippine Enhanced Defense Cooperation Agreement signed in 2014, the Philippines has granted U.S. forces access to several military bases. Amid growing concerns from China, the Philippines under President Ferdinand Marcos Jr. provided the U.S. military access to four additional Philippine base locations in April 2023, increasing the total number of U.S. access to nine bases on the Philippine archipelago.[11]

The U.S. footprint exists for historical reasons, but it is also undergirded by a strong ongoing strategic and political rationale. The United States maintains large permanent forces in South Korea and Japan because of existing alliance commitments and ongoing security threats, including North Korea's continually growing nuclear arsenal. Moreover, U.S. allies and partners in East Asia depend heavily on trade and commerce. A U.S. naval presence is thus critical in protecting sea lines of communication (SLOC) and freedom of navigation in the region. With the potential for major crises in the Taiwan Strait and on the Korean Peninsula, U.S. ground forces stationed in East Asia act as a major deterrent. They are prepared for combat operations and positioned for security force assistance should conflict break out.[12] American forces also provide humanitarian support and disaster relief fostering domestic regional support for U.S. presence. Examples include Operation Tomodachi, when U.S. forces in Japan offered humanitarian assistance following the 2011 earthquake and tsunami in Fukushima, and Operation Damayan in the Philippines, which mobilized U.S. military aircraft to transport food, relief supplies, and workers and airlift more than 5,000 stranded storm survivors following Typhoon Hayan in 2013.[13]

China's Rise and Basing Developments
Until the 2000s, the Chinese Communist Party (CCP) avoided expansionist policies that ran counter to China's strategic narrative of a "peaceful rise."[14] As China's commercial interests and military capabilities have grown, however, so too have its global political ambitions.[15] The CCP's need and desire to protect far-flung assets offer a strong strategic rationale for increasing access to ports and developing a blue-water navy that can operate globally. In its 2019 Defense White Paper, China's Ministry of Defense stated that "the People's Liberation Army (PLA) actively promotes international security and military cooperation and refines relevant mechanisms for protecting China's overseas interests. To address deficiencies in overseas operations and support, it builds 'far-seas' forces, develops overseas logistical facilities, and enhances capabilities in accomplishing diversified military tasks."[16]

A 2022 RAND study states that the deployment of PLA forces abroad "represents a significant change for a country that has for decades resisted foreign basing and access."[17] Up through the post–Cold War period to the 2000s, China frequently referred to its rise as one of "peaceful development." It therefore denied any reports regarding the presence or expansion of an overseas military presence beyond the role of peacekeeping and humanitarian assistance. This may have been the case during the era of Hu Jintao's leadership (2003–2013), when China still remained relatively weak and unable to project power beyond its immediate borders. However, China's interests, objections, and ambitions have since shifted during the past decade under Chinese President Xi Jinping's leadership. China's economic growth and global commercial interests have led the CCP to expand the PLA's operational presence well beyond its borders. To sustain its growth, China will continue to build economic ties and seek new political partners, particularly in developing countries, where Chinese money has been more welcome. Hence, Chinese overseas bases (and basing access) not only protect commercial assets but also serve the useful purpose of forging security partnerships that can ultimately help China shape a regional order more favorable to its own interests.

China's strategic interests now extend to the Middle East, sub-Saharan Africa, and Latin America. From a military standpoint, increased geopolitical rivalry with the United States and its allies has prompted the PLA to explore operational capacity beyond its own waters. However, China must also "prepare for possible contingencies along its periphery."[18] The first island chain, what we loosely interpret as East Asia, represents the zone of China's "core interests," especially from the perspective of PLA combat planning. These core interests include the Taiwan Strait and the South China Sea.

The CCP will do all that it can to prevent the United States and its allies from dominating China's SLOC and undermining China's position on Taiwan. China's development and militarization of seven artificial islands in the South China Sea since 2013 signals the seriousness of its assertive claims within its first island chain. In the past decade, China has deployed YJ-12B and YJ-62 anti-ship cruise missiles in the Spratly and Paracel islands, further reinforced with longer-range missile capabilities from the mainland.[19] The PLA has also installed radar and signals intelligence capabilities on all the islands as well as some airfields. Furthermore, the PLA's deployment of many ballistic as well as cruise missiles that can target Taiwan, Okinawa, and Guam, together with a substantially stronger (and quieter) submarine fleet, changes the military balances in the region in significant ways.

Russia as an Outlier

Great power competition may also motivate China to seek partnerships with other countries, such as Russia, to counterbalance the United States. For example, in July 2023, two Russian warships joined the PLA Navy to conduct joint exercises in the Sea of Japan. The next month, Russian and Chinese ships approached the Aleutian Islands (though in international waters).[20] Russian military bases are positioned in its far east in Vladivostok and the Kamchatka Peninsula. However, maritime disputes over the Kuril Islands with Tokyo have led Moscow to build a more permanent military presence in the area since 2015. This presence includes airstrips, military barracks, and the deployment of surface-to-air missiles in the Northern Territories of the Kuril Island chain.[21]

Despite these recent developments, Russia remains more of a peripheral player in the East Asian theater. Russian forces remain concentrated on its western front and bogged down in the war in Ukraine. Looking longer term, however, the possibility of Chinese–Russian collusion in East Asia may be of greater concern for U.S. military planners.

GEOSTRATEGIC COMPETITION AND OVERSEAS BASES IN EAST ASIA

In light of U.S.–China competition, the United States has sought to strengthen its force posture to make it "more geographically distributed, operationally resilient, and politically sustainable."[22] The Obama administration's strategic rebalance to Asia, followed by the Trump and now Biden administrations' strategies in the Indo-Pacific, have all generally followed this approach to the region. Modest steps to address the changing threat environment in East Asia and the wider Indo-Pacific over the past decade include (1) sending 2,500 marines to Darwin, Australia; (2) rotating littoral combat ships in Singapore; (3) realigning and reducing the number of marines in Okinawa while boosting U.S. posture in Guam; (4) adding prepositioned equipment and strategic assets on the Korean Peninsula while also moving the main U.S. military headquarters and army base in Korea well south of Seoul; (5) gaining greater access to bases, ports, and facilities in Southeast Asia and the Indian Ocean, including in the Philippines and in the Maldives; and (6) re-upping U.S. security commitments to the Pacific Islands.[23]

Two points are worth noting with these incremental steps. First, most of these changes except the Guam relocation involve just hundreds or at most a couple thousand U.S. personnel (or, in the case of Korea, a relatively short move of less than fifty miles from Seoul to Pyeongtaek). Second, recent adjustments in U.S. force posture under the Biden administration are taking place outside of the first island chain in the western Pacific and Indian oceans, where China has made significant progress in building ports, possibly for dual-use civilian–military purposes.

Because of the modest scale of these changes to date, a consensus appears to have emerged among defense experts that despite the strategic priority placed on the Indo-Pacific by the last three U.S. administrations, current U.S. force posture remains insufficient to meet future challenges—especially as China's military footprint begins to grow. However, it is not yet clear whether major U.S. and allied combat forces should be postured in Southeast Asia in anticipation of major operations. China's behavior to date, while of concern, does not yet justify, for example, the deployment of hundreds of surface-to-surface missiles in the Philippine Archipelago or other island nations of the western Pacific region where the U.S. military has inked new security agreements and/or additional basing access.[24] Of course, that could change should the PLA continue to threaten the use of force or actually employ kinetic operations. But pressuring Manila or another foreign capital to accept permanent and large-scale combat capabilities on their national territories could be counterproductive for alliance relations and could also risk an action–reaction spiral with Beijing.[25]

In light of our assessment of Chinese overseas basing, U.S. force posture in East Asia may in fact be broadly correct even if efforts to develop more contingent access arrangements make sense.[26] The United States has a first-mover advantage in East Asia against any potential rival. Dozens of permanent bases and established deployment patterns with up to 100,000 military personnel give the United States considerable military and political leverage in the region. The former Soviet Union never seriously challenged the United States militarily in East Asia. Although China poses a greater threat by virtue of its central location in East Asia and its large economic weight, it too faces obstacles in challenging U.S. military interests in Northeast Asia, where U.S. presence and alliance commitment is heaviest.[27] And in Southeast Asia, America's go-slow approach has so far worked—increasing American options for a crisis or conflict without spooking the neighborhood or enraging the Chinese as to produce a major Chinese effort to develop bases of its own in the region. Force posture concerns in East Asia may therefore be less about insufficient military presence and access and more about force distribution and composition.[28]

The trend lines could, of course, change; indeed, they are already gradually changing. Given the emphasis on strategic competition in the 2022 National Security Strategy, pressure may build for the military to disperse or reduce its force posture in East Asia to strengthen its position in other areas of the Indo-Pacific where China has made recent political-military advancements. Pakistan, Bangladesh, Cambodia, and Myanmar in particular appear ripe for future Chinese overseas basing or basing access.[29]

This change in approach could mean a relocation of resources to the western Pacific or South Pacific, though some of the forces could be sourced from the United States rather than Japan or South Korea. For example, some of the U.S. Marine Corps forces on Okinawa and Guam might be partially relocated, perhaps through small and modest steps in the next decade—not only to Australia, as has already been done, but also to the southern islands of the Ryukyu Islands in Japan, parts of the Philippines, and/or some of the small island nations of the western Pacific. However, for now, big transformations strike us as unnecessary. At least some of these changes should remain dependent on future Chinese behavior and the magnitude of the threat as perceived not only in Washington and Tokyo but also in Seoul, Manila, Singapore, Canberra, New Delhi, and elsewhere. Decisions about military preparations should account for what remains a fluid strategic context. For now, forward access rather than forward basing should remain the main goal in most countries.

Some changes in force mix could make sense for the United States too. Greater dispersal toward Southeast Asia and the Indian Ocean may require a different composition of forces—such as different Marine Corps forces (to include the corps' new littoral combat regiments) and a larger naval presence. This could mean a greater role for the U.S. Coast Guard in countering China's "gray zone" tactics to gain control in the South China Sea and tackle issues of concern to regional actors, including illegal fishing.[30] But again, the change can for now be modest and gradual.

American forces should also move away from depending on mega facilities with huge logistics requirements and reduce their dependence on large, fixed assets, such as long runways or large surface ships home-ported at known locations. Recent thinking from the Marine Corps makes good sense; the corps' Force Design 2030 concept emphasizes leaner logistics, smaller amphibious ships, more accurate firepower (including anti-ship missiles) together with less brute-force traditional capabilities and survivable command and control.[31]

A particularly large strategic hole in U.S. force posture exists in Southeast and South Asia, where basing access agreements remain limited. Here, China has moved out in front of the United States by building commercial ports and potentially fitting them to provide military logistics and intelligence capabilities.[32] Yet, although the United States should be wary of recent Chinese gains in the Indian Ocean and on the Pacific Islands, it is not obvious that a near-term push for a major military response would achieve desirable results. Furthermore, China may also react to any U.S. westward shift, particularly if the shift gives the United States a strategic edge in a Taiwan Strait conflict. Such actions may accelerate a regional security dilemma.[33] Any major shift away from Northeast Asia would raise significant concerns from Japan and South Korea regarding the U.S. commitment to defense and deterrence. Perhaps more important, premature U.S. efforts to prepare for sustained combat operations against China over scenarios that could emerge in places like the South China Sea could push away allies and weaken collaboration with U.S. security partners.

In light of these concerns, one option is to seek basing access rights in Southeast Asia, where the United States has built some political capital in recent years. American access to four additional Philippine base sites in 2023 was welcomed by the Biden administration as the Marcos government sought to restore U.S.–Philippine relations following a period of alliance mismanagement under former Philippine president Rodrigo Duterte (2016–2022).[34] Access to Naval Base Camilo Osias in northern Luzon has drawn particular attention from strategic planners given its relatively close proximity (about 300 miles) to Taiwan. Although Southeast Asian countries prefer not to take steps that would trigger economic punishment or military coercion from China, strengthening defense ties bilaterally (e.g., between Japan and the Philippines and Vietnam and South Korea) or multilaterally (e.g., through the Quadrilateral Security Dialogue and the U.S.–India–France trilateral framework) may ensure stability and open SLOCs, as all of these countries have an incentive to ensure open commerce and freedom of navigation. It also may make sense to base survivable platforms carrying sensors and anti-ship missiles in regions near Taiwan.[35] This could be the best near-term step among the various possible modifications to the U.S. military presence in the Indo-Pacific region that could be accomplished this decade. Right now, the ability of the United States to help defend Taiwan against an amphibious assault relies too much on vulnerable airfields in the region and potentially vulnerable aircraft carriers. Weapons systems placed on forward-stationed unmanned underwater vehicles east of Taiwan or mobile rocket–launchable and parachute-recoverable unmanned aircraft on Okinawa could help deter this contingency. Taiwan, too, needs more survivable platforms to deter this kind of assault.

Holding the Line in East Asia

Crises have often been the impetus for bringing about major change in U.S. force posture.[36] In the case of geostrategic competition and basing in East Asia, however, crises may help reinforce existing postures rather than radically transform them. For example, heightened tensions in the Taiwan Strait following U.S. Speaker of the House Nancy Pelosi's visit to Taipei in August 2022[37] and a sharp uptick in missile tests conducted by North Korea that same year have made it harder for the United States to justify any major changes to force posture in East Asia. American allies such as Japan, South Korea, and the Philippines would also unlikely welcome significant reductions in U.S. force posture in the current security climate. Furthermore, the long-term nature of competition with China will require the United States to maintain a basing hub in Northeast Asia, even if the composition of forces may change.

The U.S. presence in Northeast Asia also deters potential Russian threats in the Far East. Moscow's militarization of the Kuril Islands and maritime disputes over the islands between Japan and Russia could also escalate, potentially requiring greater U.S. military support.[38] Russian defense minister Sergei Shoigu in 2023 stated that the deployment of a coastal defense missile system in Paramushir was partly in response to U.S. efforts to contain Russia and China.[39] Joint exercises between China and Russia in the East China Sea and the Sea of Japan, as witnessed in December 2022[40] and July 2023,[41] respectively, will likely increase in the near future. Ongoing Russian violations of South Korea's air defense identification zone and bomber patrols in the East Sea, the Sea of Japan, and Japanese airspace also remain a problem.[42]

American and allied military innovations should not always emphasize troop numbers and locations but rather should focus on the actual and changing capabilities needed in the region and beyond. Is a large ground force effective against tactical nuclear and missile threats, or is there a need for greater force dispersal? Will autonomous robots and weapons help fend off attacks against a massive swarm of attack drones? In such scenarios, forward basing at large, fixed installations may not prove advantageous relative to multiple points of potential access.[43]

CONCLUSION

The U.S. basing arrangement in the Indo-Pacific region is broadly well calibrated, with a total of about 100,000 military personnel stationed or deployed in the region at any time and an emphasis on presence in Japan, South Korea, and, to a lesser extent, Guam. However, even if these big elements stay largely as they are, adjustments in the overall U.S. presence in the region may be needed in the coming years. These adjustments are related not only to locations and the greater dispersal and hardening of assets but also to combat capabilities, particularly in Southeast Asia and to the way U.S. forces partner with regional friends and allies.

The Indo-Pacific is arguably the most dynamic and strategically important maritime domain in the world with 60 percent of trade and 80 percent of the world's good flowing through the region.[44] American strategic planners may therefore be tempted to shift U.S. force posture to address growing maritime concerns. Meanwhile, Beijing will continue to blunt U.S. influence in a region where it claims itself as the natural hegemon. China's assertiveness and rising military power will thus require the United States to strengthen its own close-in air and maritime surveillance capabilities and missile defense systems. As Jonathan Stevenson argues, "selective and innovative forward deployments" could also enhance the U.S. ability to "deter or compel China."[45]

Any adjustments in force posture, however, must be developed with the assumption that U.S. bases in South Korea and Japan in the next five to ten years will largely remain unchanged. North Korea's growing missile and nuclear program and strengthened military ties between North Korea, Russia, and China undermine peace and stability in Northeast Asia. To maintain alliance credibility and commitment and to support developing security arrangements, such as U.S.–Japan–South Korea trilateral cooperation, the United States will need to retain its current force posture in South Korea and Japan. The Pentagon's focus on integrated deterrence suggests that political and military leaders understand this strategic priority.[46] The Biden administration sees China as the long-term "pacing threat" and Russia as an immediate, acute threat.[47] However, there is also increasing recognition that specific security challenges, such as escalated tensions in the Taiwan Strait and on the Korean Peninsula, are not isolated from great power geopolitical competition. Much more attention needs to be given to linkages between a Taiwan Strait conflict and contingency on the Korean Peninsula. If there is any scenario where North Korean deterrence will be affected by another contingency or failure of deterrence in the Indo-Pacific, it will be on the issue of Taiwan.[48]

Future adjustments in U.S. force posture in East Asia will need to be made, keeping in mind the need for integrated deterrence in the broader Indo-Pacific. American force posture in East Asia will continue to provide deterrence on a range of security challenges in the region. But for forces to be "combat credible" and "deter aggression in the face of the pacing threat from China and the acute threat from Russia," the United States may need to consider dispersing some of its base assets to reduce vulnerabilities against long-range precision missile strikes.[49] Here Washington might take advantage of its network of allies and partners to look for additional basing access, such as the U.S. Air Force's agile combat employment—an operational concept that relies less on large, permanent bases and more on launching and maintaining aircraft from dispersed forward operating locations "in concert with allies and partners" for projecting combat power.[50] For long-term geostrategic competition with China, U.S. force posture in East Asia may be largely right sized, but the capabilities and configuration may need adjustments as China strengthens its capabilities and gains a stronger basing foothold.

NOTES

1. We thank Isaac Kardon and Joshua White for valuable comments on earlier drafts as well as participants of the "Great Power Competition and Overseas Basing" workshop hosted by the Brookings Institution. We also thank Hanna Foreman for her valuable research assistance.

2. Becca Wasser, "The Unmet Promise of the Global Posture Review," *War on the Rocks*, December 30, 2021, https://warontherocks.com/2021/12/the-unmet-promise-of-the-global-posture-review.

3. "DoD Concludes 2021 Global Posture Review," U.S. Department of Defense, November 29, 2021, https://www.defense.gov/News/Releases/Release/Article/2855801/dod-concludes-2021-global-posture-review.

4. Stacie L. Pettyjohn, "Spiking the Problem: Developing a Resilient Posture in the Indo-Pacific with Passive Defensives," *War on the Rocks*, January 10, 2022,

https://warontherocks.com/2022/01/spiking-the-problem-developing-a-resilient-posture-in-the-indo-pacific-with-passive-defenses.

5. Chang-hee Nam, "Relocating the U.S. Forces in South Korea: Strained Alliance, Emerging Partnership in the Changing Defense Posture," *Asian Survey* 46, no. 4 (2006): 615–31; Alie Peter Neil Galeon, "US Base in Guam 50% Complete for 2024 Marine Transfer," *The Defense Post*, December 16, 2022, https://www.thedefensepost.com/2022/12/16/us-marine-guam-transfer. The process of restructuring the U.S. Marine Corps presence in the Pacific remains ongoing due to interminable delays in relocating a Marine Corps airfield from southern to central Okinawa.

6. Chris Dougherty, "Don't Trust the Process: Moving from Words to Actions on the Indo-Pacific Posture," *War on the Rocks*, February 23, 2022, https://warontherocks.com/2022/02/dont-trust-the-process-moving-from-words-to-actions-on-the-indo-pacific-posture.

7. The average number of U.S. troops in Asia from 1993 to 2001 is 79,031. Although numbers dipped to around 69,000 from 2002 to 2014, they rebounded to 77,261 in 2015. See Timothy Kane, "The Decline of American Engagement: Patterns in U.S. Troop Deployments," Hoover Institution, January 2016, 5, https://www.hoover.org/research/decline-american-engagement-patterns-us-troop-deployments.

8. Emma Chanlett-Avery and Caitlin Campbell, "U.S.-South Korea Alliance: Issues for Congress," Congressional Research Service, March 2022, https://crsreports.congress.gov/product/pdf/IF/IF11388.

9. Emma Chanlett-Avery, Christopher T. Mann, and Joshua A. Williams, "U.S. Military Presence on Okinawa and Realignment to Guam," Congressional Research Service, April 2019, https://crsreports.congress.gov/product/pdf/IF/IF10672/3.

10. "Military and Civilian Personnel by Service/Agency by State/County," U.S. Department of Defense, September 2022, https://dwp.dmdc.osd.mil/dwp/api/download?fileName=DMDC_Website_Location_Report_2209.xlsx&groupName=milRegionCountry.

11. Karen Lema, "Philippines Reveals Locations of 4 New Strategic Sites for U.S. Military Pact," Reuters, April 3, 2023, https://www.reuters.com/world/asia-pacific/philippines-reveals-locations-4-new-strategic-sites-us-military-pact-2023-04-03. The four locations include Camilo Osias navy base and Lal-lo airport in Cagayan province, Camp Melchor Dela Cruz in Isabela province, and the island of Balabac off Palawan.

12. Andrew Feickert, "U.S. Ground Forces in the Indo-Pacific: Background and Issues for Congress," Congressional Research Service, August 2022, 14, https://crsreports.congress.gov/product/pdf/R/R47096.

13. "Fact Sheet: U.S. Response to Typhoon Haiyan," White House, Office of the Press Secretary, November 19, 2013, https://obamawhitehouse.archives.gov/the-press-office/2013/11/19/fact-sheet-us-response-typhoon-haiyan.

14. Rush Doshi, *The Long Game: China's Grand Strategy to Displace American Order* (New York: Oxford University Press, 2021).

15. Leah Dreyfuss and Mara Karlin, "All That Xi Wants: China Attempts to Ace Bases Overseas," Brookings Institution, September 2019, https://www.brookings.edu/research/all-that-xi-wants-china-attempts-to-ace-bases-overseas; Isaac B. Kardon, "China's Global Maritime Access: Alternatives to Overseas Military Bases in the Twenty-First Century," *Security Studies* 31, no. 5 (2022): 1–32, https://www.tandfonline.com/doi/abs/10.1080/09636412.2022.2137429?journalCode=fsst20.

16. "China's National Defense in the New Era," Ministry of National Defense of the People's Republic of China, July 24, 2019, http://eng.mod.gov.cn/news/2019-07/24/content_4846443.htm.

17. Stephen Watts, Scott Boston, Pauline Moore, Cristina L. Garafola, and Center Arroyo, "Implications of a Global People's Liberation Army: Historical Lessons for Responding to China's Long-Term Global Basing Ambitions," RAND Corporation, 2022, 7, https://www.rand.org/pubs/research_reports/RRA1496-3.html.

18. Watts et al., "Implications of a Global People's Liberation Army," 8.

19. Gregory Poling, "The Conventional Wisdom on China's Island Bases Is Dangerously Wrong," *War on the Rocks*, January 10, 2020, https://warontherocks.com/2020/01/the-conventional-wisdom-on-chinas-island-bases-is-dangerously-wrong.

20. Dzirhan Mahadzir, "Russian, Chinese Warships Prepare for Joint Pacific Naval Exercises, *USNI News*, July 2023, https://news.usni.org/2023/07/10/russian-chinese-warships-prepare-for-joint-pacific-naval-exercises.

21. Ike Barrash, "Russia's Militarization of the Kuril Islands," Center for Strategic and International Studies, September 27, 2022, https://www.csis.org/blogs/new-perspectives-asia/russias-militarization-kuril-islands.

22. Ash Carter, "The Rebalance and Asia-Pacific Security," *Foreign Affairs*, November/December 2016, https://www.foreignaffairs.com/articles/united-states/2016-10-17/rebalance-and-asia-pacific-security.

23. Andrew Feickert, "U.S. Ground Forces in the Indo-Pacific," 12–13; Dreyfuss and Karlin, "All That Xi Wants."

24. This counters the views of other basing scholars, such as Jonathan Stevenson, who suggests placing mobile surface-to-surface precision-strike ballistic missiles, at least on a rotational basis, in the Philippines to "put at risk" Chinese military assets in the South China Sea. See Jonathan Stevenson, *Overseas Bases and US Strategy: Optimising America's Military Footprint* (Abingdon: Routledge, 2022), 73.

25. On resistance to U.S. bases in the Philippines, see Andrew Yeo, *Activists, Alliances, and Anti-U.S. Base Protests* (New York: Cambridge University Press, 2011).

26. Michael O'Hanlon, "Evolving the U.S. Base Structure in the Indo-Pacific," Brookings Institution, 2020, 3, https://www.brookings.edu/wpcontent/uploads/2020/11/FP_20201210_indo_pacific_ohanlon.pdf.

27. It is partly for this reason that China began turning its attention westward, using the Belt and Road Initiative to gain an economic foothold in Central Asia, Southeast Asia, South Asia, and beyond. It is easier for China to establish its "string of pearls" along the Indian Ocean to the Middle East in the absence of significant U.S. presence.

28. As one participant commented in the "Great Power Competition and Overseas Basing" workshop hosted by the Brookings Institution, concentrated land forces may not be immediately useful in any contingencies involving combat with China. As such, the United States may need to consider decentralizing or dispersing hubs to produce "distributed lethality" and effectively deter Chinese aggression in Taiwan or the South China Sea in the long term.

29. Cristina L. Garafola, Stephen Watts, and Kristin Leuschner, *China's Global Basing Ambitions: Defense Implications for the United States* (Santa Monica, CA: RAND Corporation, 2022).

30. Farrah Tomazin, "US to Deploy Coast Guard to Indo-Pacific in the Face of China's Tise," *Sydney Morning Herald*, May 13, 2022, https://www.smh.com.au/world/north-america/us-to-deploy-coast-guard-to-indo-pacific-in-bid-to-counter-china-s-rise-20220513-p5akys.html; Nguyen The Phuong, "The U.S. Coast Guard in the South China Sea: A Vietnamese Perspective," Institute for Southeast Asian Studies, October 6, 2022, https://www.iseas.edu.sg/articles-commentaries/iseas-perspective/2022-98-the-u-s-coast-guard-in-the-south-china-sea-a-vietnamese-perspective-by-nguyen-the-phuong.

31. United States Marine Corps, "Force Design 2030: Annual Update," June 2023, https://www.marines.mil/Portals/1/Docs/Force_Design_2030_Annual_Update_June_2023.pdf.

32. Isaac B. Kardon and Wendy Leutert, "Pier Competitor: China's Power Position in Global Ports," *International Security* 46, no. 4 (2022), 10, https://muse.jhu.edu/article/855437.

33. Van Jackson, "America's Indo-Pacific Folly: Adding New Commitments in Asia Will Only Invite Disaster," *Foreign Affairs*, March 12, 2021, https://www.foreignaffairs.com/articles/asia/2021-03-12/americas-indo-pacific-folly.

34. Cliff Venzon, "Philippines to Accelerate U.S. Defense Deal on Base Access," *Nikkei Asia*, November 15, 2022, https://asia.nikkei.com/Politics/International-relations/Philippines-to-accelerate-U.S.-defense-deal-on-base-access.

35. David Ochmanek and Michael O'Hanlon, "Here's the Strategy to Prevent China from Taking Taiwan," *The Hill*, December 8, 2021, https://thehill.com/opinion/national-security/584370-heres-the-strategy-to-prevent-china-from-taking-taiwan.

36. Stacie L. Pettyjohn and Alan J. Vick, "The Posture Triangle: A New Framework for U.S. Air Force Global Presence," Rand Corporation, 2013, https://www.rand.org/pubs/research_reports/RR402.html.

37. Huizhong Wu, Eileen Ng, and Lisa Mascaro, "US House Speaker Pelosi Arrives in Taiwan Defying Beijing," Associated Press, August 2, 2022, https://apnews.com/article/china-asia-beijing-malaysia-a5a5acc39151c99b1b4c2d69e67b133.

38. Barrash, "Russia's Militarization of the Kuril Islands."

39. "Russia Boosts Defences Near Japan, Accuses US of Expanding Asia-Pacific Presence," Reuters, March 22, 2023, https://www.reuters.com/world/russia-boosts-defences-near-japan-accuses-us-expanding-asia-pacific-presence-2023-03-22.

40. "Russia and China Hold Naval Drills, Practise Submarine Capture," Reuters, December 28, 2022, https://www.reuters.com/world/russia-china-hold-naval-drills-practise-submarine-capture-2022-12-28.

41. Kathrin Hille, "China and Russia Step Up Military Co-operation on Japan's Doorstep," *Financial Times*, July 18, 2023, https://www.ft.com/content/3a6f7efe-b064-45a7-8125-259a51df8a20.

42. Josh Smith and Hyonhee Shin, "S.Korea Scrambles Jets after Chinese, Russian Warplanes Enter Air Defence Zone," Reuters, May 24, 2022, https://www.reuters.com/world/asia-pacific/skorea-scrambles-jets-after-chinese-russian-warplanes-enter-air-defence-zone-2022-05-24.

43. New security developments in space, cyberspace, and critical and emerging technologies may also require a new way of thinking about force posture in the next decade.

44. Stevenson, *Overseas Bases and US Strategy*, 43.

45. Stevenson, *Overseas Bases and US Strategy*, 73.

46. As stated in the 2022 U.S. National Defense Strategy, integrated deterrence entails "working seamlessly across warfighting domains, the spectrum of conflict, all instruments of U.S. national power, and our network of alliances and partnerships." See Department of Defense, "National Defense Strategy," October 2022, https://www.defense.gov/News/News-Stories/Article/Article/3202438/dod-releases-national-defense-strategy-missile-defense-nuclear-posture-reviews.

47. "National Security Strategy," White House, October 12, 2022, https://www.whitehouse.gov/wp-content/uploads/2022/10/Biden-Harris-Administrations-National-Security-Strategy-10.2022.pdf.

48. Andrew Yeo, "Linkages between North Korean Nuclear Deterrence on the Korean Peninsula and Integrated Deterrence in the Indo-Pacific Region," in conference proceedings prepared for the Asian Leadership Conference, KRINS-Brookings Panel, Korea Research Institute of National Strategy, Seoul, May 17, 2023.

49. David Vergun, "Official Says Integrated Deterrence Key to National Defense Strategy," *DOD News*, December 6, 2022, https://www.defense.gov/News/News-Stories/Article/Article/3237769/official-says-integrated-deterrence-key-to-national-defense-strategy.

50. Sandeep Mulgund, "Command and Control for Agile Combat Employment," *Wild Blue Yonder*, August 30, 2021, https://www.airuniversity.af.edu/Wild-Blue-Yonder/Article-Display/Article/2753756/command-and-control-for-agile-combat-employment.

4

Military Basing and Access in the Indian Ocean Region

Strategic Asymmetries among the Major Powers

ISAAC KARDON

The sea-lanes crossing the Indian Ocean trace the maritime strategic axis of Asia. They connect the Atlantic Ocean and Mediterranean Sea to the Pacific Ocean and South China Sea, establishing the strategically vital "rimland" position around much of the Eurasian landmass.[1] This wide maritime common washes the distant shores of South and East Africa, the Middle East, and South and Southeast Asia, which together make up the Indian Ocean region (IOR). The IOR comprises not only the littoral states from South Africa to Australia but also six island nations and several French, British, and Australian territories scattered across the southern and eastern Indian Ocean.

The strategic interests of the major powers vary considerably across these different arenas, with correspondingly different requirements for military basing and access. All, however, contend with the same geostrategic reality: access and maneuver across the Indian Ocean are necessary to meet military objectives in any of its subregions—which include the Middle East and Persian Gulf, the Bay of Bengal, and the Horn of Africa. Strategic objectives vary quite considerably from state to state, but each must contend in the

Figure 4.1. Indian Ocean Maritime Zones and Choke Points.

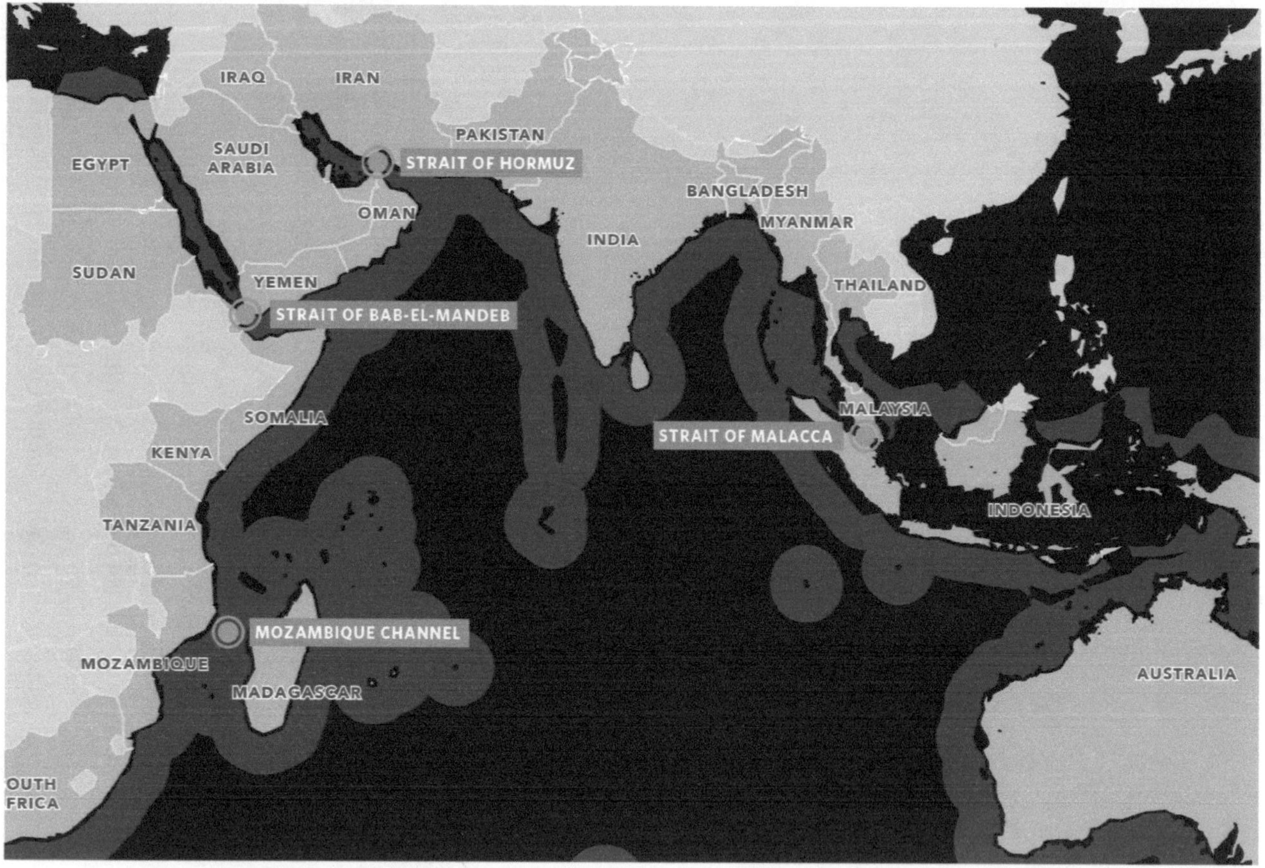

"The Strategic Importance of the Indian Ocean," Carnegie Endowment for International Peace, https://carnegieendowment.org/publications/interactive/indian-ocean-map-phase-2/.

first place with the same narrow choke points and arcing littorals that both enable and constrict flows of cargo, people, vessels, and information. Figure 4.1 illustrates the basic maritime contours of the region and highlights the choke points that define the region's strategic geography.

This chapter analyzes competitive dynamics among the major powers competing for military bases and access points in the IOR. First, it surveys the region's geography, observing the ways its maritime layout structures the basic security environment. Next, it assesses the major powers' distinct interests in the theater, focusing on the force postures and strategic interactions among the United States, the People's Republic of China (PRC), India, Australia, and France as they pursue varied military basing and access objectives in the IOR. Finally, it highlights the central competitive dynamics among these powers, emphasizing the asymmetry in Chinese and U.S. military capabilities and strategic objectives in the region. This asymmetry shows the quite distinct postures of U.S. and Chinese forces, the mix of military and commercial facilities they employ, and the economic and defense relationships that each state has cultivated across the region.

THE STRATEGIC GEOGRAPHY OF THE IOR

The Indian Ocean's maritime space is more integrated than the disparate continental subregions it connects.[2] Its main characteristic is a long, longitudinal span across the southern flank of Eurasia bisected in its northern sector by the Indian subcontinent. Its northern tier traces several distinct marginal seas: the Gulf of Aden, the Arabian Sea, the Gulf of Oman, the Persian Gulf, the Bay of Bengal, and the Andaman Sea. The vast southern tier, by contrast, is open ocean—save for the far-flung territories of the French Southern and Antarctic Lands, Australia's Indian Ocean Territories, and the British Indian Ocean Territories of the Chagos Archipelago, notably including the critical strategic hub at Diego Garcia.[3]

From a military basing and access standpoint, the IOR is constricted by key choke points at its eastern and western approaches and to its key gulfs and bays. The flow and positioning of any naval fleet in the region will be determined in large part by whomever controls and monitors these narrow access corridors. These are the efficient routes for navigation and power projection, but they also create vulnerabilities to interdiction and thus present themselves as the focal point in security competition for facilities and security partnerships. The most significant among these are the following.

Bab-el-Mandeb Strait–Red Sea–Suez Canal

This connected set of waterways creates the northwesterly access point to the IOR. It runs from the Mediterranean through Suez and exits the Red Sea via the Bab-el-Mandeb at the Horn of Africa. It is the dominant route for trade between Europe and Asia and has long been treated as a strategic waterway by external powers that continue to pursue access to ports and bases in the Red Sea and eastern Mediterranean. The *Ever Given* blockage in the canal in the spring of 2021 illustrated the vital economic importance of this series of choke points for global trade and reminded observers of the extraordinary strategic impact that such a constriction could impose if it were to happen under wartime conditions.[4]

Malacca–Sunda–Makassar–Lombok–Ombai–Wetar–Torres Strait

The short hyphen in the middle of "Indo-Pacific" is misleading. It elides the long, punctuated nature of the sea-lanes connecting these two oceans. The ostensible pivot between the Indian and Pacific oceans is actually a constricting complex of straits and channels created by the Malay Peninsula, the Indonesian archipelago, and Australia. Defining the far east of the Indian Ocean basin, these land features channelize all of the sea-lanes to and from East Asia and the Pacific into a small number of narrow tracks. This has implications for trade and military flows and is especially salient on questions of energy security. The so-called Malacca Dilemma—Beijing's anxiety that the PRC's energy and other vital commodity flows from the IOR can be interdicted by hostile forces—is one acute political problem created by this regional geographic reality.[5]

Strait of Hormuz–Gulf of Oman

As the sole maritime entrance to the Persian Gulf and its vast hydrocarbon wealth, the Strait of Hormuz (accessed via the Gulf of Oman) is a uniquely vulnerable and consequential choke point. Dominated by Iran's long coastline along its northern tier and the Arabian peninsula along the south, it is a site of acute interest for all major powers but with access limited only to those states contiguous to it or with agreements to position themselves in those countries. The Strait of Hormuz and the Persian Gulf have been and are likely to remain points of regional contestation and geostrategic competition. Yet each of the major powers in the region has different priorities when it comes to securing access to the Persian Gulf. In the past, this included supporting combat operations in Afghanistan and Iraq (the

United States) and consolidating transport infrastructure and establishing shipping and supply lines to the region (China).

MILITARY POSTURES AND BASING INTERESTS IN THE IOR

Each of the major powers is heavily invested in protecting its interests in the IOR, but each has allocated its investments in different ways when it comes to military basing and access. Geography, as ever, establishes the primary conditions for these strategic decisions: distant powers (e.g., the United States, the United Kingdom, and France) require installations on foreign soil to sustain operations of any scale in the region. Local powers (e.g., India, Iran, the Gulf states, and Australia) are resident and may project power in the region from their home territories. China lies somewhere in between due to its contiguity to several IOR nations (i.e., India, Pakistan, and Myanmar) but is also limited by the circuitous maritime transits required to access the region. Before turning to their competitive dynamics, some baseline analysis of each major player's interests and posture will establish the geostrategic setting.

United States

America's global alliance commitments and long-standing defense policy require the United States joint force to project combat power in every world region. In practice, this has meant a significant military footprint in the IOR, concentrated especially in the greater Middle East, where the U.S. military has been deployed in combat operations nearly continuously since the end of the Cold War. With dedicated facilities in Bahrain, Qatar, the United Arab Emirates (UAE), Oman, Djibouti, and elsewhere, forward-deployed and rotational U.S. forces field significant air, land, sea, and space capabilities in the western Indian Ocean.

Substantially less U.S. force is deployed to the southern and eastern subregions, with two notable exceptions. The joint U.S.–U.K. installation at Diego Garcia provides logistical and communications support to U.S. operational forces deployed forward in the IOR and has been indispensable for virtually all U.S. missions in the region since the 1970s.[6] At the region's easternmost point, the U.S. Navy also has a rotational presence for an aircraft carrier and littoral combat ships at Singapore's Changi Naval Base (though these are Seventh Fleet assets that operate mainly in the Pacific).

The basic mission set for which bases are required has varied over the years, with the greater Middle East consuming the majority of U.S. effort and resources in the early part of the twenty-first century. Higher present priorities placed on deterring Iran in the region and competing with China globally have placed U.S. basing needs in flux.

China

Compared to the U.S. posture in the region, China is (and will likely remain) "underweight" on military basing—even as it doggedly pursues agreements and installations across the IOR. With neither legacy force deployments nor continuous security commitments to allies or partners in the region, China's main line of effort has been to build its economic access to regional markets and resources. Beijing's threat perceptions, however, have changed in a new era of great power strategic competition.

During China's now closed "period of strategic opportunity,"[7] Beijing relied almost exclusively on the United States and its maritime partners to invest in the regional security and stability necessary to sustain essential commodity shipments flowing back to the mainland.[8] Beijing now perceives a significantly greater threat from the United States and is meanwhile more capable of protecting its own overseas interests. Its leaders are therefore making concerted efforts to establish a basing and logistics network in the region.

The People's Liberation Army (PLA) base at Djibouti is the first of its type for China and probably not the last. However, this lone outpost on the far western edge of the theater lies at the end of tenuous external lines. With no mutual support from other dedicated Chinese military facilities in the region, the Djibouti base is isolated and operationally quite limited. As currently configured, the "Djibouti overseas support base" may well be best suited for the counter-piracy, peacekeeping, humanitarian assistance, disaster relief, and other noncombat missions that PRC spokespeople somewhat implausibly suggest are its sole intended purposes.[9]

China's economic dependence on foreign trade across vulnerable IOR sea-lanes creates a security challenge for its leadership. Globalization entails some level of vulnerability for Chinese assets and citizens abroad and makes protection of the sea-lanes connecting them back to the Chinese mainland a necessity. Dispersed in resource-rich but stability-challenged locales, China's "overseas interests" face persistent risk of disruption, crisis, and a range of threats from natural disasters to civil war.[10] Perhaps most pressing, greater military competition or outright conflict with the United States makes Chinese leadership intent on insulating their critical transportation channels from threat of interdiction and sanction.

Lacking a network of bases from which to operate forward in the region, China's growing naval operations have made extensive use of PRC-owned and -operated commercial facilities across the IOR.[11] For the PLA Navy (PLAN), this means developing the capabilities and installations necessary to meet a requirement to provide "open seas protection" in the "far seas."[12] The priority theater for this mission involves the sea lines of communication (SLOCs) connecting East Asia to the western Indian Ocean and East Africa. This "maritime lifeline" conveys existentially important maritime trade (especially natural resources) to the PRC's population-rich, resource-poor eastern seaboard.[13] For PLAN leadership, this entails a requirement to develop a force posture and fleet suited to defend IOR sea-lanes and project regional power sufficient to protect Chinese assets. Lacking a legacy network of bases, however, China has leveraged an existing network of some twenty-five port assets across the region to make up for some of the logistical challenges of operating out of area in the IOR.[14]

India

The Indian subcontinent is the eponymous and most conspicuous feature in the IOR. Bisecting the northern Indian Ocean, it quite literally shapes the theater. India is the regional power of most consequence in the IOR and is actively building itself into a "net security provider" in the region. It is doing so in close cooperation with Quadrilateral Security Dialogue ("Quad") nations—the United States, Australia, and Japan—as well as with France and other maritime partners.[15] India is also increasingly cooperative and collaborative—if nonaligned—with a range of U.S. efforts to balance China.

India's military presence and capability in the major littoral areas of the IOR are considerable due to a significant geographic "home field advantage" and deep-seated influence in regional states.[16] Beyond the concentrated Indian forces on the subcontinent, Port Blair is India's easternmost and only tri-service theater command, located in the Andaman and Nicobar Islands. With a capable force proximate to the Strait of Malacca, India expresses its security interests into the Southeast Asian region and positions itself to better observe and address growing PLA activity into the Indian Ocean.

India has watched keenly as China has dramatically expanded its operational repertoire in the IOR over the course of the past decade. The PLA's carrier program, its submarine deployments, and its growing sophistication on regional logistics and intelligence, along with many other steady advances in capability and capacity, have long been close concerns of the

Indian naval and defense community. Fatal clashes with PLA forces at Galwan in the summer of 2020, however, have brought a more adversarial stance toward China into mainstream Indian foreign and even economic policy discourse. Still, the degree to which India has been willing to participate in more security-oriented aspects of the Quad or any outright military balancing against China is limited by India's sense of its national interest.[17] In particular, Indian leaders are constrained by caution about provoking unnecessary hostile PRC reactions, tempered by respect for the long-term challenge of contending with the economic leader in the region, a nuclear power that will maintain a permanent position on India's northern boundary—and, increasingly, along its maritime periphery.

Australia

At the eastern end of the Indian Ocean, Australia is one of only two naturally "Indo-Pacific" nations (alongside Indonesia). The Indian Ocean theater is thus a direct and increasingly high Australian priority, particularly when it comes to China and cooperation with Quad partners. In recent years, burgeoning Australia–India ties under the banner of the Quad framework have brought significant Australian attention to a range of strategic IOR issues in particularly close coordination with India.[18] Meanwhile, Australia's "Indian ocean island step-up" to the South Pacific mirrors and complements India's outreach to the vitally important island nations of the region.[19] The growing comity and cooperation between these two resident IOR nations is one of the most notable regional obstacles to Chinese basing efforts.

France

French territories across the western and southern Indian Ocean make it a resident power in the region of a sort. Its renewed attention to the "Indo-Pacific" as a "priority for France" includes a planned deployment of the *Charles de Gaulle* carrier strike group in the Indian Ocean to complement a growing range of naval and maritime security operations from France's scattered island territories, which provide points d'appui for sophisticated French forces to contribute critical capacity, maritime domain awareness, and diplomatic weight toward regional security cooperation.[20]

United Kingdom

The United Kingdom is a major player in the wider European "Indo-Pacific tilt."[21] The Australia–U.K.–U.S. (AUKUS) framework is an important emerging vector of U.K. security interest in the region. Even with limited capacity in this distant theater, the United Kingdom is fundamentally important to Indian Ocean basing considerations because it hosts the vital American logistics support base at Diego Garcia. This arrangement has not yet been explicitly challenged in Britain's sovereignty dispute with Mauritius, but access must be carefully attended and managed.

COMPETITIVE BASING DYNAMICS AND IMPLICATIONS FOR U.S. POLICY

Surveying the major powers' basing interests and activities in the IOR, a striking asymmetry is laid bare. On one side is the United States, with a robust basing network concentrated in the western Indian Ocean. American power is embedded within a network of alliances and partnerships and has routinely been employed in combat and noncombat joint operations across the region. On the other side of the picture is China, leading with its economic engagement and lagging with its military force posture. That these are not symmetrically competitive positions is the basic basing dynamic that should inform future efforts to shore up U.S. interests in the IOR. Four particular insights emerge from this way of viewing geostrategy in the IOR:

1. *Sheer economic heft produces China's primary competitive edge in the region; U.S. efforts must offset regional states' forgone gains from trade and investment with the PRC with something more than just military capability.* Even as it seeks basing and other access arrangements, China does so in pursuit of a relatively modest (if rapidly evolving) set of military objectives. These revolve around protecting seaborne trade and sustaining China's overall *economic* access to the region. China's economic weight is its primary power instrument in the region and is likely to remain effective as a carrot to reward those willing to cooperate; it is always handy as a stick to deny market access or otherwise divert trade and investment flows.[22]

   Any successful U.S.-led effort to counter PLA military inroads in the IOR must therefore provide explicit value to offset forgone economic gains from trade with China. In defense partnerships, this will mean exploring new areas of arms sales, technology sharing, security assistance, military exercises, and naval interoperability. But these defense partnerships are only part of the problem motivating regional states, so these initiatives will need to be nested in broader economic and diplomatic outreach.

By contrast to the U.S. defense-forward posture in the region, China will likely remain competitive in theater largely on the strength of its status as the leading IOR trading nation. Beijing leverages trade flows as a source of considerable leverage in its relations. By cultivating close commercial and diplomatic ties with nations across the IOR, China positions itself to keep these states "onsides" in the event of greater strife and efforts to sanction or interdict PRC trade across the IOR. As such, even U.S. allies and partners show varied levels of comfort in joining U.S. efforts to overtly balance China. This regional ambivalence needs to be priced in and offset by countervailing (if not equivalent) economic incentives from the United States.

As a rule, states are not interested in alienating China as an economic partner. There is a major payoff for U.S. policy in calibrating efforts to engage the right nations in the right initiatives that do not exceed their appetites for competing with China. Various permutations of India, Australia, France, the United Kingdom, and Japan constitute a core of strong states with capable navies and significant—but far from complete—overlap in their threat perceptions of China. Multilateral maritime security initiatives (on counter-piracy, sea-lane protection, maritime domain awareness, and so on) will not overtly counter China's military basing and access across the IOR, but they will build a constituency of states cooperating toward a more secure region. Growing PLA capabilities and activities will look even more conspicuous against the backdrop of a robust regional maritime security architecture.

2. *China provides regime security for like-minded authoritarian rulers; it is not offering an alternative to U.S.-provided regional security.* There is no law dictating that China must inevitably fill a vacuum left by the disengaging U.S. forces in the region. Even stipulating that the U.S. role as regional security provider is waning, there is little appetite among regional states for simply substituting China in place of the United States. Not only does China lack the security interests, capabilities, and military relationships in the region that would be required to play that external balancing role, but it is evidently pursuing an alternative, asymmetric set of strategic objectives. The basing and access requirements for "far seas protection" (e.g., noncombatant evacuation, convoy, and anti-piracy operations) are relatively modest in comparison to those

involved in forward power projection, which include diverse joint strike packages, amphibious capabilities, and all manner of other combat operations. China's lower requirements reflect its strategic limitations. They are in part a result of Beijing's reluctance to engage militarily overseas unless discrete PRC assets are directly threatened. As currently practiced, Chinese foreign policy has little appetite for direct military risks in the region's roiling conflicts. PLA forces will likely remain well removed from the kinetic fray in the unfolding conflict in Gaza. Any such commitment would be a radical departure from the policy line and strategy centered on securing access to markets and resources, not intervening in distant conflicts.

By contrast to the U.S. role as a long-term external security provider in the IOR, China's nascent security partnerships involve no countervailing Chinese offer to provide military aid to allies in distress, to deter hostile actors, or to secure the free flow of hydrocarbons. Instead, the PRC explicitly seeks to protect certain narrowly defined equities: its citizens, its economic assets, and its sea lines of communication. As such, it engages in largely transactional military relationships—and not only or even especially with counterpart militaries but with security agencies and police forces in countries that in many cases see China's draconian surveillance and social control as a great accomplishment in governance rather than as an infringement of human rights and civil liberties.[23] China's exports of surveillance, policing, and other social control–oriented technologies are China's differentiated "great power public good" on offer to the region. On balance, these may help autocrats stay in power and diminish human rights for their subjects.[24] However unpalatable this may be, PRC-provided *regime* security is not necessarily in direct competition with U.S.-provided *regional* security.

3. *The "Djibouti model" is probably not a template for future PLA bases in the IOR.* The establishment of the first overseas PLA base at Djibouti in 2017 generated an expectation of future Chinese bases across the IOR. Nearly seven years on, the lack of any additional bases is a telling indication of the rare opportunity presented by one small but highly permissive host nation on the Horn of Africa. The base became a reality as the result of a rare alignment of several stars: the UN authorization for a multilateral anti-piracy mission aligned perfectly with Djibouti's existing status as a multilateral military hub, hosting not only U.S. and European forces but even Japan's first overseas base. Under general cir-

cumstances of lesser competitive pressure and foreign scrutiny on China's military activities abroad in the period 2015–2017, this was truly a rare and perhaps non-replicable opportunity.[25]

Chinese officials have reportedly sought agreements to build and operate additional military facilities in the region, with the most advanced negotiations evidently under way in the UAE.[26] Beijing may yet succeed on the strength of its tremendous economic bargaining leverage, but to do so, it will have to overcome concerted efforts by an increasingly attentive United States that still wields substantial military and political influence with allies and partners across the region. These relationships narrow the field for Chinese efforts to obtain further military access to facilities in the region.

4. *The different strategic circumstances reigning in the IOR make the "Indo" in "Indo-Pacific" appear ill-calibrated to the geostrategic demands of the theater.* The "free and open Indo-Pacific" framework championed by the United States and Japan has understandably skewed toward the western Pacific, the theater where open conflict with China is most conceivable. This may well be an appropriate strategic emphasis but requires further thought on what links these two great oceans. From the PRC perspective, surveying "the two oceans" that most affect its destiny, the Indian Ocean is the logistical rear. In the event of conflict in the Pacific, the IOR is the theater through which Beijing will need to protect critical flows of fuel, food, and other vital commodities for the war effort. Defending these sea-lanes is thus the essential "strategic task" for the PLA in the Indian Ocean, where it is not postured to fight an offensive campaign.

Some military capability—and thus basing and access—is necessary for China to secure flows of vital resources to the mainland in support of efforts in the western Pacific, the primary war-fighting theater. Degrading Beijing's confidence that a major campaign in the western Pacific could be sustained from Indian Ocean supply lines for a protracted period will enhance deterrence. One means toward this end is enhanced regional maritime security cooperation, already in progress under the auspices of the Quad (plus), AUKUS, India–Israel–U.S.–UAE (I2U2), India–France, and several other existing or aspirational partnerships among various configurations of regional actors. These are not exercises in standing up a military or naval force to counter a rising China but rather investments in building a cooperative, multilateral IOR.

All told, surveying the region's maritime geography offers a framework for more clearly understanding the strategic threats and opportunities that inexorably draw the major powers to the IOR. This geostrategic competition is marked by the clear asymmetries in the objectives for which the various powers are competing. Chinese maritime power is indeed disruptive, and its basing and access arrangements are changing the strategic calculus for regional players. However, the robust economic foundations of China's access to the region should give caution to those who expect a purely military counterbalance to be effective.

NOTES

1. This term derives from Nicholas Spykman, whose geographic analysis prioritized the maritime "rimland" as the dominant strategic position in Eurasia. He considered the South China Sea as the "Asiatic Mediterranean," the central medium of trade, communication, and strategic power projection on the eastern end of Eurasia, balanced by the Mediterranean on the western end. See Nicholas J. Spykman, *The Geography of the Peace* (New York: Harcourt, Brace, 1944), 40–41, 54–55; for a more recent analysis in this vein, see Geoffrey Gresh, *To Rule Eurasia's Waves: The New Great Power Competition at Sea* (New Haven, CT: Yale University Press, 2020); see also Robert S. Ross, "The Geography of the Peace," *International Security* 23, no. 4 (1999), 81–118.

2. *China's Influence in South and Central Asia, Panel IV—Maritime Competition in the Indian Ocean: Testimony before the U.S.-China Economic and Security Review Commission*, 117th Cong. 12 (2022) (statement of Darshana Baruah, Fellow, Carnegie Endowment for International Peace), https://www.uscc.gov/sites/default/files/2022-05/Darshana_Baruah_Testimony.pdf.

3. Mauritius disputes British sovereignty over the Chagos Archipelago (where Diego Garcia is located). An advisory opinion by the International Court of Justice in 2019 found Britain's claim illegal; negotiations between the two states are ongoing. See *Legal Consequences of the Separation of Chagos Archipelago from Mauritius in 1965*, Advisory Opinion, International Court of Justice General List no. 169 (February 25, 2019); U.K. Parliament, Statement of James Cleverly, Secretary of State for Foreign, Commonwealth and Development Affairs (November 3, 2022), https://questions-statements.parliament.uk/written-statements/detail/2022-11-03/hcws354.

4. See Lincoln F. Pratson, "Assessing Impacts to Maritime Shipping from Marine Chokepoint Closures," *Communications in Transportation Research* 3 (December 2023), https://doi.org/10.1016/j.commtr.2022.100083.

5. Ian Storey, "China's 'Malacca Dilemma,'" *China Brief* 6, no. 8 (April 12, 2006), https://jamestown.org/program/chinas-malacca-dilemma.

6. The facility provides "critical support to US and allied forces forward deployed in the Indian Ocean, while supporting multi-theater forces operating in the

CENTCOM, AFRICOM, EUCOM, and PACOM areas of responsibilities in support of overseas contingency operations." "Navy Support Facility Diego Garcia: In-Depth Overview," *Department of Defense Military Installations*, https://installations.militaryonesource.mil/in-depth-overview/navy-support-facility-diego-garcia#:~:text=over%202%2C000%20civilians.-,Location,an%20area%20of%206%2C720%20acres (accessed January 10, 2023).

7. The "period of strategic opportunity" is an idea originating in the Deng Xiaoping era to describe the basically benign international security environment that China perceived beginning as Soviet power waned in the 1980s. The National Party Congress of the Twentieth Central Committee of the Chinese Communist Party confirmed that this prior judgment has been supplanted by a much more malign view of China's international security environment. See David Finkelstein, "China's Party Congress Report Highlights New Challenges," Center for Naval Analyses, October 20, 2022, https://www.cna.org/our-media/indepth/2022/10/chinas-party-congress-report-highlights-new-challenges.

8. Some 80 percent of China's imported oil and large and growing proportions of its critical and rare earth minerals must transit the Indian Ocean from Africa and elsewhere in the IOR. Data from https://oec.world.

9. "Djibouti: Chinese Military's First Overseas Support Base," PRC Ministry of National Defense, April 23, 2019, http://eng.mod.gov.cn/news/2019-04/23/content_4840097.htm.

10. In 2015, the PLA's officially designated "strategic tasks" expanded to include "safeguarding China's overseas interests." "China's Military Strategy," State Council Information Office of the People's Republic of China (SCIO), May 27, 2015, https://english.www.gov.cn/archive/white_paper/2015/05/27/content_281475115610833.htm. For a 2021 amendment to national legislation that codified "safeguarding overseas interests" as a core mission of the PLA, see "Law of the People's Republic of China on National Defense 2020 Revision," 13th National People's Congress, 24th session, December 26, 2020, article 22 (amendment effective January 1, 2021), http://www.npc.gov.cn/englishnpc/c23934/202109/567129ffe3144ccb9ff358fed798b9e3.shtml.

11. For PLAN port calls at facilities owned and operated by PRC firms, see the data appendix to Isaac Kardon and Wendy Leutert, "Pier Competitor: China's Power Position in Global Ports," *International Security* 46, no. 4 (Spring 2022), https://dataverse.harvard.edu/dataset.xhtml?persistentId=doi:10.7910/DVN/LL9BKX.

12. Michael Swaine, "The PLA Navy's Strategic Transformation to the Far Seas: How Far, How Threatening, and What's to Be Done?," Carnegie Endowment for International Peace, May 7, 2019, https://carnegieendowment.org/2019/05/07/pla-navy-s-strategic-transformation-to-far-seas-how-far-how-threatening-and-what-s-to-be-done-pub-80588; Jennifer Rice and Erik Robb, "The Origins of 'Near Seas Defense and Far Seas Protection,'" *CMSI China Maritime Report*, no. 13 (February 2021), https://digital-commons.usnwc.edu/cmsi-maritime-reports/13/#:~:text=This%20report%20traces%20the%20origins,and%20maritime%20rights%20and%20interests.

13. See Kardon and Leutert, "Pier Competitor," 24–26.

14. See Isaac B. Kardon, "China's Global Maritime Access: Alternatives to Overseas Military Bases in the 21st Century," *Security Studies* 31, no. 5 (2022): 885–916; see also Leah Dreyfuss and Mara Karlin, "All That Xi Wants: China's Attempts to Ace Bases Overseas," Brookings Institution, September 2019, https://www.brookings.edu/wp-content/uploads/2019/09/FP_20190930_china_basing_karlin_dreyfuss.pdf.

15. Darshana Baruah, "India in the Indo-Pacific: New Delhi's Theater of Opportunity," Carnegie Endowment for International Peace, June 2020, https://carnegieendowment.org/files/Baruah_UnderstandingIndia_final1.pdf; see also Darshana Baruah, "Maritime Competition in the Indian Ocean," testimony for the U.S.-China Economic and Security Review Commission, May 12, 2022, https://carnegieendowment.org/2022/05/12/maritime-competition-in-indian-ocean-pub-87093.

16. Baruah, "India in the Indo-Pacific," 18–25.

17. Ashley Tellis, "America's Bad Bet on India: New Delhi Won't Side with Washington against Beijing," *Foreign Affairs*, May 1, 2023, https://www.foreignaffairs.com/india/americas-bad-bet-india-modi.

18. See Radhey Tambi, "Islands of Opportunity: Australia and India's Chance to Cooperate," Lowy Institute, December 5, 2022, https://www.lowyinstitute.org/the-interpreter/islands-opportunity-australia-india-s-chance-collaborate; Darshanah Baruah, "Australia-India Naval Cooperation and the Islands of the Indo-Pacific," *War on the Rocks*, May 27, 2020, https://warontherocks.com/2020/05/australia-india-and-the-islands-of-the-indo-pacific.

19. See Baruah, "Australia-India Naval Cooperation and the Islands of the Indo-Pacific."

20. Kosuke Takahashi and Ridzwan Rahmat, "French Navy Outlines Indo-Pacific Commitment," *Jane's Defence Weekly*, November 10, 2022, https://www.janes.com/defence-news/news-detail/french-navy-outlines-indo-pacific-commitment; the French also announced plans to deploy this strike group to the Pacific. See Xavier Vavasseur, "French Navy Plans Aircraft Carrier Mission to the Pacific in 2025," *Naval News*, July 22, 2022, https://www.navalnews.com/naval-news/2022/07/french-navy-aircraft-carrier-mission-pacific-in-2025/#:~:text=The%20French%20Navy%20(Marine%20Nationale,carrier%20strike%20group%20in%202025.&text=One%20of%20the%20focus%20of,a%20French%20Navy%20Command%20source, and Gresh, *To Rule Eurasia's Waves*, 128–72.

21. Ben Barry, Bastian Giegerich, Euan Graham, and Ben Schreer, "The UK Indo-Pacific Tilt: Defence and Military Implications," *IISS Research Papers*, June 8, 2022, https://www.iiss.org/blogs/research-paper/2022/06/the-uk-indo-pacific-tilt.

22. See, e.g., Tenny Kristiana, "China's Carrot and Stick Game on Terminal High Altitude Area Defense (THAAD) System Deployment," *Studies on Asia* 6, no. 1 (2021): 55–71, and Audrye Wong, Leif-Eric Easley, and Hsin-wei Tang, "Mobilizing Patriotic Consumers: China's New Strategy of Economic Coercion," *Journal of Strategic Studies*, May 8, 2023, https://doi.org/10.1080/01402390.2023.2205262.

23. On China's surveillance technology exports, see Sheena Chestnut Greitens, "Dealing with Demand for China's Global Surveillance Exports," Brookings Insti-

tution, April 2020, https://www.brookings.edu/research/dealing-with-demand-for-chinas-global-surveillance-exports.

24. Greitens, "Dealing with Demand for China's Global Surveillance Exports."

25. See Peter Dutton, Isaac Kardon, Conor Kennedy, "Djibouti: China's First Overseas Strategic Strongpoint," *CMSI China Maritime Report* no. 6, April 3, 2020, 3–9, https://digital-commons.usnwc.edu/cmsi-maritime-reports/6/.

26. Warren P. Strobel and Nancy A. Youssef, "F-35 Sale to U.A.E. Imperiled over US Concerns about Ties to China," *Wall Street Journal*, May 25, 2021, https://www.wsj.com/articles/f-35-sale-to-u-a-e-imperiled-over-u-s-concerns-about-ties-to-china-11621949050. Iran, Pakistan, Sri Lanka, Myanmar, the Seychelles, and others have also been regarded as potential PLA basing sites. See the serial reporting in U.S. Department of Defense, "Report on Military and Security Developments Involving the People's Republic of China," Office of the Undersecretary of Defense, November 29, 2022, https://www.defense.gov/News/Releases/Release/Article/3230516/2022-report-on-military-and-security-developments-involving-the-peoples-republi.

5

Overseas Basing Logistics at a Crossroads in the Middle East, Sub-Saharan Africa, and the Western Indian Ocean

Strategic Asymmetries among the Major Powers

JASON B. WOLFF[1]

The 2022 National Security Strategy affirms that the overall strategic goal of the United States is a free, open, prosperous, and secure international order, but China and Russia are increasingly challenging this goal by promoting their own agendas.[2] The United States has outlined its actions and leadership role in response to the rise of China's military power and Russia's recent aggression in Europe. However, to succeed, it will need to rely heavily on new and existing global partnerships and alliances. These relationships provide vital overseas basing and access, enabling the United States to project power to deter strategic threats or disrupt terrorist threats. A key aspect of projecting this type of power is the ability to use military force when deemed necessary, as described in the 2022 National Defense Strategy.

The National Defense Strategy outlines the U.S. military's role and force structure needed to maintain and gain war-fighting advantages while limiting those of U.S. competitors. Its framework dictates how the Department of Defense (DOD) should manage the rise of China and deter Russian aggression, but the DOD has limited resources and must focus on more than just these top two priorities. The DOD must also protect against threats from North Korea, Iran, violent extremist organizations, and transboundary challenges, such as pandemics and global climate change. These significant issues, most of which are beyond U.S. borders, impact multiple regions and drive insecurity from a regional to a global scale. Reaching globally beyond U.S. borders requires leveraging limited resources from strategic locations that can move to a crisis at a moment's notice when needed. The U.S. military can and does project power globally, and this capability plays a pivotal role in providing international security. Additionally, permanently assigned overseas military forces provide strategic basing and power projection platforms for quick-response options at a global point of need. These relationships with host nations are key to remind adversaries of the U.S. commitment to mutual defense treaties.

Since the drawdown from Afghanistan and Iraq, the United States has committed most of its overseas forces to European bases and the Indo-Pacific in locations concentrated in the Northern Hemisphere. The DOD determined this force posture by conducting the 2021 Global Posture Review, the results of which yielded incremental increases in force posture in both Europe and Indo-Pacific regions. The actions taken in Europe include increasing the posture of the U.S. Army by 500 personnel in Germany and creating a Multi-Domain Task Force and Fires Command. These units work together to provide command and control and integration support with other U.S. Army, joint, and multinational fires capabilities. This enables synchronization across cyber, air, land, sea, and space for lethal and nonlethal effects. The Indo-Pacific saw increasing support for the Republic of Korea, which received the permanent stationing of a U.S. Army rotational artillery division headquarters.[3] This headquarters unit provides robust joint command and control, allowing more integration and deconfliction of missions with army units and allied forces stationed on the peninsula. These moves now seem like minor steps in the grand strategy of great power competition when compared to sending a temporary but indefinite surge of 20,000 extra U.S. military personnel into Europe. This response, beginning in February 2022 and with no end in sight, was to support Ukraine and provide additional space, land, air, maritime, and cyber capabilities to assure allies and deter Russia.[4]

In the Middle East, sub-Saharan Africa, and the western Indian Ocean, the United States maintains bases in Bahrain, Diego Garcia, Djibouti, Jordan, Kuwait, Oman, Qatar, Saudi Arabia, Turkey, and the United Arab Emirates. By comparison, China has one base in Djibouti, and Russia holds two in Syria. The presence of Chinese and Russian military bases does not appear to influence or incentivize neighboring countries. This is evidenced by the fact that there are no new bases currently being constructed by or for China or Russia in these regions. If the establishment of Chinese and Russian military bases were to offer major benefits such as economic growth or international prestige for host countries, one would expect a long line of potential customers among regional actors.

Despite the absence of significant Russian and Chinese overseas bases, some modest efforts to acquire (or for host countries to provide) basing access have been made. For example, since 2019, Russia has been in talks with Sudan to explore the establishment of a naval base along the Red Sea. This deal, with options to base up to four navy ships and 300 Russian troops, still needed ratification by the civilian government as of February 11, 2023.[5] The four-year delay illustrates the current geopolitical situation for Russia and lack of incentive from the Sudanese government to move forward on the deal, although the delay does not totally exclude the possibility of Russian bases on the Red Sea in the future. The Chinese are also said to have plans for naval bases at seaports in Gwadar in Pakistan and Hambantota in Sri Lanka, but there is no evidence of military construction or a public declaration of a military basing agreement by either host country.[6] There is evidence of Chinese firms offering loans and taking operational control of the Hambantota port facilities with a ninety-nine-year lease in 2017.[7]

China is taking a more aggressive economic rather than a military approach to increase its presence and access in the region. Beijing is building infrastructure through public–private financing and is constructing railways, power grids, and strategic seaports to cultivate trade growth.[8] Reuters reported that Chinese banks already have a very measurable lead with financing, providing $23 billion from 2007 to 2020. This contrasts with the relatively much smaller amount of $1.9 billion provided by the United States through the U.S. International Development Finance Corporation during that same period of time.[9] In addition to moneylending, China is actively pursuing mineral rights for long-term use and developing commercial markets for its finished products.[10] Such practices give China an advantage in a competitive economic trade space. This also makes it extremely difficult for the United States to request military access or basing options when they do not have a sufficient economic footprint to leverage.

Meanwhile, Russia's efforts focus on providing military aid; this has worked to provide Russia access in a limited capacity in Iran, Madagascar, Mozambique, and Syria. Moscow's soft power efforts also include increasing its influence through regional cooperation in multilateral forums. They are making measurable progress. In November 2021, for example, Russia became a dialogue partner in the Indian Ocean Rim Association. This partnership allows Russia to have a greater stake in the Indian Ocean and East African coastal affairs.[11] Although Russia's moves to join the association appear calculated, it has made little to no additional progress in these regions since the ongoing war in Ukraine started.

As the United States evaluates its resources and force posture in response to military and geoeconomic challenges from China and Russia, it is at a crossroads; Washington cannot place a base in every partner nation to keep pace with or deter its competitors. The United States must look to strengthen the ties that create partnerships and not deepen the divides that separate them. The United States currently looks at overseas basing as being entirely a military function, and it needs to start leveraging the United States Agency for International Development (USAID), the U.S. defense and commercial industry, and their allies for access. This agency, in particular, can build relationships and advance U.S. national security into new areas, driving development previously closed due to a lack of resources.[12]

Thus, a new, broader approach to U.S. overseas basing is worth considering, an approach that includes more robust logistics networks spread across multiple countries and strategic locations. The United States must critically look at how it is going to establish new bases using the lens of logistics. The planners must consider the size of operations or mission volume to determine if there are surges or a constant flow. These requirements will drive the capabilities needed and transportation access required over and through land, air, and sea-lanes. An evaluation of infrastructure, transportation assets, and local industrial manufacturing is also needed to determine if local support is available and viable to sustain robust military operations.

OVERSEAS BASING

According to the DOD, an installation is "a military base, camp, post, station, yard, center, homeport facility for any ship, or other activity under the jurisdiction of the DOD, including leased space, which is controlled by, or primarily supports DOD's activities. An installation may consist of one or more sites."[13] American overseas basing can be defined as sustained military forces on an installation with equipment located together in a geographic location outside of the U.S. mainland and its territories. An installation's capabilities may include, among others, security cooperation assistance, humanitarian aid, logistics support, and combat power.

The U.S. overseas basing formula is to build installations, move in forces, and provide equipment to make the forces operational as fast as possible. The faster the construction, the faster the United States can bring military power to bear. However, the formula has not always succeeded. In Afghanistan, rapid build-a-base tactics were used continuously from 2001 until the U.S. withdrawal of forces in 2021, but once a base is completed, sustainment starts immediately. The underlying Afghan economy was too fragile and could not support sustainment operations. There was insufficient capacity to produce the required items locally at the quantities and levels of quality required to support the combat forces.

To enable sustainment, the United States spent incredible amounts of money to bring all classes of supplies—from bottled water, food, and rations to miscellaneous supplies/humanitarian items—into the country. This means importing a tremendous quantity of clothing and equipment and fuel for vehicles plus hydraulic lubricants and coolants, construction lumber, barbed wire, metal fence and barrier materials, and all types of rockets, bullets, explosives, and ammunition. Shampoo, toothpaste, and toilet paper are personal demand items/hygiene products, while tanks, Humvees, and trucks are examples of major end items. Medication, bandages, medical devices, and blood are considered medical supplies and equipment, and spare parts, engines, tires, and radios are repair parts and components. Washington spent more than twenty years and $837 billion arming, equipping, and constructing a multitude of forward operating bases in Afghanistan that were then mostly abandoned or destroyed (only a handful of bases were turned over to the host nation).[14]

The United States also shares several base facilities with allies and partners in the Middle East. These installations are typically dual use, as they are military capable but also generally used for commercial operations. For example, the Kuwait International Airport is also home to the Al-Mubarak Air Base, which supports the U.S. 386th Air Expeditionary Wing and the 5th Expeditionary Air Mobility Squadron.[15] As noted earlier, the

United States cannot rely on current basing practices that are manpower and resource intensive—even if successful in some ways—to keep pace with China and deter Russia in the Middle East, sub-Saharan Africa, and the western Indian Ocean.

THE ADDED POWER OF ROBUST LOGISTICS NETWORKS

The United States must take a "whole-of-government" approach to basing and not view its military bases just as U.S. outposts.[16] A central pillar of this approach should be robust logistics networks that aim to sustain access through transportation infrastructure and industrial development rather than just military operations. Logistics networks can drive down costs and help reduce war-fighting requirements in a region. They also simultaneously increase U.S. presence and influence in multiple regions and add resiliency at multiple locations in a country or region instead of at a few bases. This robust logistics network strategy focuses on access, infrastructure development, and growth of the industrial complex in locations able to reach multiple regions and is not solely reliant on military operations for sustainment.

Access

Thinking not just in the short term but also in the long term, the United States will require air, land, and water access to project power, including sea and intercoastal routes. The concept of access is the ability to move or transit into, out of, and through another sovereign country's territory. Examples of access include flying through another country's airspace, sailing through its waters, landing in the country at a port of debarkation, and conducting over-the-shore land movements. Permission to access the country is called "clearance."

Every country has unique clearance approval processes for transporting commodities and people through customs and immigration. Clearance approval includes meeting requirements for weapons, ammunition, and hazardous materials. The U.S. military wants to know the limitations, restrictions, and conditions to avoid violations that can delay cargo for days to months if not handled properly. Following the clearance process and collaborating with the host country are essential. It can ease barriers, reduce delays, and accelerate delivery times by submitting the paperwork correctly and on time. More important, in times of crisis, a country can waive or eliminate clearance requirements for a good partner. Qatar waived specific clearance requirements when assisting in the humanitarian evacuation from Afghanistan.[17]

Building robust logistics networks can streamline the clearance processes and build familiarization for both countries to accomplish this process better. As relationships with host countries strengthen, the ability to have access is vital. An in-depth evaluation needs to be conducted to confirm if the United States needs to maintain a military base to have access. Based on this, maintaining an installation, forces, or equipment in a country could become optional if access is granted and there are robust logistics networks in place.

The United States can leverage its multiple organizations by having a presence, prior analysis, and multiple evaluations of logistics and transportation into and out of this part of the world. Almost all cargo requires multiple transmodal operations to the destination and the last tactical mile. This means requiring one or more modes of transportation. When it requires changing modes of transportation, additional infrastructure and transportation assets are required. The United States can learn from its past twenty-five years in these regions and focus on locations that provide optimal logistic basing opportunities now or in the future. The optimal solutions can be determined by using a logistic matrix of infrastructure, transportation assets, and defense and industrial manufacturing capabilities that can reduce their supply chains. The United States must realize the need to invest militarily and commercially in these key areas over the next twenty years or longer with allies and partners in order to have these capabilities to ensure security. More important, continued investment and growth will be required to keep the competition at bay.

Transportation Infrastructure
Building robust logistics networks and sustaining access in the Middle East, sub-Saharan Africa, and the western Indian Ocean requires having substantial infrastructure at sea and aerial ports as well as facilities that enable inland ground transportation. Two of the most strategic sea-lanes for shipping run through and along the coast of sub-Saharan Africa. They are of global consequence since one represents a gateway to the Suez Canal and the other a gateway to the Cape of Good Hope. The Middle East is a central geolocation; from this region, one can reach two-thirds of the world's population with an eight-hour flight, allowing for rapid responses to multiple situations.[18] Given the varying opportunities in the regions, the most ideal

placement of bases and infrastructure will always require in-depth analysis and planning. The United States must pursue options that will impact today and remain viable for fifty years. Host nation facilities already in existence or easily modified for operations would provide optimal solutions for limited resources. However, the United States must act now and aggressively for the next five years before the competition has a monopoly and the initiative is lost to competitors forever.

Both seaports and aerial ports have advantages and disadvantages to consider. Seaports allow bulk delivery but have limitations or constraints due to the requirements for inland transportation, including vital intermodal connections that utilize ships, roadways, railways, pipelines, and airports. In addition, multiple uncontrollable factors impact seaports, including seasonal weather conditions and wave and tide cycles that change the depth of the sea floor. These and other complex factors affect access to channels, including the need for tugboats, which can result in ships having less space to maneuver. The capability to download petroleum products and chemicals from tankers requires transfer stations, adding more complexity in a crowded area. A seaport with piers, cranes, and material handling equipment is required to accommodate the roll-on/roll-off prepositioned support ships carrying tracked vehicles or tanks, all critical factors for U.S. forces. Additionally, there are only a few seaports that can accommodate a vessel as large as an aircraft carrier or as specialized as a submarine for rearming in these regions.

Aerial ports allow swift delivery, but aircraft delivery is in limited quantities compared to sea vessels. Moreover, just like seaports, aerial ports need intermodal connections for inland transportation and must contend with uncontrollable factors: seasonal weather, altitude above sea level, and co-location to deserts, oceans, and mountains can all affect flying conditions. In prioritizing the placement of air bases in the Middle East, sub-Saharan Africa, and the western Indian Ocean, the United States must thoroughly evaluate its aircraft options, existing runway lengths, and weight tolerances. It must also consider hangar dimensions and available warehouse space. To expedite this, the U.S. Air Force has established standard air mobility planning factors to help determine optimal locations for what the U.S. commander foresees as their requirement for aircraft.[19] For example, planning factors for the large C-17A transport aircraft include a maximum range of 2,500 nautical miles, up to 160,000 pounds of cargo, and eighteen pallet positions (storage space units). Compared to the smaller C-130J transport aircraft with a range of 1,500 nautical miles, it can accommodate 30,000 pounds of cargo and six pallet positions. Essentially, the type of aircraft used can dictate how many bases are needed and at what location the support must be available.

Furthermore, the logistical needs for supporting a single base versus multiple regional bases are vastly different. The cost is not "U.S. only" in equipment and staffing, but the host nation must provide additional liaisons and support at each location. The goal is to leverage existing aerial ports or build the minimum required infrastructure at strategic locations with partner nations.

The ports also require ground transportation infrastructure to enable the movement of people and commodities into and out of ports for inland transportation and intermodal connections. Essential ground infrastructure includes roads, rail, and pipelines. Nevertheless, multiple uncontrollable factors also impact ground infrastructure. Roadways are the most susceptible to weather conditions; terrain features like mountains, river crossings, and deserts change daily. Many developing countries still have limited paved or concrete roads and less commercial trucking capacity than seen in developed countries. Furthermore, they have fewer railways, and the pipeline systems required for tankers to move fuel or chemicals are often found only at major seaports.

Overall, the importance of infrastructure cannot be stressed enough for the ability to conduct and sustain successful humanitarian, security, and military operations in any location. These regions have limited infrastructure that can be improved and should not deter US. involvement but rather encourage more involvement to ensure proper infrastructure development. Key advancements and partnerships can be created by the United States utilizing private corporations and proven successful industrial planning, design, and development procedures to make a location desirable for global trade. This type of critical assistance in improving infrastructure could also accelerate a country's industrial development as long as there are enough transportation assets to maximize the infrastructure.

Transportation Assets

Transportation assets are motor vehicles and other support equipment that move cargo and people. The baseline needs to be the assets available organically in the country that can be rented, bought, or donated for use by U.S. forces and not what the United States can bring into the country.

The United States needs to look at its requirements for vehicle fleets, rail system resources, material handling equipment, and personnel required against what is actually available and what can be provided and maintained in working condition.

Tractor and trailer trucking systems are the building block of the U.S. transportation system in the continental United States. The U.S. standard eighteen-wheeler configurations are not available in these regions, nor are there multiple configurations of trailers. The supply of flatbed trailers, refrigerated trailers (reefers) for produce and medicines, drop-deck (stepdeck) trailers for outsized items, tankers to move fuel and chemicals, and double drop (lowboy) trailers to move large machinery/equipment are limited.[20] These assets are always a constraining planning factor for any large surge of capacity or planning for extended time frames. The truck fleets and freight trailers that can move cargo must be explored if they are available to the U.S. military for use and if the vehicles and drivers are qualified to move explosives or hazardous materials. Many countries do not have large commercial fleets but do have individual owners, as experienced in Iraq and Afghanistan in the early 2000s.

The rail systems evaluation needs to encompass all railcar types and an understanding of how to utilize the boxcar, flatcar, gondola, refrigerated car, tanker, and intermodal, or well, car. They all have distinct roles, and a basic understanding demonstrates the complexity of moving cargo by rail. Boxcars are used to carry most palletized materials and items needing protection from weather. Flatcars are for military vehicles, tractors, steel beams, pipes, and lumber. Gondolas will carry bulk items, such as aggregate needed for building foundations and scrap metal. Refrigerated boxcars carry food items and medicines. Tankers carry fuel or chemicals including liquid or compressed gas. Intermodal, or well, cars are specially designed for intermodal shipping containers.[21] These cars must be organic to the host country and are not a military asset that can be moved into theater.

To make this all work, the United States must have qualified personnel to schedule, unload/load, and deliver the cargo or civilian professionals in sufficient quantity. The United States also requires the correct material handling equipment, including forklifts in warehouse/cargo yards, cranes on piers, and container handlers for intermodal containers in cargo/rail yards. Most items can be provided by commercial agents, but there is special equipment used to load U.S. military planes provided and manned by U.S. Air Force personnel.[22] These are the 60K Tunner or 25K Halvorsen aircraft cargo loaders.

These loaders are also able to load foreign military or commercial aircraft, such as the AN 295, A40CM, and B747. There are allied and commercial solutions available if the 60K Tunner or 25K Halvorsen aircraft loader becomes a limiting factor, depending on the mission and capability required.[23]

Industrial Development

New or established industrial manufacturing will substantially impact standing up or sustaining any base. The fewer items a unit must bring to a location, the more cost effective it is to deploy and sustain the unit. The United States should evaluate whether the host country has industrial infrastructure that can support the manufacturing of military products if required and whether it has a professionally trained workforce. However, even if a partner nation does not have these elements, kick-starting its industrial development can often be done and is best done through incremental steps.

The active development of more local support capabilities providing food, medicine, and commercial products for military, humanitarian, and civilian purposes can be an excellent first step to building an industrial manufacturing base. For example, the purification and bottling of water is a proven entry-level business endeavor that can kick-start industrial development. In Afghanistan, the Aria Water Plant was a joint venture of private Afghan funders and the U.S. Army's 10th Sustainment Brigade soldiers. The plant was started and completed in six months, producing nearly 400,000 bottles of water a day once all four production lines were at capacity. More of this type of industrial development could have provided local support capabilities and would have saved the United States and nongovernmental organizations millions of dollars per year.[24] These crossover products from military to humanitarian and civilian use can be the first step to building up a manufacturing economy.

The start of military manufacturing could open doors for the utilization of products by U.S. forces and their allies, but a faster way to have compatible logistic networks is to have a host nation achieve direct participation in U.S. Foreign Military Sales (FMS) programs. When a country participates in FMS programs, it receives transferred defense articles, services, and training that the DOD acquires for its own use.[25] This helps minimize incompatibility and maximize interoperability. This could allow the United States a smaller logistical footprint if it has access to host nation support.

Suppose a country is not in the FMS program. In that case, the option of Direct Commercial Sales allows international partners to obtain U.S.

defense services and articles to start the foundation of a shared logistics network providing materials and services. The increased participation in these programs could help establish new partnerships in multiple locations and thereby build up redundancies in U.S. and partner nation logistics networks. It could also help nurture long-term partnerships and interoperability.[26] Another bonus to having a logistic network with the United States is that it could open the door to partnerships with NATO countries that are already compatible with U.S. logistics. Shared logistics systems provide a common operating picture that limits the competition space among partners. They also further reduce the ability of China or Russia to entice nations to their sphere of influence.

THE WAY FORWARD

The United States must bring as many groups and organizations to the table as possible to build a robust logistics network in each of these regions. This means breaking down the silos, which can begin by integrating with the Department of State and utilizing the Global Fragility Act to draw their attention to key countries in the sub-Saharan region, for example. This requires a total government approach while leveraging commercial partners to get the geopolitical goals aligned with the military goals and the funds needed to integrate with regional and global markets economically and politically. The United States must make its mission, vision, and plans known to host nations and their allies and partners, and it must allow others to join and contribute to the development of these countries and their economies. The United States has not leveraged Great Britain, Germany, France, or Japan despite the joint military ventures and other government interactions.

In pursuing long-term partners, the United States can offer benefits and resources to regional actors that China and Russia cannot. The United States can train, equip, and educate regional partners in U.S. and coalition professional military training environments at a scale and diversity not currently demonstrated or sustained by China and Russia.

The United States must increase the coalition of partner nations in Southern Hemisphere regions to build more viable and robust logistics networks. It is already committed to military basing in Diego Garcia and Djibouti from these locations; the United States can project combat power and humanitarian assistance from these locations (and from its Middle East bases if required). In pursuing long-term partnerships, Washington must strategically focus on allies that could provide the best return on investment to oppose the competition from China and Russia. It must also capitalize on regional partnerships, including by leveraging the momentum from the United States–Africa Leaders Summit 2022. The United States has an open door to start or strengthen partnerships with the African leaders who attended the summit, which aligns with the established fifty-year master plan and blueprint for Africa to become a global social and economic powerhouse (called Agenda 2063). These U.S. partnerships could help African countries accelerate their Agenda 2063 economic goals by jointly establishing logistics networks that will, in turn, help them develop more industrial manufacturing and infrastructure.[27]

The United States must bring multiple groups and organizations to the table to build robust logistics networks within the regions (the Middle East, sub-Saharan Africa, and the western Indian Ocean) and between them. In doing so, the U.S. government should break down its internal institutional silos. For example, the DOD, the Department of State, and the Office of the U.S. Trade Representative should work together to ensure participation in and execution of the African Growth and Opportunity Act within economic markets. This effort and other actions could encourage allies to join and contribute to developing the Middle East, sub-Saharan Africa, and western Indian Ocean countries with interconnected, robust logistics networks and to grow their economies.

CONCLUSION

The United States cannot meet the National Security Strategy and National Defense Strategy goals and sustain them in the future by relying on current overseas basing practices. It will fail. Today, only a new strategy of robust logistics networks involving access, infrastructure, industrial development, and partnerships can keep pace with China and deter Russia. The best logistical network locations are on the trade routes located near the east coast of sub-Saharan Africa and the western Indian Ocean, bordered by the Middle Eastern countries in this area. The United States will require secure access to this vital crossroad to project power globally and sustain its presence across multiple regions.

NOTES

1. The views expressed herein are solely those of the author and do not necessarily represent the views of the U.S. government or the Brookings Institution.

2. "National Security Strategy," White House, October 2022, 11, https://www.whitehouse.gov/wp-content/uploads/2022/10/Biden-Harris-Administrations-National-Security-Strategy-10.2022.pdf.

3. Todd South, "Army Division Artillery Headquarters Moves from JBLM to South Korea Permanently," *Army Times*, September 9, 2021, https://www.armytimes.com/news/your-army/2021/09/09/army-artillery-headquarters-moves-from-jblm-to-south-korea-permanently.

4. "Fact Sheet—U.S. Defense Contributions to Europe," U.S. Department of Defense, June 29, 2022, https://www.defense.gov/News/Releases/Release/Article/3078056/fact-sheet-us-defense-contributions-to-europe.

5. Sam Magdy, "Sudan Military Finishes Review of Russian Red Sea Base Deal," Associated Press, February 11, 2023, https://apnews.com/article/politics-sudan-government-moscow-803738fba4d8f91455f0121067c118dd.

6. Amy Hawkins and Helen Davidson, "China May be Planning Overseas Naval Bases in Asia and Africa, Say Analysts," *The Guardian*, July 27, 2023, https://www.theguardian.com/world/2023/jul/27/china-building-overseas-naval-bases-across-asia-and-africa-say-analysts.

7. Hawkins and Davidson, "China May Be Planning Overseas Naval Bases in Asia and Africa, Say Analysts."

8. Brian Gicheru Kinyua, "Is China Using Africa to Shape a New Global Maritime Order?," *The Maritime Executive*, September 24, 2020, https://maritime-executive.com/editorials/is-china-using-africa-to-shape-a-new-global-maritime-order.

9. Andrea Shalal, "Chinese Funding of Sub-Saharan African Infrastructure Dwarfs That of West, Says Think Tank," Reuters, February 9, 2022, https://www.reuters.com/markets/us/chinese-funding-sub-saharan-african-infrastructure-dwarfs-that-west-says-think-2022-02-09.

10. Antony Sguazzin, "China May Have Created a Trap for Itself with African Lending," *The Japan Times*, December 18, 2022, https://www.japantimes.co.jp/news/2022/12/18/asia-pacific/china-debt-trap-diplomacy.

11. Sankalp Gurjar, "Russia's Indian Ocean Pivot," *Deccan Herald*, November 23, 2021, https://www.deccanherald.com/opinion/russias-indian-ocean-pivot-1053726.htm.

12. "Policy Framework," United States Agency for International Development, March 2023, https://www.usaid.gov/policy/documents/mar-23-2023-usaids-policy-framework.

13. "Base Structure Report—Fiscal Year 2018 Baseline a Summary of the Real Property Inventory Data," U.S. Department of Defense, September 30, 2017, https://www.acq.osd.mil/eie/Downloads/BSI/Base%20Structure%20Report%20FY18.pdf.

14. Special Inspector General for Afghanistan Reconstruction, "What We Need to Learn: Lessons from Twenty Years of Afghanistan Reconstruction," August 2021, 1, https://www.sigar.mil/pdf/lessonslearned/SIGAR-21-46-LL.pdf.

15. "Al-Mubarak, Air Base Kuwait International Airport, 29°14'15"N 47°58'26"E," GlobalSecurity.org, accessed October 28, 2022, https://www.globalsecurity.org/military/facility/kuwait-iap.htm.

16. Rebecca Bill Chavez, "Ensure a Whole-of-Government Approach," Atlantic Council, May 31, 2022, https://www.atlanticcouncil.org/in-depth-research-reports/books/allies-ensure-a-whole-of-government-approach.

17. "The United States and Qatar: Strategic Partners Advancing Peace and Security," U.S. Department of State, November 20, 2022, https://www.state.gov/the-united-states-and-qatar-strategic-partners-advancing-peace-and-security.

18. Scott Mayerowitz, "Middle East Becomes the World's New Travel Crossroads," *USA Today*, March 4, 2013, https://www.usatoday.com/story/todayinthesky/2013/03/04/middle-east-becomes-the-worlds-new-travel-crossroads/1961565.

19. Air Force Pamphlet (AFPAM) 10–403, "Air Mobility Planning Factors," Department of the Air Force, October 24, 2018, https://static.e-publishing.af.mil/production/1/af_a3/publication/afpam10-1403/afpam10-1403.pdf.

20. ATS, "What Are the Common Trailer Types Used in the Trucking Industry?," accessed July 5, 2023, https://www.atsinc.com/blog/trailer-types-shipping-industry.

21. Union Pacific, "What Are All of the Different Rail Car Types?," January 18, 2022, https://www.up.com/customers/track-record/tr181121_rail_car_types.htm.

22. Air Mobility Command, "Tunner 60K Loader," retrieved July 5, 2023, https://www.amc.af.mil/About-Us/Fact-Sheets/Display/Article/144023/tunner-60k-loader.

23. JBT AeroTech, "Halvorsen 3 Pallet Loaders," accessed July 5, 2023, https://www.jbtc.com/aerotech/products-and-services/defense-aviation-ground-equipment/cargo-loaders/halvorsen-3-pallet-loaders.

24. Michael Rautio, "State-of-the-Art Bottled Water Plant Opens in Afghanistan," Joint Logistics Command, January 8, 2007, https://www.afcent.af.mil/Units/455th-Air-Expeditionary-Wing/News/Display/Article/275413/state-of-the-art-bottled-water-plant-opens-in-afghanistan.

25. "Foreign Military Sales FAQ," Defense Security Cooperation Agency, accessed October 28, 2022, https://www.dsca.mil/foreign-military-sales-faq.

26. "Foreign Military Sales FAQ."

27. U.S. Department of State, "U.S.-Africa Leaders Summit Overview," accessed December 16, 2022, https://www.state.gov/africasummit.

6

Strategic Competition for Overseas Basing in Sub-Saharan Africa

DAWN C. MURPHY[1]

Sub-Saharan Africa is a vast region encompassing forty-nine countries.[2] It is strategically located on the Indian and Atlantic oceans with close proximity to a number of key sea lines of communication (SLOCs). At 9.4 million square miles, this resource-rich region contains almost three times the landmass of the United States. With 1.2 billion people and relatively high population growth rates, it provides substantial current and future market opportunities for goods and services.

Historically, sub-Saharan Africa suffered through colonization at the hands of European powers and was a battlefield for competition between the Soviet Union and the United States during the Cold War. During the early post–Cold War era, great power competition in sub-Saharan Africa faded into the background, and U.S. attention to the region tended to focus on nontraditional security concerns, including terrorism, piracy, and the resolution of civil wars and interstate conflicts that threatened the stability of the region and civilian populations. Non-security issues, such as economic development, human rights, disease prevention, and humanitarian response, were also often emphasized.

In recent years, sub-Saharan Africa has once again emerged as an arena of strategic economic, political, and potentially military competition between the United States, China, and Russia. Washington is now tracking current and future Chinese and Russian military threats in this often-forgotten region. One particularly important element of those threats is overseas basing. As Chinese and Russian economic, political, and security interests and behavior in sub-Saharan Africa increase, there are concerns that these strategic competitors will desire to expand their basing footprint in the region to protect their regional and global interests. There are also worries that increasing Chinese and Russian economic and political influence on the continent may result in a willingness of local countries to allow them to establish bases there. A future expanded Chinese and Russian basing infrastructure could facilitate their ability to project and maintain military power at greater distances and ultimately interfere with the United States' and its allies' and partners' military operations in potential conflict scenarios. These bases could also put the United States and its allies' and partners' homelands further at risk during a war over issues such as Taiwan or territorial disputes in the East China Sea or South China Sea. As U.S.–China and U.S.–Russia relations deteriorate, these worries become more pronounced and urgent to address.

THE RISING POWER OF CHINA IN SUB-SAHARAN AFRICA

Over the past thirty years, China's footprint in sub-Saharan Africa has significantly expanded. China envisions itself as a leader of the Global South, of which sub-Saharan Africa is an important part. It views the region as one with great potential for economic engagement and South–South cooperation and values support from its forty-nine countries in the international system.

Arguably, China is now the region's most important economic partner. Today, it is the top trading partner with the region and increasingly eclipses other great powers in economic relations and influence.[3] China's trade with sub-Saharan Africa is three times greater than U.S. trade with the region. China imported $83 billion worth of goods (versus the United States at $25 billion) from the region in 2022.[4] Most of those imports are energy and minerals. China's exports to the region also exceed those of the United States. They were $74 billion in 2022 versus $21 billion for the United States.[5] Foreign direct investment (FDI) flows from the People's Republic of China (PRC) to the region are five times those of the United States. In 2021, China's FDI flows were approximately $5 billion, while U.S. FDI flow into the region was zero or perhaps even negative.[6] American and Chinese FDI stocks in 2021 were equal at $44 billion.[7]

China is also an increasingly influential political actor in sub-Saharan Africa. For more than twenty years, the PRC has leveraged the Forum on China–Africa Cooperation (established in 2000) to facilitate all types of multilateral cooperation with the entire continent, including sub-Saharan Africa. It also established strategic partnerships with the African Union and a number of countries across the region, including all of the anchor states. Through its special envoys for Africa (established in 2007) and the Horn of Africa (established in 2022), the PRC works to serve as a mediator and attempts to address hot spot issues it views as essential to maintaining regional peace and security.

Sub-Saharan Africa is also an important region for China's global political initiatives. Since 2015, it has been an integral region for China's Belt and Road Initiative. More recently, sub-Saharan Africa is a key region of emphasis for Beijing's Global Development Initiative, Global Security Initiative, and the Global Civilization Initiative.[8]

China's current and potential basing objectives should be examined within this broader shifting geostrategic context. Beijing's economic and political influence has undoubtedly grown in the region over the past two decades. It is now the region's most important economic partner, and its political influence on the continent rivals or surpasses Washington.

In contrast with its economic and political engagements in sub-Saharan Africa, China's military footprint in the region is still limited: it consists primarily of a base in Djibouti, participation in UN peacekeeping operations and multilateral anti-piracy missions in the Gulf of Aden, and relatively low volumes of conventional arms sales over time compared to those of other great powers.[9] It is also reported that China maintains embedded People's Liberation Army training for local military forces in the Democratic Republic of Congo and a military training school in Tanzania to support domestic security in those countries.[10]

China's current and likely future basing interests in sub-Saharan Africa include securing and maintaining access to resources and markets and safeguarding its citizens and businesses abroad.[11] Those bases could provide the PRC with a platform for collecting information about U.S. military operations in sub-Saharan Africa.[12] Beijing may also pursue the ability to project and maintain military power from the region into the Atlantic or Indian ocean to support future potential conflict scenarios with the United States.[13]

Before 2017, China pursued an explicit policy of no foreign basing. Although a number of Chinese military facilities in the South China Sea predating Djibouti had base-like qualities, the facility in Djibouti is China's first and, to date, only declared overseas base.[14] In November 2015, China signed a ten-year contract with the Djibouti government and announced it was establishing an installation in Djibouti to resupply Chinese navy ships participating in Gulf of Aden anti-piracy missions.[15]

China's military personnel initially deployed to the Djibouti base in July 2017 and conducted their first live-fire exercise later that year.[16] China's base will reportedly host thousands of troops, but as of 2022, only 400 marines were stationed there.[17] The base has an operational pier likely able to accommodate aircraft carriers, other large combat ships, and submarines.[18] It has a heliport but does not yet have a dedicated runway for other aircraft.[19]

Immediately after its founding, China's Djibouti base resulted in tensions between the United States and China. For example, in May 2018, the United States issued a démarche to China over incidents of lasers pointed from the Chinese base at military aircraft that resulted in eye injuries to U.S. pilots. China denied those allegations.[20] In 2019, the U.S. Department of Defense (DOD) again expressed concern that China had constrained international airspace by blocking American aircraft from flying over the Chinese base, firing lasers at American pilots, and flying drones to interfere with U.S. missions. It also accused China of intrusion activity and attempts to gain access to Camp Lemonnier. In response, China denied those allegations and complained that low-flying U.S. aircraft had been conducting spy missions near its base.[21]

According to Chinese Communist Party officials, China established the base in Djibouti for several reasons. The location enhances China's ability to protect the SLOCs in the Middle East and Africa and supports its navy's participation in anti-piracy activities. As asserted by the Chinese Ministry of Defense, the location also ensures that China can contribute to regional peacekeeping and humanitarian assistance.[22] For several years before establishing this base, the United States and other countries encouraged China to stop free riding and contribute more global public goods. Arguably, China positioned itself to protect the region's SLOCs to potentially provide these public goods, especially if the United States were to cease its protection of these SLOCs or other powers were to threaten China's access to them.

The location also enables China to better protect its citizens and businesses in sub-Saharan Africa. Several Chinese white papers, government statements, and China's 2015 National Security Law (clauses 28 and 30) call for protecting its citizens abroad.[23] Based on its experience evacuating more than 35,000 citizens from Libya in 2011 and more than 600 from Yemen in 2015, China determined that it needed a more permanent presence to facilitate future civilian evacuations from conflict zones in the Middle East and Africa.[24] Beijing explicitly refers to these experiences as a reason for establishing the base in Djibouti.[25] That said, the DOD argues that there is not yet any indication that the PRC is actually using the Djibouti base for that purpose.[26]

In choosing Djibouti as a base location, China may have been attempting to demonstrate that it is a responsible power by positioning its base in a country that already hosts a wide range of countries with interests in the geostrategic location of Djibouti. With several other countries already hosting and planning bases in Djibouti in 2017, Beijing may have perceived the country as a nonthreatening location for its own base, especially given China's experience with conducting multilateral anti-piracy activities with many of those same countries. The United States, France, Italy, and Japan all have bases in Djibouti. The U.S. base, Camp Lemonnier, is the headquarters of the U.S. Africa Command Joint Task Force for the Horn of Africa and houses more than 4,000 U.S. and allied personnel (versus only 400 personnel at the Chinese base as of 2022). France's base, Aerienne 188, is home to French as well as Spanish and German forces.[27] Through a joint agreement, the Indian navy now has access to Japan's base in Djibouti.[28] Saudi Arabia is also in the process of establishing a base in the country.[29] Although the PRC's original intent may have been to demonstrate that it is a responsible power by selecting Djibouti as a basing location, proximity to so many other bases now also provides China with the opportunity to collect information about military activities of a number of other external countries operating in the region, including the United States.

Geographically, China's Djibouti base is in sub-Saharan Africa, but its existence can be understood only in the broader context of Beijing's interests in both the Middle East and Africa. It can be argued that China at the time chose Djibouti because Iran would not positively perceive a Chinese base in an Arab country and, similarly, other Arab countries would see a base in Iran as threatening.[30] Establishing the base in Djibouti gave China the benefits of proximity to the Middle East without having to choose sides in the region; in other words, it allowed China to maintain its delicate balancing act with all the region's powers and not infringe on the U.S. sphere of influence.

Although the PRC does not frame the Djibouti base in terms of power projection, this base is significant because it highlights China's emerging ability to deploy and sustain a military presence far from its mainland.[31] The DOD increasingly expresses concerns that this base and future Chinese bases in sub-Saharan Africa could serve that purpose.[32]

China has yet to announce any further plans for basing in sub-Saharan Africa, but speculation about the potential for basing activity is growing. The Pentagon recently stated that China is "likely already considering and planning for additional military logistics facilities to support naval, air, and ground projection."[33] It asserts that in Africa, Beijing is likely considering military logistics facilities in Angola, Equatorial Guinea, Kenya, Mozambique, Namibia, Nigeria, Seychelles, and Tanzania and is most interested in military access along the SLOCs from China to Africa and the Strait of Hormuz. According to media reports, China may also be pursuing a base in Madagascar.[34]

THE DISRUPTIVE POWER OF RUSSIA

In comparison with China and the United States, Russia's economic and political activities in sub-Saharan Africa are limited. Russia's imports from the region are a meager $7 billion, and it exports only $1.5 billion per year to the continent.[35] Russian FDI is minuscule, representing less than 1 percent of total FDI going into Africa.[36] As discussed earlier in the chapter, Beijing and Washington are much more significant economic actors on the continent. Russia recently established a Russia-Africa Economic and Humanitarian Forum (2019) and conducts some limited trade and economic relations with sub-Saharan Africa, but its economic and political presence in Africa is dwarfed by China.[37]

Russia's security behavior in the region tends to be opportunistic, ad hoc, profit seeking, and destabilizing.[38] Russia's military activities include mostly serving as the region's top supplier of conventional arms; deploying Wagner Group mercenaries—who have close ties to Russia's military intelligence agency—to the Central African Republic, Madagascar, Mali, Mozambique, and Sudan to protect regimes in power there;[39] and pursuing a formal base in Sudan.[40]

In 2020, it was made public that Russia was entering into an agreement with Sudan for a military base that would host up to 300 personnel and four naval vessels. If the deal moves forward, it would be Russia's first base in sub-Saharan Africa since the fall of the Soviet Union. Its purpose will be to maintain Russian ships, support anti-piracy missions in the Red Sea, and provide potential control over the SLOCs passing through the Red Sea.[41] After the 2021 coup in Sudan, the base agreement reportedly was on hold,[42] but neither the Russian government nor the Sudanese government has confirmed a pause in planning.[43] That said, reporting and analysis as of 2023 indicated that despite Russia's military involvement in Ukraine and instability in Sudan, this base project was still being pursued.[44]

Before Russia's invasion of Ukraine, there was speculation that Moscow would pursue naval facilities in Somaliland and Eritrea.[45] It was also reported that Russia attempted to negotiate with the Djibouti government for a base before those talks stalled.[46] These efforts and the plan for a base in Sudan indicate that Russia may want to project force in the Red Sea along the strategic maritime choke hold of the Bab-el-Mandeb Strait from Djibouti to Yemen.[47]

In the wake of the recent death of Wagner leader Yevgeny Prigozhin, many of Russia's paramilitary organization security activities and other military engagements in Africa are reportedly in the process of reorganization and may be absorbed by the Russian military.[48] It is still too early to assess the impact of those changes on Russia's security behavior in sub-Saharan Africa.[49] For now, Moscow is focused mostly on the war in Ukraine and reassessing how to interact with Africa through Wagner, but in the future, its broader basing aspirations in the region may be fully rekindled and actualized. If that happens, Russia would be better positioned to project and maintain military power off the Horn of Africa.

THE ENDURING POWER OF THE UNITED STATES

Although it is now increasingly surpassed by China's economic presence and challenged by China's political behavior in the region, the United States maintains robust economic and political relations with sub-Saharan Africa. Details of U.S. trade and FDI with the region compared to China were discussed earlier in the chapter. Recent examples of high-profile U.S. engagements with the region to attempt to maintain economic and political influence include the Prosper Africa Initiative (2019) to promote trade with and investment in the region[50] and the United States–Africa Leaders Summit (2019 and 2022) aimed at strengthening ties with African partners across functional areas.[51]

To protect its security interests, the United States seeks primarily to preserve strategic access to the continent; to counter threats to U.S. persons, facilities, and interests from violent extremist organizations or other maligned actors; and to prevent and respond to humanitarian and other crises.[52] The primary security policies of the United States to pursue those interests in sub-Saharan Africa are seeking political solutions to conflicts in the region through African-led efforts, combating terrorism that threatens U.S. citizens and businesses in the region, mitigating humanitarian crises, and investing in local and regional peace building and peacekeeping to prevent future conflicts.[53]

The United States is also increasingly emphasizing Africa's importance for competing with China and Russia across all functional areas and preventing the growth of influence and power projection of both countries from the continent. The United States increasingly expresses concerns that a Chinese basing presence in sub-Saharan Africa could directly threaten the United States' and its allies' and partners' abilities to conduct military operations in potential future conflict scenarios. This includes conflict in the Taiwan Strait and sovereignty disputes in the East China Sea or South China Sea.

Compared to China and Russia, the United States has a more substantial but still limited security footprint in sub-Saharan Africa. In 2020, it had approximately 5,000 service members and 1,000 civilians and contractors on the continent.[54] As noted earlier, the United States has a permanent base in Camp Lemonnier in Djibouti with more than 4,000 U.S. and allied personnel. It also has troops deployed in Kenya, Somalia, and West Africa (mainly in Niger), focused on counterterrorism operations. Personnel in Niger conduct a wide range of activities, including intelligence, surveillance, and reconnaissance flights from a U.S. Air Force facility.[55] The United States also provides logistical support to French counterterrorism operations in Mali.[56] In addition, Congress has authorized the DOD to deploy U.S. special operation forces in support of "foreign forces, irregular forces, groups, or individuals engaged in supporting or facilitating ongoing military operations" to combat terrorism. The DOD does not generally disclose the scope or location of those authorized activities.[57]

Today, most of the U.S. military presence in sub-Saharan Africa is focused on counterterrorism activities, but like China's base in Djibouti and Russia's potential future bases in the region, the U.S. base in Djibouti could be leveraged for the United States to enhance its ability to project and maintain military power in the Bab-el-Mandeb Strait between Djibouti to

Yemen, off the Horn of Africa, and into the Indian Ocean. It also provides the United States with additional opportunities to collect information on the military activities of China and other countries with a basing presence in Djibouti.

GEOSTRATEGIC COMPETITION, RISKS, AND CHALLENGES FOR THE UNITED STATES

China's economic and political engagement and influence in sub-Saharan Africa are growing rapidly, Russia continues to build its security relations in the region, and the United States increasingly views the region through a lens of strategic competition with China and Russia. Current and future basing by China and Russia in the region could enhance their ability to project and maintain military power that threatens the United States' and allies' and partners' military objectives in possible future conflict scenarios. That said, compared to other regions, sub-Saharan Africa is not a high strategic priority for China, Russia, or the United States. Most of the vital interests of these powers are in Asia, Europe, the Western Hemisphere, and the Middle East. Despite that obvious fact, in recent years, U.S. concerns about additional Chinese and Russian basing in sub-Saharan Africa have grown. Those U.S. anxieties are driven by China's and Russia's apparent increased desire and capability to project power and the threats that their rising influence in certain regions pose to the United States and its allies and partners.

Two geographical locations, in particular, are highlighted in U.S. government reports to Congress and media reporting about potential future locations of Chinese bases: the Indian Ocean coast of East Africa and the Atlantic coast of West Africa. The primary risk to the United States from China's base in Djibouti and other potential bases in sub-Saharan Africa is that they could enable Beijing to project power in a conflict and potentially control key SLOCs around the region. China's base in Djibouti provides it with potential leverage over the SLOCs transiting the Red Sea and enhances Beijing's ability to project power more in the Middle East and the Indian Ocean. Potential future bases in Kenya, Madagascar, Seychelles, or Tanzania could also endanger access to key SLOCs along the east coast of Africa, enhance China's power projection in the Indian Ocean and the Indo-Pacific region more broadly, and intensify competition between China and India.[58] Any of those bases could increase China's ability to threaten U.S. partner India in a conflict scenario.

The potential for Chinese basing on the Atlantic coast of Africa is another important although limited risk to the United States and several of its NATO allies. The U.S. Africa Command commander General Stephen Townsend testified in 2022 about China's potential basing arrangements on the west coast of Africa, especially Equatorial Guinea.[59] A possible Chinese naval facility was identified as the most significant Chinese security threat for the United States in the region because of its proximity to the United States and because it would provide China with the capability to rearm and repair naval vessels during a U.S.–China armed conflict.[60] Townsend stated that "a permanent Chinese naval presence in West Africa would almost certainly require the Department to consider shifts to U.S. naval force posture and pose increased risks to freedom of navigation and the U.S. ability to act."[61] In February 2022, senior U.S. diplomatic officials traveled to Equatorial Guinea to convince the country not to sign a basing agreement with China.[62] Other potential basing locations on the Atlantic coast of Africa, such as Nigeria, could pose similar challenges.

The main threat posed by Chinese basing in Equatorial Guinea or Nigeria is that it would provide China with naval access to the Atlantic for ships and submarines to project and maintain military power. This would increase the PRC's ability to threaten the homeland of the United States and NATO countries and their military activities in the Atlantic Ocean during a conflict scenario.

The threat of Russian basing in sub-Saharan Africa, compared to the PRC, is less of a risk for the United States. It has not yet established a base, and it appears that Russia has mostly paused its basing activity in sub-Saharan Africa for now due to its focus on Ukraine and developments with the Wagner Group. That said, Russia's long-planned facility in Sudan and other potential bases on the Horn of Africa, including in Eritrea and Somaliland, could threaten longer-term U.S. interests by providing Russia the opportunity to project power in key SLOCs transiting the Red Sea.

Another potential risk (or opportunity) for the United States in relation to basing in sub-Saharan Africa will be Sino–Russian relations on the continent. Depending on how Russia behaves in sub-Saharan Africa and the broader overall dynamics of Sino–Russian relations, Beijing–Moscow relations could become either closer or more strained on the continent. In recent years, China and Russia have largely coexisted in this region with relatively little friction between them. If their actions become more coordinated, as we have seen in other regions like the Middle East, their joint efforts and potential bases to project power together could pose risks to U.S. interests. Nevertheless, Russia's focus on creating instability in Africa and China's desire for stability in the region to support its economic and political interests may in the future create tensions between them in sub-Saharan Africa. Geopolitical divisions between Beijing and Moscow could provide an opportunity for the United States to ensure that they do not join forces on the continent.

POLICY IMPLICATIONS

Multiple policy implications flow from the geostrategic competition, risks, and challenges for the United States. At this point, Chinese economic, political, and security influence in sub-Saharan Africa and its current and future basing poses a potential threat to U.S. regional and global interests. China is identified as the pacing challenge by the U.S. government. In contrast, Russia has a smaller set of security interests in the region, and it is currently distracted by the war in Ukraine. Consequently, its behavior in the region is primarily disruptive. As a result, this section focuses on the policy implication of the behavior of the primary strategic competitor to the United States in the region: China.

The first policy implication is that Washington must prioritize its concerns about Chinese basing globally and in sub-Saharan Africa. Chinese basing in Asia, Europe, the Western Hemisphere, and the Middle East is a much more significant threat to the United States and its allies and partners, and the United States should therefore focus on those regions. Preventing Chinese basing in sub-Saharan Africa should be a lower priority relative to other geographic regions.

In sub-Saharan Africa, the top priority of the United States should be to limit new Chinese basing activity that could significantly impact access to the Strait of Hormuz, SLOCs in the Indian Ocean (such as bases in Kenya, Madagascar, the Seychelles, or Tanzania in East Africa), and bases that would enable it to further project and maintain power in a conflict with India—a key U.S. partner in the Indian Ocean region.

The second priority should be to limit Chinese bases that could provide Chinese ships and submarines access to the Atlantic with closer proximity to the United States and its NATO allies' homeland and military activities (e.g., bases in Equatorial Guinea and its neighboring countries on the west coast of Africa, such as Nigeria).

Other potential basing locations in the region, such as Angola and Namibia or other countries in southern or central Africa, should be less of a concern. They do not pose a significant threat to key SLOCs in the Middle East or Indian Ocean or substantially improve China's power projection capability in the Indian Ocean toward India or in the Atlantic Ocean toward the United States and NATO countries.

Going forward, as additional potential basing locations are identified, U.S. concerns about them should be driven by the following questions: Does basing in that country provide China with greater power projection capability over key SLOCs in the Middle East and the Indian Ocean? Does it provide China with a substantially greater ability to threaten the U.S. homeland or the homeland of U.S. allies and partners if a conflict scenario emerges? Does it provide the PRC with a greater ability to threaten the military activities of U.S. allies and partners in a conflict scenario? Does the United States have significant military cooperation with the potential host country? If yes, would a Chinese base in the country risk the transfer of sensitive military technology or information to the PRC? If the answer to all of those questions is no, Chinese basing in those sub-Saharan African countries should not be a particular concern for the United States. Examples of countries that would fall into that category at this point would include Angola, Namibia, or other countries in southern or central Africa.

The second policy implication is that the United States should not focus solely on military basing. Although basing is important, policymakers should consider the broader range of military capabilities that China can gain in sub-Saharan Africa through other types of military agreements, cooperation, and port access. Beijing does not necessarily need bases to project power and threaten SLOCs in the future.[63] For example, joint exercises with countries in the region, military aspects of strategic partnerships, the potential military use of commercial ports, and security cooperation in the Forum on China–Africa Cooperation and with the Africa Union should all be examined.[64]

Third, the United States should pursue opportunities for cooperation. Additional Chinese basing in sub-Saharan Africa is a legitimate concern. But to some degree and in some areas, Chinese and U.S. security interests in the region overlap and are complementary. The shared interests of the United States and China in sub-Saharan Africa include maintaining access to SLOCs around the continent, combating terrorism, fighting piracy in the Gulf of Guinea and Gulf of Aden, ensuring stability in and between countries throughout the region, and providing humanitarian assistance. These interests drive both of them to maintain a basing presence in the region. Shared interests offer significant opportunities for cooperation in sub-Saharan Africa between the United States and China in an era of strategic competition. In fact, sub-Saharan Africa may be one of the most promising regions for potential cooperation. Where possible, the United States should pursue these opportunities for cooperation with China to minimize the potential for competition and conflict between these two great powers in this region. The United States and China could conduct joint counterterrorism operations. They could cooperate through multilateral mechanisms to fight piracy in the Gulf of Guinea. They could jointly engage in humanitarian relief or conflict mediation efforts between states. Of all the regions in the world, sub-Saharan Africa may provide some of the most significant opportunities for security cooperation. Leveraging these opportunities may not only help address common security challenges on the continent but also help build trust between the United States and China and help manage the overall relationship in the region and globally. If China feels more confident that its security interests on the continent are protected, it may have less of a motivation to pursue additional bases.

CONCLUSION

Increasingly, China is sub-Saharan Africa's most important economic and political partner, and its influence is starting to eclipse that of the United States. China and Russia have different interests and capacities in sub-Saharan Africa. China's economic and political interests and footprint have rapidly expanded in sub-Saharan Africa, but its strategic focus remains elsewhere globally. Its security interests in the region are limited, primarily seeking to secure and maintain access to resources and markets and safeguard its citizens and businesses abroad. Today, it has one base in Djibouti, but the United States fears that it is pursuing bases in other countries on the continent. In the future, China may desire to project and maintain military power to threaten the United States and its allies and partners in conflict scenarios.

Russia, with more limited economic and political stakes in the region, is more opportunistic. It tends to pursue its security interests in an ad hoc fashion, often through undertaking profit-seeking and destabilizing activities. It does not yet have a base in the region, but it has expressed an interest in pursuing one or more in the future. It also interacts with a number of countries in the region through its Wagner Group.

The United States has an enduring economic and political role in the region. It maintains a permanent base in Djibouti, an air force facility in Niger, and troops in Kenya and Somalia and has authorized special operations forces to support counterterrorism missions in other countries in sub-Saharan Africa.

Compared to other regions, sub-Saharan Africa is not a high strategic priority for China, Russia, or the United States. Most of the vital interests of these powers are in Asia, Europe, the Western Hemisphere, and the Middle East. As a result, this chapter argues that preventing Chinese basing in sub-Saharan Africa should not be a high priority for the U.S. government. That said, in recent years, U.S. concerns about Chinese and Russian basing in sub-Saharan Africa are growing. In light of those worries, the U.S. government should prioritize its concerns in the region. Its primary focus should be on limiting Chinese basing in East Africa that threatens the SLOCs in the Middle East and Indian Ocean and that enables the PRC to project power toward India. The secondary focus should be on limiting Chinese bases on the Atlantic coast of Africa with closer proximity to the United States and NATO. In general, however, Chinese basing in southern and central Africa should not be a major concern for the United States.

Finally, Washington should seek opportunities for cooperation with Beijing in the region, based on their numerous shared security interests there. This may provide one of the few remaining opportunities for these two great powers to build trust and demonstrate to themselves that they are able to work together to provide public goods and address shared challenges in the international system. In general, states in sub-Saharan Africa do not want to pick sides between Washington and Beijing. In the security realm, the United States and China do not necessarily need to force them to choose.

NOTES

1. The author thanks Isaac Kardon and Andrew Yeo for their valuable comments on drafts of this work as well as participants in the "Great Power Competition and Overseas Basing" workshop hosted by the Brookings Institution for their insights. The views expressed in this policy brief are those of the author and do not reflect the official policy or position of the National Defense University, the Department of Defense, or the U.S. government.

2. For the purposes of this policy brief, sub-Saharan Africa includes all the countries in Africa except for Egypt and the African Maghreb countries of Algeria, Libya, Morocco, and Tunisia. Those North African countries are considered to geographically belong to the greater Middle East.

3. Phillip Meng, "China Isn't the Only Asian Country Expanding Its Trade with Africa," Atlantic Council, July 31, 2023, https://www.atlanticcouncil.org/blogs/econographics/china-isnt-the-only-asian-country-expanding-its-trade-with-africa.

4. International Monetary Fund, Direction of Trade Data, https://data.imf.org, accessed October 11, 2023.

5. International Monetary Fund, Direction of Trade Data.

6. "Data: Chinese Investment in Africa," China-Africa Research Initiative, http://www.sais-cari.org/chinese-investment-in-africa.

7. "Data: Chinese Investment in Africa."

8. For a discussion of China's cooperation forums, special envoys, and the Belt and Road Initiative in sub-Saharan Africa, see Dawn C. Murphy, *China's Rise in the Global South: The Middle East, Africa, and Beijing's Alternative World Order* (Redwood City, CA: Stanford University Press, 2022), chaps. 4, 5, and 9.

9. For a discussion of China's military activity in sub-Saharan Africa, see Murphy, *China's Rise in the Global South*, chap. 8.

10. "Military and Security Developments Involving the People's Republic of China," U.S. Department of Defense, 2023, 156, https://www.defense.gov/News/Releases/Release/Article/3561549/dod-releases-2023-report-on-military-and-security-developments-involving-the-pe.

11. For a more detailed discussion of China's interests in sub-Saharan Africa, see Murphy, *China's Rise in the Global South*, chap. 3.

12. "Military and Security Developments Involving the People's Republic of China," 2023, 155.

13. "Military and Security Developments Involving the People's Republic of China," 2023, 154–56.

14. This section on China's base in Djibouti draws heavily from Murphy, *China's Rise in the Global South*, chap. 8.

15. Jane Perlez and Chris Buckley, "China Retools Its Military with a First Overseas Outpost in Djibouti," *New York Times*, November 27, 2015, https://www.nytimes.com/2015/11/27/world/asia/china-military-presence-djibouti-africa.html.

16. "China's Engagement in Djibouti," Congressional Research Service, September 4, 2019, https://crsreports.congress.gov/product/pdf/IF/IF11304.

17. "Military and Security Developments Involving the People's Republic of China," U.S. Department of Defense, 2022, https://www.defense.gov/News/Releases/Release/Article/3230516/2022-report-on-military-and-security-developments-involving-the-peoples-republi; Peter A. Dutton, Isaac B. Kardon, and Conor M. Kennedy, "Djibouti: China's First Overseas Strategic Strongpoint," U.S. Naval War College Digital Commons, April 2020, 30, https://digital-commons.usnwc.edu/cmsi-maritime-reports/6. Some estimates indicate that more than

10,000 troops could ultimately be housed at the base compared to 4,000 at the U.S. base, Camp Lemonnier.

18. "Military and Security Developments Involving the People's Republic of China," 2022, 144.

19. Dutton et al., "Djibouti," 31.

20. "China Denies Using Lasers on US Aircraft in Djibouti," Associated Press, May 6, 2018, https://apnews.com/fd24e1e1004743d6a20343d890ff4f5f/China-denies-using-lasers-on-US-aircraft-in-Djibouti.

21. David Brennan, "US Commander Says China Tried to Sneak into American Military Base in Africa," *Newsweek*, June 18, 2019, https://www.newsweek.com/u-s-china-sneak-military-base-africa-djibouti-1444542.

22. Jeremy Page, "China to Build Naval Hub in Djibouti," *Wall Street Journal*, November 26, 2015, https://www.wsj.com/articles/china-to-build-naval-logistics-facility-in-djibouti-1448557719.

23. Gabriel Collins and Andrew Erickson, "Djibouti Likely to Become China's First Indian Ocean Outpost," *China Signpost*, July 11, 2015, https://www.chinasignpost.com/2015/07/11/djibouti-likely-to-become-chinas-first-indian-ocean-outpost.

24. Shannon Tiezzi, "US General: China Has 10 Year Contract for First Overseas Military Base," *The Diplomat,* November 26, 2015, https://thediplomat.com/2015/11/us-general-china-has-10-year-contract-for-first-overseas-military-base. The Libya evacuation was the People's Liberation Army's most extensive overseas evacuation since the founding of the PRC.

25. Based on author interviews of Chinese government officials and scholars about the time the base was founded.

26. "Military and Security Developments Involving the People's Republic of China," 2023, 155.

27. Dietmar Pieper, "How Djibouti Became China's Gateway to Africa," *Spiegel Online,* February 8, 2019, https://www.spiegel.de/international/world/djibouti-is-becoming-gateway-to-africa-for-china-a-1191441.html.

28. Huma Siddiqui, "India and Japan Cement Defence Ties!," *Financial Express*, September 20, 2020, https://www.financialexpress.com/business/defence-india-and-japan-cement-defence-ties-ink-landmark-acsa-pact-india-to-get-access-to-djibouti-in-africa-2079896.

29. "Saudi Arabia Is Latest Nation to Build Military Base in Djibouti," CGTN, June 15, 2023, https://africa.cgtn.com/saudi-arabia-is-latest-nation-to-build-military-base-in-djibouti.

30. Based on author interviews with Middle Eastern and African government officials and scholars around the time the base was established. Although in recent years there have been reports that China has increasingly reached out to the United Arab Emirates and Iran for potential basing opportunities in the region, China continues to be cautious to not be seen as picking sides in the Middle East.

31. Bates Gill, *Daring to Struggle: China's Global Ambitions under Xi Jinping* (Oxford: Oxford University Press, 2022), 127.

32. "Military and Security Developments Involving the People's Republic of China," 2023, 154–56.

33. "Military and Security Developments Involving the People's Republic of China," 2023, 154–56.

34. Dipanjan Roy Chaudhury, "China Eyes Military Base in Indian Ocean Region in Madagascar," *The Economic Times*, July 20, 2022, https://economictimes.indiatimes.com/news/defence/china-eyes-military-base-in-indian-ocean-region-in-madagascar/articleshow/93008091.cms?from=mdr; *China's Influence in South and Central Asia, Panel IV—Maritime Competition in the Indian Ocean: Testimony before the U.S.-China Economic and Security Review Commission*, 117th Cong. 12 (2022) (statement of Darshana Baruah, Fellow, Carnegie Endowment for International Peace), https://www.uscc.gov/sites/default/files/2022-05/Darshana_Baruah_Testimony.pdf.

35. "Direction of Trade Data," International Monetary Fund, https://data.imf.org.

36. Joseph Siegle, "Decoding Russia's Economic Engagements in Africa," African Center for Strategic Studies, January 6, 2023, https //africacenter.org/spotlight/decoding-russia-economic-engagements-africa.

37. "Second Summit Economic and Humanitarian Forum Russia-Africa," Russia-Africa Summit, https://summitafrica.ru.

38. For an excellent analysis of Russia's basing outside the former Soviet Union and its opportunistic and ad hoc behavior, see Emily Holland, "Opportunistic Basing: Russian Foreign Policy and Overseas Military Facilities' (working paper, 2023).

39. Joseph Siegle, "Russia and Africa: Expanding Influence and Instability," in *Russia's Global Reach: A Security and Statecraft Assessment*, ed. Graeme P. Herd (Garmisch-Partenkirchen: George C. Marshall European Center for Security Studies, 2021), 80–90; General Stephen J. Townsend, "Investing in America's Security in Africa: A Continent of Growing Strategic Importance," testimony before the House Armed Services Committee, March 15, 2022, https://www.armed-services.senate.gov/imo/media/doc/AFRICOM%20FY23%20Posture%20Statement%20%20ISO%20SASC%2015%20MAR%20Cleared.pdf; Federica Saini Fasanotti, "Russia's Wagner Group in Africa: Influence, Commercial Concessions, Rights Violations, and Counter Insurgency Failure," Brookings Institution, February 8, 2022, https://www.brookings.edu/blog/order-from-chaos/2022/02/08/russias-wagner-group-in-africa-influence-commercial-concessions-rights-violations-and-counterinsurgency-failure.

40. Holland, "Opportunistic Basing."

41. Holland, "Opportunistic Basing."

42. Amy Mackinnon, Robbie Gramer, and Jack Detsch, "Russia's Dreams of a Red Sea Naval Base Are Scuttled—for Now," *Foreign Policy*, July 15, 2022, https://foreignpolicy.com/2022/07/15/russia-sudan-putin-east-africa-port-red-sea-naval-base-scuttled.

43. Holland, "Opportunistic Basing."

44. Mathieu Droin and Tina Dolbaia, "Russia Is Still Progressing in Africa. What's the Limit?," Center for Strategic and International Studies, August 15, 2023, https://www.csis.org/analysis/russia-still-progressing-africa-whats-limit; Samy Magdy, "Sudan Military Finishes Review of Russian Red Sea Base Deal," Associated Press, February 11, 2023, https://apnews.com/article/politics-sudan-government-moscow-803738fba4d8f91455f0121067c118dd.

45. Siegle, "Russia and Africa."

46. Holland, "Opportunistic Basing."

47. Siegle, "Russia and Africa."

48. Anton Troianovski, Declan Walsh, Eric Schmitt, Vivian Yee, and Julian E. Barnes, "After Prigozhin's Death, a High-Stakes Scramble for His Empire," *New York Times*, September 8, 2023, https://www.nytimes.com/2023/09/08/world/europe/prigozhin-wagner-russia-africa.html.

49. Joseph Siegle, "Inflection Point for Africa–Russia Relations after Prigozhin's Death," Africa Center for Strategic Studies, September 6, 2023, https://africacenter.org/spotlight/inflection-point-for-africa-russia-relations-after-prigozhins-death.

50. "Prosper Africa," Prosper Africa, https://www.prosperafrica.gov.

51. "U.S.-Africa Leaders Summit," U.S. Department of State, https://www.state.gov/africasummit.

52. Townsend, "Investing in America's Security in Africa."

53. "National Security Strategy," White House, October 2022, 44, https://www.whitehouse.gov/briefing-room/statements-releases/2022/10/12/fact-sheet-the-biden-harris-administrations-national-security-strategy.

54. "Sub-Saharan Africa: Key Issues and U.S. Engagement," Congressional Research Service, February 2021, 16, https://crsreports.congress.gov/product/details?prodcode=R45428. The total includes all of the U.S. Africa Command personnel, not just those in sub-Saharan Africa.

55. "Sub-Saharan Africa," 17.

56. "Sub-Saharan Africa," 18.

57. "Sub-Saharan Africa," 19.

58. Darshana Baruah, "Maritime Competition in the Indian Ocean," testimony for U.S.-China Economic and Security Review Commission, May 12, 2022, https://carnegieendowment.org/2022/05/12/maritime-competition-in-indian-ocean-pub-87093.

59. Townsend, "Investing in America's Security in Africa."

60. Michael M. Phillips, "China Seeks First Military Base on Africa's Atlantic Coast: Alarmed Officials at the White House and Pentagon Urge Equatorial Guinea to Rebuff Beijing's Overtures," *Wall Street Journal*, December 5, 2021, https://www.wsj.com/articles/china-seeks-first-military-base-on-africas-atlantic-coast-u-s-intelligence-finds-11638726327.

61. Townsend, "Investing in America's Security in Africa."

62. Michael M. Phillips, "U.S. Aims to Thwart China's Plan for Atlantic Base in Africa: An American Delegation Wants to Convince Equatorial Guinea against Giving Beijing a Launchpad in Waters the U.S. Considers Its Backyard," *Wall Street*

Journal, February 11, 2022, https://www.wsj.com/articles/u-s-aims-to-thwart-chinas-plan-for-atlantic-base-in-africa-11644607931.

63. For great work on this issue, see Isaac B. Kardon, "China's Global Maritime Access: Alternatives to Overseas Military Bases in the Twenty-First Century," *Security Studies* 31, no. 5 (October 2022): 885–916; Isaac Kardon, "China's Ports in Africa," National Bureau of Asian Research, May 2022, https://www.nbr.org/publication/chinas-ports-in-africa; and Isaac B. Kardon and Wendy Leutert, "Pier Competitor: China's Power Position in Global Ports," *International Security* 46, no. 4 (April 2022): 9–47, https://direct.mit.edu/isec/article-abstract/46/4/9/111175/Pier-Competitor-China-s-Power-Position-in-Global?redirectedFrom=fulltext.

64. For a discussion of security aspects of the Forum on China–Africa Cooperation, see Murphy, *China's Rise in the Global South*, chap. 4.

7

International Ordering and Great Power Competition

Lessons from Central Asia's Post–Cold War Basing Relations

ALEXANDER COOLEY

In June 2014, U.S. officials handed back control of the Manas Transit Center, an air base in Kyrgyzstan that had supported its operations in Afghanistan since 2001, to the Kyrgyz government. The handoff was framed as a geopolitical victory for Russia, an ally of the small Central Asian state.[1] The base itself was a logistics, not combat, hub. However, it had been a regular source of geopolitical intrigue and hard bargaining over access rights and quid pro quos. Investigative reports revealed how Kyrgyz officials sought to politically and economically benefit from the base and the regional geopolitical rivalry it generated.[2] With U.S., Russian, and Chinese security facilities present in Central Asia, the region presents a striking illustration of how even relatively small facilities can become entangled in local politics, escalating regional great power rivalries.

Central Asia's base politics reveals that overseas U.S. basing agreements and their underlying bargains are embedded in a broader ecology of "international orders" and emerging geopolitical counterorders, pushed by strategic competitors including China and Russia. This chapter is divided into theoretical and empirical sections. The first part explores how foreign military bases are implicated in and help to constitute three important dimensions of international orders: security communities, goods substitution (public, private, and club goods) and provision, and the political principles and governing practices that bind sending and receiving states. In the initial post–Cold War period, when the U.S.-led liberal international order was globally dominant, the United States was able to secure overseas basing rights by integrating host countries within its security network, offering various economic and political goods, and championing the virtues of political liberalism.

The second part of the chapter uses post-Soviet Central Asia as a regional test case to explore how the rise of China and Russia as influential revisionist powers has complicated and challenged U.S. leadership and its basing access. It explores how Moscow and Beijing integrated their basing footprint within their own regional security architectures and how these great power rivals sought to buttress their own basing initiatives by providing economic and political support to the Central Asian regimes. Furthermore, it examines how both Russia and China publicly opposed Western calls for greater democracy and human rights protections by Central Asia's authoritarian regimes. By the time the United States was withdrawing from Afghanistan in 2021, Russia and China had effectively pressured the Central Asian states to deny even temporary basing rights to the United States to facilitate its regional exit.

CHANGING NORMS OF SOVEREIGNTY, INTERNATIONAL ORDERS, AND FOREIGN MILITARY BASING

In recent years, scholars have shed light on foreign military basing as a particular form of sovereign practice. These changing norms of sovereignty are often associated with or embedded in particular international orders. Sebastian Schmidt has explored how modern sovereign basing agreements between a host and a sending country—where the foreign military presence does not interfere with domestic authority structures of the host—in the U.S. case was a pragmatic solution to the problem of redefining the status of its enduring security presence from the wartime era within allies and occupied states.[3] Prior to World War II, the United States routinely inserted clauses in agreements governing its deployments that allowed it the right to interfere in the domestic sovereign affairs of its hosts, such as the infamous Platt Amendment that first governed the U.S. military presence in Guantanamo Bay, Cuba.[4]

But sovereign basing norms have also been implicated in changing norms and international ordering of decolonization in the 1950s and 1960s. While European colonial powers let go of previous imperial holdings, they often did so with the provision that they retain basing rights for a certain period of time as well as other property rights, such as mining or commodity concessions.[5] For example, France granted independence to a dozen sub-Saharan colonies in 1960, retaining basing rights in all of them for an initial period of ten years. However, over time, base hosts gained increased bargaining leverage to either expel or restrict the activities of sending states.[6] In short, the particular sovereign norms that scholars of foreign military basing have delineated are often part of a broader international order.

Three distinct features integrate a basing host into the broader international and regional ordering architectures and infrastructures of the base host: (1) broader security institutions and common security narratives, (2) base-related goods provision and substitution, and (3) the regime types of base hosts.

SECURITY INSTITUTIONS AND SECURITY NARRATIVES

Basing agreements themselves are often embedded within a greater overall security framework, such as an alliance (NATO), a common defense treaty, or a security community. How basing agreements are presented and legally justified domestically in the host is often critical for maintaining domestic legitimacy and enduring commitment. Invoking a common security threat is usually necessary but often insufficient for gaining the consent of a host country's public to accept an enduring foreign military presence. For example, U.S. bases in Italy during the Cold War and post–Cold War eras have routinely been referred to almost exclusively as NATO facilities, whereas the basing agreements in Greece and Spain in the 1980s, renewed under fiery socialist prime ministers who publicly opposed membership in NATO, were designated as Greek and Spanish facilities, respectively.[7] In Greece, elites openly dismissed the direct Soviet threat but saw maintaining U.S. bases as critical for ensuring that Washington keep a check on rival Turkey's military ambitions.[8] The Turkish government has always distinguished between U.S. bases serving U.S. or bilateral purposes, which it has periodically halted, and the NATO or multilateral function of the U.S. presence in

Incirlik. As Yeo has explored, a common security purpose that is publicly articulated by elites in both the host and the sending state can be critical for maintaining public support for the facility amid vocal social protests.[9] The management of base-related crises and accidents can also feed and intensify contending narratives surrounding the security purposes and mission of the U.S. presence abroad.

Accordingly, revisionist competitors can politicize and target the overall security framework of a U.S. overseas basing agreement. Revisionist competitors can employ either "brokering" or "wedging" strategies or a combination of both.[10] Brokering involves trying to embed the target country in a new framework of bilateral or regional security cooperation controlled by the revisionist power. For example, Russia's Collective Security Treaty Organization presents itself as a NATO-style body guarding against transnational and territorial threats in Eurasia, but the treaty also includes a clause prohibiting members from stationing foreign military troops without the consent of the other treaty members. Wedging is the inverse—undermining support in the host country for security cooperation with the United States by, for example, supporting anti-U.S. political factions, anti-base movements, or base-related disinformation campaigns. For example, both Russia (especially in the U.S. Black Sea bases hosted by Romania and Bulgaria) and China (attempting to play on Okinawan divisions with mainland Japan over the U.S. bases on the island) have used social media to disseminate anti-U.S. disinformation in an attempt to delegitimize the U.S. overseas presence among local populations.

BASES AND GOODS SUBSTITUTION

A second area where basing relations are implicated in international ordering is in the array of goods associated with agreements. As David Lake explores in his account of the underlying dynamics of U.S. global hierarchy, the underlying bargain between the United States and its security clients was one of providing security—as measured and substantiated by U.S. troops abroad—in exchange for concessions elements of their sovereignty and political autonomy.[11] Indeed, major security clients, especially major base hosts such as Germany, Korea, and Japan, subsidize the presence of U.S. forces by paying substantial amounts of Host Nation Support—a fact framed by former U.S. president Trump as an example of allies "taking advantage" of the United States.[12]

However, with other categories of base hosts, the sending country has needed to offer other types of goods and assets—including club goods or private payoffs to regimes—as a partial quid pro quo for establishing and maintaining basing rights. In the U.S. case, a number of allies that initially provided basing facilities for minimal quid pro quo in the 1950s and 1960s (including Greece, Spain, Turkey, and the Philippines) in the 1970s and 1980s demanded escalating packages of rents and other aid for ceding basing rights.[13] Base-related goods included security assistance (Military Assistance Programs) and weapons sales on concessionary terms (Foreign Military Financing) as well as more direct forms of economic payments.[14] In some cases, the United States used its hegemonic leadership position in international financial institutions to push for the disbursal of goods such as development assistance and financial packages as more indirect forms of quid pro quo. For example, in the Philippines, as part of its support for anti-communist Ferdinand Marcos, the United States provided large rental packages for its military bases but also supported major international financial institutions, such as the World Bank and International Monetary Fund lending to Manila.[15] Similarly, when the French secured basing rights from its African colonies in 1960s, they kept the newly independent regimes in the Franc Zone by demanding they continue to use the former metropole currency.[16]

Providing public, club, and private goods is an important way in which base hosts can take advantage of ordering mechanisms to establish and sustain basing deals. It follows that competing great powers can use the counterordering mechanism of "goods substitution"[17]—and the offer of providing rival or competing goods of comparable quality (development aid packages, debt relief, and infrastructure upgrades) and/or less intrusive political conditions (no human rights clauses or anti-corruption oversight) to undermine the status of an existing basing deal or offer new incentives to establish their own bases. At the extreme, strategic competitors can deny the United States basing and access rights by outbidding the goods that U.S. policymakers are willing and able to provide in exchange for basing rights. Moscow has periodically used economic crises as an opportunity to try to obtain access from small states on the margins of the U.S. security community, though most of these efforts have been unsuccessful. For example, following the 2008 financial crisis, Russia approached the government of Iceland with the prospect of extending an emergency loan to the cash-strapped country in exchange for being granted access to the old U.S. basing facility at Keflavik airport.[18]

ORDERING PRINCIPLES AND REGIME TYPES

Basing deals advance prevailing norms about what constitutes legitimate forms of political governance and social practices between the sending and the hosting regime. In the case of the American-led hegemonic system, political liberalism has been a major—but not exclusively so—political ordering principle, establishing the idea that governments should protect a minimal set of rights among citizens. Of course, U.S. policy in practice has often not reflected these values—especially in supporting right-wing dictatorships.[19] But Cold War basing relations were deeply enmeshed in global ideological competition: U.S.-allied regimes and security clients received U.S. assistance and goods by burnishing their anti-communist commitments, just as the Soviet Union tried to advance socialism in the Third World by aiding the rise of self-identifying Marxist-Leninist regimes and integrating these allies and clients into a network of communist military assistance, development, and technical expertise.[20] American officials supported the authoritarian practices of certain base hosts such as Franco's Spain and South Korea under military rule, making the U.S. military itself susceptible to political backlash during democratization and demands for renegotiations of politically sensitive elements of these deals.[21] But conservatives in the United States during the Cold War claimed that maintaining relations with right-wing authoritarian regimes was practically necessary. Jean Kirkpatrick's famous essay argued that by aggressively pushing U.S. allies and security clients to improve their human rights practices, the Carter administration had allowed more unfriendly ideological forces—communism and Islamic militants—to seize power in Chile and Iran.[22]

Still, some political practices and agreements with base hosts have proven unacceptable as prevailing social norms change. Ingimundarson has revealed how in 1951 the United States initially went along with the Icelandic government's secret demand to ban the stationing of African American soldiers on its territory, a practice that was publicly denied by both sides until it was lifted in the 1970s in response to U.S. presidential pressure.[23] Even in the classic authoritarian case of Marcos in the mid-1980s, most U.S. officials saw a tipping point internally after which base access was likely to be jeopardized by continuing to side with Marcos over his main political opponent Cori Aquino. To a large extent, this drove U.S. officials to facilitate the 1986 exit and exile of the Philippine autocrat.

The end of the Cold War elevated the importance of political liberalism and liberal values as the main basis for security partnership and basing relationships. Throughout the 1990s, the unipolar moment and accompanying international order saw political liberalism and democratic principles ascendant. The era saw the unprecedented post-communist transitions (economic and political), the expansion of transatlantic institutions along liberal principles, and U.S.-led military interventions in the Balkan Wars. NATO completed its largest enlargement in 2004 by adding ten new members, mostly post-communist states, all having undertaken a number of liberal reforms that included ensuring civilian control over the military, guaranteeing minority rights and media freedoms, and transparency in legislative bodies.[24]

But the events of 9/11 and the onset of the Global War on Terrorism had transformative effects on the global salience of political liberalism. Not only did the U.S. officials make the case that terrorists and terrorist suspects, as enemy combatants, were not entitled to certain constitutional protections, but, as Kim Lane Scheppele observed, the 2000s saw a range of anti-Constitution measures adopted around the world by governments that included increasing their surveillance over citizens, empowering security services, and creating a parallel set of legal processes outside of the criminal code.[25] Moreover, governments used this new political framework to brand political opponents and sometimes entire classes of citizens as terrorists or extremists. More broadly, the protection of regime security and anti-terrorism have been widely promoted, among other illiberal norms, within new regional security arrangements led by both Russia and China, such as the Shanghai Cooperation Organization (SCO),[26] in addition to the counter-norms of "civilizational diversity," associated with China, and the importance of traditional values, often pushed by Russia.[27] Finally, the so-called Color Revolutions (2003–2005) in Eurasia and the Arab Spring (2011–2013) in the Middle East—where authoritarian governments were toppled following democratic protests while being viewed in the West as democratic protests and uprisings—were framed by Moscow, Beijing, and other regional actors as illegitimate regime changes instigated by the West.

In sum, foreign military basing relations are implicated in important aspects of international orders that include security communities, goods substitution, and political norms of regime types. The particular configuration of a prevailing order may enable certain basing agreements to be established and maintained in some eras and challenged in others. Moreover, viewing foreign military basing arrangements as implicated in a wider set of international ordering activities helps us to see the likelihood of how great power competitors or revisionist challengers might adopt the practice of basing and how these agreements might be implicated in their counterordering challenges to U.S. hegemony and influence.

INTERNATIONAL ORDERS AND FOREIGN MILITARY BASES IN POST–COLD WAR CENTRAL ASIA

We can see illustrations of these international ordering dynamics and revisionist challenges in the evolving base politics of post–Cold War Central Asia—the region comprising the five former Soviet republics turned independent states of Kazakhstan, Kyrgyzstan, Tajikistan, Turkmenistan, and Uzbekistan. Central Asia is an instructive region for observing changing regional ordering dynamics and basing practices over four distinct phases: (1) post-Soviet independence and state building (1991–2001), (2) U.S. hegemony and broad acceptance of U.S. bases (2001–2004), (3) contestation of liberal ordering and competitive counterordering projects (2004–2014), and (4) ascendant revisionism by Russia and China, intensification of regional engagement, and active blocking of new U.S. basing requests (2014–2021).

The 1990s: Managing Post-Soviet Extrication and Soviet Basing Legacies

Until the events of September 11, 2001, the post-Soviet Central Asian states were relatively removed from major conflicts or geopolitical turmoil. Throughout the 1990s, all of the Central Asian states attempted to strengthen their sovereignty and independence by developing a range of external ties to both Western and Asian partners while still remaining deferential to Russia on most security-related matters. Regional cooperation and integration were limited, constrained by patrimonial politics and concerns about regime autonomy and security. In terms of basing posture, Russia initially retained a monopoly on the region's Soviet-era legacy bases, the most significant of which was in Tajikistan's capital of Dushanbe, where Moscow maintained 5,000 troops of the 201st Motorized Division, its largest military base outside of the territory of the Russian Federation, which had intervened decisively on behalf of the nascent Tajik government during the Tajik Civil War in 1992.[28] Russia also maintained a network of missile testing facilities at Kasputin Yar in northern Kazakhstan and operated the space-launch facility at Baikonur in Kazakhstan via an initial twenty-year lease that was agreed on in 1994.[29] The Russian bases generated little political attention or controversy during the 1990s.

2001–2005: U.S. Intervention in Afghanistan and the Global War on Terrorism

This relative tranquility would change overnight following the events of 9/11, as Central Asia became the front line of the Global War on Terrorism and a logistical key to Operation Enduring Freedom in Afghanistan. American planners concluded an agreement in October 2001 with the government of Uzbekistan to use a Soviet-era air base, for noncombat support missions, near the city of Khanabad (known as Karshi-Khanabad or "K2") in the south of the country, close to the Afghan border.[30] A few weeks later, the United States reached an agreement with the government of Kyrgyzstan to use a portion of the civilian international airport of Manas in Kyrgyzstan, near the capital of Bishkek, for refueling and staging flights into Afghanistan. Along with these basing deals, the United States signed a number of agreements with all of the Central Asian states securing overflight rights, emergency landing, and refueling agreements, though many of these were kept secret. In addition, two other NATO powers concluded their own enduring bilateral basing arrangements with Central Asian hosts: Germany contracted with the government of Uzbekistan to use a facility at Termez on the Afghan border (the first time Germany had established an overseas military base since World War II), while France agreed with the government of Tajikistan to use a portion of the international airport of the capital Dushanbe, as seen in figure 7.1.

Critically, in this initial phase, both Russia and China supported—or at least did not publicly object to—U.S. and allied basing deals. China used the U.S.-led Global War on Terrorism to frame its own crackdown and efforts to erase the cultural identity of the Uyghur population in its western province of Xinjiang.[31] Russian president Vladimir Putin even downplayed the prospect of geopolitical competition with the United States and affirmed the sovereign rights of the Central Asian states to conclude such security arrangements.[32] This accommodating position would change within eighteen months as Russian analysts and security officials began to publicly speculate that the United States, following the end of major combat operations in Afghanistan, was maintaining its basing presence in Central Asia. Indeed, Moscow established its own air base in Kant, Kyrgyzstan, in October 2003,

Figure 7.1. Map of Major NATO and Russian Military Bases and Facilities in Central Asia, c. 2003.

Adapted from Alexander Cooley, *Great Games, Local Rules: The New Great Power Contest in Central Asia* (Oxford: Oxford University Press, 2014).

just a few kilometers away from Manas, under the auspices of the Russian-led Collective Security Treaty Organization.

2005–2014: Contested Regional Orders—Competing Security Communities and Counterordering Efforts

In the mid-2000s, geopolitical tensions over the U.S. presence intensified while the United States struggled to reconcile its promotion of democracy and liberal ordering principles with the authoritarianism and cronyism of the Central Asian governments. Russia exploited these tensions by denouncing liberal political norms and supporting the authoritarian practices of the Central Asian governments in a bid to weaken U.S. regional influence.

The war in Iraq and the Bush administration's pursuit of the "Freedom Agenda," endorsing regime change for the purposes of democratization, alarmed the Central Asian governments. So did the onset of the Color Revolutions, which brought street protests following flawed national elections and toppled corrupt governments in Georgia (2003), Ukraine (2004), and Kyrgyzstan (2005), replacing them with self-styled reformers who publicly expressed the wish to orient more toward the West and away from Russia.³³ The relationship with Uzbekistan became strained as President Islam Karimov's rule grew increasingly repressive. In May 2005, the Uzbek security services fired on a protesting crowd that had assembled in the eastern city of Andijon, killing hundreds in what became known as the "Andijon massacre." The Uzbek government insisted that the victims were members of a militant Islamic group, while international human rights organizations insisted that these protestors were ordinary citizens demonstrating against government policies.³⁴

The aftermath of Andijon soon took a geopolitical turn as well, as both Russia and China publicly supported Karimov's actions, whereas the European Union and the United States imposed sanctions on Uzbek government officials and called for an international investigation into the events. As relations between the United States and Uzbekistan rapidly deteriorated in the wake of Andijon, Beijing and Moscow used the annual meeting of the SCO (formed in 2001) to call for greater non-Western influence in the region's security and, adopting China's security agenda, to combat the "three evils" of terrorism, separatism, and extremism.³⁵ At its annual summit in July 2005, the SCO issued a now infamous communique that noted that the situation in Afghanistan had been stabilized and that the "foreign" (i.e., American) military bases stationed in member states should be put on a timetable for withdrawal.³⁶ Just days later, after the United States backed a UN plan to not repatriate some Uzbek refugees from Andijon who had fled to neighboring Kyrgyzstan, the government of Uzbekistan notified the United States that it was terminating the base lease and effectively evicting U.S. forces from K2.³⁷ A few months later, Uzbekistan formally joined the Russian-led Collective Security Treaty Organization in what was widely viewed as a geopolitical victory for Moscow.³⁸

As the base in Uzbekistan became a lightning rod of tensions over Central Asian authoritarianism and Russian and Chinese security initiatives, Manas in Kyrgyzstan became embroiled in a series of corrupt Kyrgyz regimes demanding increasing quid pro quo and private goods from U.S. planners. The status of the base became highly charged following the ouster of Kyrgyz president Askar Akayev in March 2005 by interim acting president Bakiyev, who demanded that the United States increase its rental payment for the use of Manas 100-fold—from \$2 million to \$200 million annually. A deal in July 2006 extended the U.S. lease at Manas until 2010, raising base rent to \$17 million annually, with the U.S. side also committing to provide an annual total of $150 million in aid and assistance to Kyrgyzstan as tacit quid pro quo.[39]

Dissatisfied with the agreement, a dramatic base bidding war ensued in early 2009 as Russia attempted to bribe the Kyrgyz president to close the base by offering an emergency $2 billion economic relief package. The announcement set off a frenzied response, and the U.S. side concluded another new deal to keep the base open, valid until 2014, under which Manas would be referred to as a "transit center" and the annual rent would be raised from $17 million to $63 million.[40] Bakiyev's regime would collapse the following year in 2010, and acting premier Roza Otunbayeva announced that she would honor the basing agreement despite popular perceptions that its operations—especially the lucrative fuel contracts—had served to line the pockets of the Bakiyev family. On this point, former U.S. secretary of defense Robert Gates referred to the government of Bakiyev as "amazingly corrupt" and Manas as a site of "grand extortion."[41] The Kyrgyz government maintained its commitment to allow the base until 2014; however, U.S. officials were unsuccessful in their attempts to extend the lease for an additional year.

2014–2021: Russia's and China's Greater Eurasia and Counter-Liberal Order

The last U.S. forces departed Manas well in advance of the July 2014 deadline, marking the end of the U.S. basing presence in Central Asia. The year 2014 also marked a significant shift in the geopolitical orientation of the region, with Russia and China intensifying their regional economic and security engagement. Russia intensified its relations with the Central Asian states following its annexation of Crimea—including accelerating the establishment of the Eurasian Economic Union—while China has prioritized investing in Central Asia through its Belt and Road Initiative (three of six initiative routes pass through Central Asia).[42]

Indeed, recent security initiatives from the Chinese People's Liberation Army appear to have made China the new basing power in the region. According to a pair of investigative stories, the government of Tajikistan has, since 2016, allowed China to maintain a small group of Chinese paramilitary forces at a remote facility near the Afghan border.[43] Under the reported terms of the agreement, China is allowed to station personnel at the facility and to patrol broad swaths of the Tajik–Afghan border. Along with Chinese upgrades of Tajik border posts, these Chinese units appear to be focused on controlling border crossings and possible infiltration into China. In October 2021, the Tajik parliament transferred full control of the facility to China and approved the construction of a second Chinese-funded facility.[44] Chinese economic engagement in Tajikistan also increased, with 80 percent of the Central Asian country's new debt from 2007 to 2018 originating from Chinese state creditors.[45] In 2016, China established a new regional security organization, the Quadrilateral Cooperation and Coordination Mechanism, which includes itself, Tajikistan, Afghanistan, and Pakistan and whose purpose is to enhance regional security cooperation on counterterrorism, joint training, and border management issues. Russia did not oppose the Chinese facility, suggesting that earlier predictions that Moscow's and Beijing's jockeying for influence in Central Asia might undermine their so-called axis of convenience appear unwarranted.[46]

China's and Russia's growing regional influence also afforded them the leverage to prevent the United States from securing contingency basing rights from the Central Asian states in support of withdrawing its forces from Afghanistan. In April 2021, General Kenneth McKenzie—head of U.S. Central Command—publicly announced that the United States was exploring securing basing in Central Asia as part of its preparation to reposition troops and plan for contingencies.[47] A subsequent report noted that U.S. defense officials were eager to secure bases for "troops, drones, bombers and artillery," with administration officials preferring to negotiate a deal with Uzbekistan or Tajikistan.[48] An investigative story later reported that, at his first summit with U.S. president Joe Biden in June 2021, Putin had rejected any role for U.S. military forces in Central Asia, undercutting the U.S. military's options to base drones and counterterrorism forces to support the withdrawal, reportedly asserting that "China would reject it as well."[49]

As the U.S. withdrawal accelerated, both China and Russia apparently increased their consultations with the Taliban and conducted border exercises with the Central Asian forces in an attempt to manage the border instability and regional uncertainty caused by the disintegrating Afghan National Army, which had resulted in hundreds of Afghan troops fleeing into Tajikistan and Uzbekistan. Moscow's and Beijing's regional assertiveness underscores that Central Asia is no longer hospitable to a U.S. basing presence and no longer influenced mainly by the U.S.-led international order. I summarize the relative efficacy and success of Russian and Chinese regional counterordering efforts in table 7.1.

Table 7.1. Scorecard of Select Counterordering Efforts and Status of U.S. Bases in Central Asia.

Features of U.S.-led International Order	Revisionist Actions from Russia and China + Challenges	Outcome and Assessment
Overseas Bases and U.S.-led Security Organizations U.S. bases in Uzbekistan (2001–2005) and Kyrgyzstan (2001–2014) Part of U.S.-led OEF coalition and ISAF mission	New Alternative Security Organizations CSTO (2002), SCO (2001), and QCCM (2016); support Russian bases in Kyrgyzstan (2003–) and Tajikistan; Chinese base in Tajikistan (2016–)	Co-existed with U.S. bases in 2003–2014; deepened in 2014–2021 without U.S. presence; and denied U.S. contingency basing requests in 2021
Regional Public and Club Goods U.S. economic and security assistance to Central Asia: IMF and World Bank loans	Goods Substitution: Alternative sources of regional public goods; offer comparable goods with fewer conditions Russia's attempt to bribe Bakiyev to close Manas in 2009 with $2bn emergency assistance package	Unsuccessful 2009 Russian Effort: Kyrgyzstan renegotiates Manas agreement with U.S. for more rent and name change Successful 2014 Russian Pressure: Kyrgyzstan terminates Manas lease; Russian debt write-off conditioned on base removal
Political Values U.S. emphasizes joint commitment to GWOT, opposition to Taliban, and some liberal values	China and Russia criticize destabilizing consequences of political liberalism + U.S. support for democratization Russia and China back Karimov's Andijan crackdown while U.S. and EU are critical	Successful: Uzbekistan evicts U.S. forces from K2; joins CSTO in 2006 (until 2012)

Permission by author.

CONCLUSION

The rise and decline of the U.S. basing presence in Central Asia—and the expansion of the Russian and Chinese security footprint—offer some insights into the broader question of how strategic competition might impact regions in which the United States once exerted considerable leverage, in part because of its legacy deployments. Although the U.S. military presence in Central Asia became significant for operations in Afghanistan in 2001, Russia and China increased their influence and leverage over the Central Asian states by establishing new security organizations, providing more economic goods, and supporting their nondemocratic political practices. Accordingly, the presence of U.S. forces not only spurred security concerns but also drove Moscow and Beijing to establish and deepen new forms of ordering in the region. As a result, Russia and China now wield more regional levers of influence over the Central Asian states than the United States. Such new ordering initiatives now increasingly characterize the governance of other regions, such as the Middle East or Latin America, where once-dominant U.S.-led international ordering is facing new alternatives.

The Central Asian case also suggests that the United States will find it increasingly difficult to compete or outbid competitors for basing access as states find regional alternatives to the security initiatives, public goods, and political norms of the liberal international order. Even small and relatively weak countries will be empowered to drive harder bargains to allow the United States access. Finally, in Central Asia itself, rather than attempt to dislodge Russia and China from the region, U.S. officials would be better served to maintain non–base-related security cooperation with Central Asian militaries as well as increase their own investments in visible regional public goods, such as media, education, and public health, that promote U.S. soft power.

NOTES

1. Olga Dzyubenko, "U.S. Vacates Base in Central Asia as Russia's Clout Rises," Reuters, June 3, 2014, https://www.reuters.com/article/us-kyrgyzstan-usa-manas/u-s-vacates-base-in-central-asia-as-russias-clout-rises-idUSKBN0EE1LH20140603.

2. John F. Tierney, "Mystery at Manas: Strategic Blind Spots in the Department of Defense's Fuel Contracts in Kyrgyzstan. Report of the Majority Staff," U.S. House of Representatives Committee on Oversight and Government Reform, December 1, 2010, https://apps.dtic.mil/sti/citations/ADA535786.

3. Sebastien Schmidt, *Armed Guests: Territorial Sovereignty and Foreign Military Basing* (Oxford: Oxford University Press, 2020).

4. Jonathan M. Hansen, *Guantánamo: An American History* (New York: Hill and Wang, 2011), chap. 4.

5. Alexander Cooley, "Foreign Bases, Sovereignty and Nation-Building after Empire: The United States in Comparative Perspective," in *The Imperial Roots of the Contemporary Global Order*, ed. Sandra Halperin and Ronen Palan (Cambridge: Cambridge University Press, 2017), 173–96.

6. Alexander Cooley and Hendrik Spruyt, *Contracting States* (Princeton, NJ: Princeton University Press, 2009).

7. On the different legitimation strategies employed in U.S. bases in southern Europe, see Alexander Cooley, *Base Politics: Democratic Change and the US Military Overseas* (Ithaca, NY: Cornell University Press, 2008).

8. Eirini Karamouzi, "Negotiating the American Presence in Greece: Bases, Security and National Sovereignty," *International History Review* 44, no. 1 (May 2021): 129–44, https://doi.org/10.1080/07075332.2021.1925327.

9. Andrew Yeo, *Activists, Alliances, and Anti-US Base Protests* (Cambridge: Cambridge University Press, 2011).

10. On brokering and wedging, see Alexander Cooley and Daniel Nexon, "'The Empire Will Compensate You': The Structural Dynamics of the U.S. Overseas Basing Network," *Perspectives on Politics* 11, no. 4 (December 2013): 1034–50, https://www.cambridge.org/core/journals/perspectives-on-politics/article/empire-will-compensate-you-the-structural-dynamics-of-the-us-overseas-basing-network/13A040F9E14540969BAF778BA021D75E.

11. David A. Lake, *Hierarchy in International Relations* (Ithaca, NY: Cornell University Press, 2011).

12. Jeffrey W. Hornung and Scott W. Harold, "Amid COVID-19, the US Needs to Host Nation Support Talks," *The Diplomat*, June 12, 2020, https://thediplomat.com/2020/06/amid-covid-19-the-us-needs-to-rethink-its-approach-to-host-nation-support-talks.

13. John McDonald and Diane Bendahmane, *US Bases Overseas: Negotiations with Spain, Greece, and the Philippines* (Boulder, CO: Westview Press, 1990).

14. Robert E. Harkavy, *Bases Abroad* (Oxford: Oxford University Press, 1989; Stockholm: SIPRI, 1989), 340–56.

15. Raymond Bonner, *Waltzing with a Dictator: The Marcoses and the Making of American Policy* (New York: Times Books, 1987).

16. Rawi Abdelal, *National Purpose in the World Economy* (Ithaca, NY: Cornell University Press, 2001).

17. See Morten Skumsrud Andersen, Alexander Cooley, and Daniel H. Nexon, eds., *Undermining American Hegemony: Goods Substitution in World Politics* (Cambridge: Cambridge University Press, 2021).

18. Rebecca Adler-Niden, Benjamin Decarvalho, and Halvard Leira, "Goods Substitution at High Latitude: Undermining Hegemony from Below in the North Atlantic," in Andersen et al., *Undermining American Hegemony*, 151–76.

19. David F. Schmitz, *The United States and Right-Wing Dictatorships, 1965–1989* (Cambridge: Cambridge University Press, 2006).

20. See Yordanov's account of Cold War relations in the Horn of Africa: Radoslav A. Yordanov, *The Soviet Union and the Horn of Africa during the Cold War: Between Ideology and Pragmatism* (Lanham, MD: Lexington Books, 2016).

21. See discussions in Cooley, *Base Politics*, and Kent E. Calder, *Embattled Garrisons: Comparative Base Politics and American Globalism* (Princeton, NJ: Princeton University Press, 2007).

22. Jean Kirkpatrick, 'Dictatorships and Double Standards," *Commentary* 68, no. 5 (1979): 34.

23. Valur Ingimundarson, "Immunizing against the American Other: Racism, Nationalism, and Gender in US-Icelandic Military Relations during the Cold War," *Journal of Cold War Studies* 6, no. 4 (2004): 65–88.

24. Rachel A. Epstein, *In Pursuit of Liberalism: International Institutions in Postcommunist Europe* (Baltimore: Johns Hopkins University Press, 2008).

25. Kim Lane Scheppele, "Law in a Time of Emergency: States of Exception and the Temptations of 9/11," *University of Pennsylvania Journal of Constitutional Law*, no. 6 (2003): 1001.

26. Stephen Aris, "The Shanghai Cooperation Organisation: 'Tackling the Three Evils.' A Regional Response to Non-Traditional Security Challenges or an Anti-Western Bloc?," *Europe-Asia Studies* 61, no. 3 (2009): 457–82; Roy Allison, "Regionalism, Regional Structures and Security Management in Central Asia," *International Affairs* 80, no. 3 (2004): 463–83.

27. Alexander Cooley, "Authoritarianism Goes Global: Countering Democratic Norms," *Journal of Democracy* 26, no. 3 (2015): 49–63.

28. Barnett Rubin, "The Fragmentation of Tajikistan," *Survival* 35, no. 4 (1993): 71–91.

29. Alexander Cooley, "Imperial Wreckage: Property Rights, Sovereignty, and Security in the Post-Soviet Space," *International Security* 25, no. 3 (2000): 100–127.

30. Alexander Cooley, *Great Games, Local Rules: The New Great Power Contest in Central Asia* (Oxford: Oxford University Press, 2012), 30–50.

31. Sean R. Roberts, *The War on the Uyghurs: China's Internal Campaign against a Muslim Minority* (Princeton, NJ: Princeton University Press, 2021).

32. "President Announces Reduction in Nuclear Arsenal," White House, November 13, 2001, https://georgewbush-whitehouse.archives.gov/news/releases/2001/11/20011113-3.html.

33. Lincoln A. Mitchell, *The Color Revolutions* (Philadelphia: University of Pennsylvania Press, 2012).

34. Rachel Denber and Iain Levine, "'Bullets Were Falling Like Rain': The Andijan Massacre, May 13, 2005," Human Rights Watch, 2005, https://www.hrw.org/report/2005/06/06/bullets-were-falling-rain/andijan-massacre-may-13-2005#:~:text=the%20Andijan%20massacre-,Executive%20Summary,eastern%20Uzbek%20city%20of%20Andijan.

35. Aris, "The Shanghai Cooperation Organisation."

36. C. J. Chivers, "Central Asians Call on U.S. to Set a Timetable for Closing Bases," *New York Times*, July 6, 2005, https://www.nytimes.com/2005/07/06/world/asia/central-asians-call-on-us-to-set-a-timetable-for-closing-bases.html.

37. Alexander Cooley, "Base Politics," *Foreign Affairs* 84, no. 6 (2005): 79–92, https://www.foreignaffairs.com/articles/russia-fsu/2005-10-01/base-politics.

38. Matteo Fumagalli, "Alignments and Realignments in Central Asia: The Rationale and Implications of Uzbekistan's Rapprochement with Russia," *International Political Science Review* 28, no. 3 (2007): 253–71.

39. Alexander Cooley, "Manas Hysteria," *Foreign Policy*, April 12, 2010, https://foreignpolicy.com/2010/04/12/manas-hysteria.

40. Tierney, "Mystery at Manas."

41. Robert Gates, *Duty: Memoirs of a Secretary at War* (New York: Vintage Books, 2015), 194–95.

42. Marcin Kaczmarski, "Two Ways of Influence-Building: The Eurasian Economic Union and the One Belt, One Road Initiative," *Europe-Asia Studies* 69, no. 7 (2017): 1027–46.

43. Gerry Shih, "In Central Asia's Forbidding Highlands, a Quiet Newcomer: Chinese Troops," *Washington Post*, February 18, 2019, https://www.washingtonpost.com/world/asia_pacific/in-central-asias-forbidding-highlands-a-quiet-newcomer-chinese-troops/2019/02/18/78d4a8d0-1e62-11e9-a759-2b8541bbbe20_story.html; Craig Nelson and Thomas Grove, "Russia, China Vie for Influence in Central Asia as U.S. Plans Afghan Exit," *Wall Street Journal*, June 18, 2019, https://www.wsj.com/articles/russia-china-vie-for-influence-in-central-asia-as-u-s-plans-afghan-exit-11560850203.

44. "Tajikistan Approves Construction of New Chinese-Funded Base as Beijing's Security Presence in Central Asia Grows," RFE/RL, October 28, 2021, https://www.rferl.org/a/tajikistan-approves-chinese-base/31532078.html.

45. "Belt and Road Initiative Increases Sovereign Debt Risks in Tajikistan," Global Risk Insights, July 23, 2018, https://globalriskinsights.com/2018/07/belt-and-road-initiative-increases-sovereign-debt-risks-in-tajikistan.

46. See Bobo Lo, *Axis of Convenience: Moscow, Beijing, and the New Geopolitics* (Washington, D.C.: Brookings Institution Press, 2009).

47. Eric Schmitt, "General Warns of Challenges to Tracking Terrorist Threat in Afghanistan after U.S. Exists," *New York Times*, April 20, 2021, https://www.nytimes.com/2021/04/20/us/politics/biden-afghanistan-withdrawal-terrorism.html?searchResultPosition=1.

48. Vivian Salama and Gordon Lubold, "Afghan Pullout Leaves U.S. Looking for Other Places to Station Its Troops," *Wall Street Journal*, May 8, 2021, https://www.wsj.com/articles/afghan-pullout-leaves-u-s-looking-for-other-places-to-station-its-troops-11620482659?mod=searchresults_pos3&page=1.

49. Michael R. Gordon, "Putin Rejected Role for U.S. Forces Near Afghanistan at Summit with Biden," *Wall Street Journal*, August 19, 2021, https://www.wsj.com/articles/putin-rebuffed-u-s-plans-for-bases-near-afghanistan-at-summit-with-biden-11629398848.

8

Great Power Competition and Overseas Basing in the Arctic

JEREMY GREENWOOD[1]

AN ARCTIC HEATING UP

Temperatures, competition, and interest in the Arctic have been heating up at an unprecedented rate over the past decade. Nowhere else in the world does geostrategic competition in the twenty-first century so clearly overlap with the two other largest challenges facing society: climate change and economic stability. The Arctic is both a geopolitical hot spot and home for the United States and its NATO allies. Meanwhile, Russia occupies almost 50 percent of the landmass and has some form of sovereign rights and jurisdiction to the majority of the water column above the Arctic Circle. These rights include control of resources ranging from oil and natural gas to fisheries and minerals on the seabed. Although not an Arctic nation, China has demonstrated an unwavering commitment to a "Polar Silk Road" that has the potential to open new sources for natural resources, enhance its influence in the region, and strengthen its ties to Russia.

The release by the United States of its updated National Strategy for the Arctic Region in October 2022, alongside the Biden administration's elevation of the Arctic as a priority region in its 2022 National Security Strategy, drives home this point.[2,3] Due to climate change, the world is beginning to perceive the Arctic as an ever-expanding operational domain where freedom of access or defense of territory (depending on one's national perspective) will be necessary in the coming decades. Meanwhile, new sources of natural resources will be available to those with the jurisdiction, access, or technology to reach them. To respond to this perceived new reality, the basing requirements of the great powers in the Arctic, including the United States, will begin at home, utilize partnerships and access agreements with strategic partners, and tend to have a blend of dual civil–military use.

RUSSIA'S ARCTIC BASING IS EXISTENTIAL TO ITS SURVIVAL (AND ALWAYS HAS BEEN)

Much has been made about Russia's "military buildup" in the Arctic region and its renewal of old military bases along its northern coastline.[4] It is estimated that Russia has nearly thirty military or dual-use facilities in active use or under construction north of the Arctic Circle, to include air bases, naval ports, radio/communications facilities, or military nuclear facilities.[5] Some of these facilities are quite elaborate and militarily capable facilities where significant investments have been made to project Russian military power well into the central Arctic Ocean.[6] Russia's bases inside the Arctic Circle outnumber NATO's by about a third, according to data compiled by the International Institute for Strategic Studies and Reuters.[7]

Of course, Russia has always been an Arctic nation and has prioritized the Arctic since the sixteenth century and the conquest of Siberia.[8] Today, the Arctic is an essential access point for Russian naval assets in and around the Kola Peninsula and critical to its ability to maintain a second-strike capability in the unlikely event of nuclear conflict with the West.[9] It views the Arctic as one of the largest fronts in its competition with Europe and NATO forces, and the likely accession of Sweden and Finland to NATO will only intensify that view. To say that Arctic basing or militarization is new would be to completely overlook the Cold War–era strategic nuclear posturing between the United States and the Soviet Union. The North American Aerospace Defense (NORAD) command was created in the 1950s to address the very real Cold War threat of Soviet nuclear forces launching an attack over the shortest distance from Soviet airspace to North America: over the Arctic.[10] A large bulk of NORAD infrastructure is still focused in the U.S. and Canadian Arctic to conduct early warning and interdiction of Russian military assets into the U.S. and Canadian Air Defense Identification Zone.[11,12]

While Russian air forces continue to test and prod U.S. and Canadian air defenses in the Arctic on an almost monthly basis, the real objective of Russian military basing in the Arctic is the protection of sovereign rights to land-based minerals and resources, offshore oil and natural gas, and the protection of the Northern Sea Route (NSR) as a viable maritime "toll road" for commerce, as seen in figure 8.1.[13] This was explicitly stated by Russia's senior Arctic officer, Ambassador Nikolai Korchunov, who stated as recently as October 2022 that "we will take military measures to prevent threats to navigation along the NSR."[14]

While the war in Ukraine remains a drain on Russian military assets from all theaters of operation, there is reason to believe that the Arctic will remain a priority region for the Russian military, so it should not be assumed that significant capability will be lost there in the near term. As Rebecca Pincus of the Wilson Center has stated, "While the war in Ukraine has impacted Russia's low-end military capabilities and capacity, in the Arctic, it retains a seriously formidable set of high-end capabilities."[15] The threat of ground invasion from the Arctic is remote, however.

Figure 8.1. Map Showing the Northern Sea Route, the Northwest Passage, and the Transpolar Sea Route.

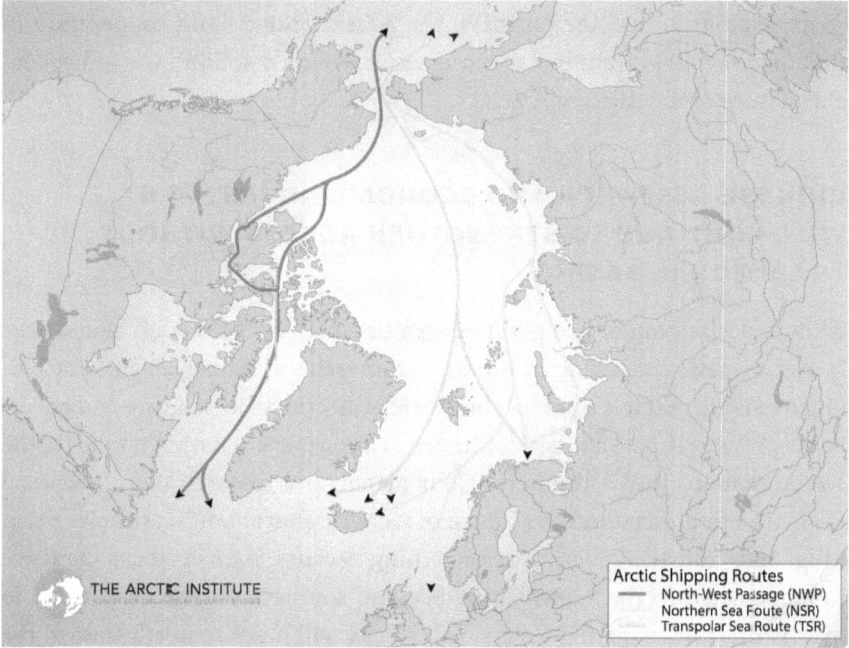

Malte Humpert, the Arctic Institute.

Even assuming that the Russian military has siphoned significant ground resources from their northern frontier for the war effort in Ukraine, they will still maintain enough ability to defend their core economic interests at sea and along the immediate shoreline.[16]

Perhaps the most important implication of Russian military buildup in the Arctic is that the Russians may actually find the rules-based international order favorable to their interests, at least in the Arctic region. Whether it is the UN Charter, the UN Convention on the Law of the Sea (UNCLOS), or customary international law, the current order grants Russia wide swaths of territory, sovereign rights and interests, and influence. Its continued efforts to keep its prior chairmanship of the Arctic Council relevant, despite the temporary withdrawal of all other members, is reflective of this fact.[17] Ambassador Korchunov put it clearly, speaking right after the announcement of a pause: "It is of utmost importance to safeguard the project activities of the Arctic Council in order to be able to pick up where we paused and step-up cooperation."[18] Russia's chairmanship of the council ended in May 2023, and Norway's assumption of that leadership role seems to have opened the door to a limited resumption of cooperation with Russia on narrow areas of non–security-related issues that are critical to the success of the Arctic Council's consensus-based governance.[19] If Russia manages to successfully reintegrate itself into the norms of the Arctic Council and cooperation in that forum yields circumpolar successes, it will only solidify the indispensable nature of the Russian Arctic.

CHINESE RESEARCH AND ECONOMIC INVESTMENT WILL CONTINUE TO STRENGTHEN ACCESS WITHOUT TRADITIONAL BASING

China's declaration of being a "near-Arctic state" in 2018 set off alarm bells in Arctic states, including in Russia. It represents a clear-eyed goal for Beijing to ensure that it is a part of the future of Arctic policymaking and governance.[20,21] As climate change continues to impact every nation on Earth, the Arctic remains the bellwether for our planet, and research there is critical for China to understand the future of its agricultural landscape, city planning, and industrial policy for the coming decades. As fish stocks continue to be depleted in the South China Sea and southern Pacific Ocean due to overfishing and warming waters, fish stocks will migrate north toward the central Arctic Ocean, challenging a growing middle class hungry for more expensive proteins. As technology improves, deep-seabed mineral nodules in the Arctic Ocean floor may become economically feasible as a new source for the world's currently depleting stocks of critical minerals. And in the short term, gas and oil supplies must be diversified to prevent any stranglehold by the United States and its allies determined to use blockades in any conflict, making Russia's northern Arctic coastline a strategic priority for access and possible transport through pipelines to China.

To be clear, China likely has no plans to build traditional military bases or outposts in the Arctic, though it will seek occasional military access rights within existing Russian bases for People's Liberation Army (PLA) Navy ships and aircraft operating in support of research missions or possible joint exercises with Russia in the NSR. These missions will demonstrate Beijing's ability to project power into the Arctic in a limited way, designed primarily to protect its research and commercial interests but also to demonstrate an ability to threaten the U.S. homeland when appropriate. The more durable Chinese military presence in the Arctic will most likely remain in the form of dual-purpose facilities operating as research stations or economic investments.

As laid out in China's 2018 Arctic White Paper, "States from outside the Arctic region do not have territorial sovereignty in the Arctic, but they do have rights in respect of scientific research, navigation, overflight, fishing, laying of submarine cables and pipelines in the high seas and other relevant sea areas in the Arctic Ocean, and rights to resource exploration and exploitation in the Area, pursuant to treaties such as UNCLOS and general international law. In addition, Contracting Parties to the Spitsbergen Treaty enjoy the liberty of access and entry to certain areas of the Arctic, the right under conditions of equality and, in accordance with law, to the exercise and practice of scientific research, production and commercial activities such as hunting, fishing, and mining in these areas."[22]

These "rights" described by Beijing will be protected by China's consistent presence in the Arctic via research stations, icebreaker deployments, and certainly some military asset deployments.[23] In Sweden, China has operated the Remote Sensing Satellite North Polar Ground Station in Kiruna, north of the Arctic Circle, since 2016. China also signed an agreement with Finland in 2018 to establish a joint research center in Sodankyla, northern Finland, for Arctic space observation and data-sharing services. In Karholl, northern Iceland, the China-Iceland Arctic Science Observatory has been operational since 2018. And China's Yellow River Research Station sits on the strategic Svalbard Islands off Norway's northwestern coast.[24] Each of these facilities may be capable of dual civilian–military use for communications, targeting, logistics/resupply, and intelligence.

Additionally, Chinese economic investment has been a key part of Arctic infrastructure development in both Russia and the Allied Arctic, including Canada, Iceland, and Norway. These investments will almost certainly provide additional support for Chinese presence in the Arctic. As Rush Doshi, a senior official at the National Security Council, noted in a comprehensive report on China in the Arctic, "Several Chinese infrastructure projects that have little economic gain have raised concerns about strategic motivations and dual-use capabilities. These include efforts by a former Chinese propaganda official to purchase 250 square kilometers of Iceland to build a golf course and airfield in an area where golf cannot be played and later to buy 200 square kilometers of Norway's Svalbard archipelago. Chinese companies have also sought to purchase an old naval base in Greenland; to build three airports in Greenland; to build Scandinavia's largest port in Sweden; to acquire (successfully) a Swedish submarine base; to link Finland and the wider Arctic to China through rail; and to do the same with a major port and railway in Arkhangelsk in Russia."[25]

These investments and dual-use facilities create a dilemma for U.S. and NATO planners who have recently declared that China's "stated ambitions and coercive policies challenge our interests, security, and values."[26] Additionally, should the Chinese and Russian militaries enhance their cooperation—which is already at an uncomfortable level for the United States—these facilities will become only more risky to allied interests. And while it is clear that China is using Russia to gain a foothold in the Arctic, it remains to be seen how deep and far that marriage of convenience will go. There have been widespread reports of Russian weariness over too much Chinese investment or control of Russian Arctic assets, as Moscow does not wish to be so obvious in its subordination to investment from Beijing.[27]

The war in Ukraine and the punishing sanctions against Russia from the West may have changed this calculus for Moscow, however, making them more willing to increase dependence on Beijing. Trade between the two countries, which reached a record $190 billion in 2022, increased by another 39 percent in the first quarter of 2023 compared with the same period in 2022. Russian raw material exports to China and imports of Chinese goods have sharply increased.[28] While it is likely that Russia will increase its trade and military dependence on China, it is too early to measure how much leverage Russia maintains with its Arctic access and rather abundant natural resources. And while many have concluded that Russia will become some sort of vassal state of China, it is safe to say that Russia will maintain a strong leadership role in the Arctic for the long term and that policymakers cannot turn all of their attention on China's Arctic ambitions as the largest threat to peace and security in that region.

THE UNITED STATES AS AN ARCTIC NATION: RELUCTANCE TO ACTION

As an Arctic state itself, the last bold move by the United States in the Arctic was its 1867 purchase of Alaska. For the most part, initial U.S policy toward the Arctic was one of ambivalence as a region of limited strategic priority—for good reason, as it was generally considered to be peaceful and too treacherous to be used as a serious front in any war. While Japan did manage to invade the Aleutian Islands in the territory of Alaska during World War II, it was of limited value to the Axis powers and never presented a real threat to the U.S. mainland. All of that changed after World War II, when the Cold War with the former Soviet Union introduced a new terrifying reality: the intercontinental ballistic missile, which can fly across the Arctic in hours or minutes, and a hostile superpower located just a few miles from U.S. territory across the Bering Strait.

NORAD continues to maintain a robust early warning and detection capability in the Arctic, with the United States and Canada actively committed to modernizing and upgrading its capabilities.[29] The United States has also demonstrated a commitment to modernizing existing military bases in the U.S. Arctic, with the recent arrival of an F-35A wing permanently stationed at Eielson Air Force Base in Alaska and the activation of the 11th Airborne Division at Fort Wainwright.[30,31] Additionally, the new U.S. National Strategy for the Arctic Region calls for the completion of a deepwater port in Nome, Alaska, that would open access for future U.S. naval assets, including the U.S. Coast Guard's planned Polar Security Cutter.[32,33] This port expansion project is still in the design phase, however, and its completion date is far from certain.[34] Similarly, the Coast Guard's widely anticipated Polar Security Cutter program is significantly behind schedule, with the Commandant of the Coast Guard testifying in April 2023, "I would give you a date if I had one. I don't have a definitive date from my team."[35,36]

Arctic deployments by the United States will also rely heavily on NATO allied nations, as seen in the biennial Exercise Cold Response, last conducted in 2022 with Norway, or the 2020 deployment of U.S. and U.K. surface warships to the Barents Sea for the first time since the 1980s.[37,38]

Perhaps the strongest sign of U.S. commitment to overseas access arrangements in the Arctic is demonstrated in the recently revised U.S.-Norway Supplementary Defense Cooperation Agreement, which allows for the United States to build facilities and have unimpeded access to three Norwegian military bases: Rygge Military Air Station south of Oslo, Sola Military Air Station on the southwestern coast, and Evenes Military Air Station and Ramsund Naval Station in the far north.[39,40] This agreement will greatly enhance the sustainability of U.S. presence in the European Arctic and facilitate cold-weather training for U.S. forces, which will strengthen NATO's joint capability in the High North.

U.S. POLICY MOVING FORWARD—MAINTAINING A PEACEFUL ARCTIC WITH GUARANTEED ACCESS

Former Commandant of the U.S. Coast Guard Admiral Karl Schultz was fond of saying that in the Arctic, "presence equals influence. If we don't have a presence there, our competitors will."[41] With its annual deployment of icebreakers and other research vessels to the Arctic each year and its increased scientific and economic investments in the region, China is in a position to have more operational presence in the Arctic than the United States will—for some time.[42] Russia has made it very clear that its future depends on the extraction and sale of fossil fuels, which makes the Arctic an essential part of its foreign policy. It has undertaken a significant investment in Arctic infrastructure and the military capability to defend it.

The United States is awakening to this reality, and though its process is slow, the trajectory is sound. The Biden administration's elevation of the Arctic in the 2022 National Security Strategy as a strategic priority is a positive development. The release of an updated National Strategy for the Arctic only confirms the importance of the region. Implementation of these strategies, however, will be key to the future of U.S. Arctic policy and place the United States on a more solid footing in the strategic competition for Arctic influence. Movement in the following areas would signal a solid implementation:

- Foreign policy begins at home, and nowhere is that as true as it is in the Arctic.[43] Targeted and expedited sustainable investments in Alaska are the first steps to a sound U.S. Arctic policy. There is a desperate need for deepwater ports, roads, communications infrastructure, upgraded airfields, and relocation of threatened infrastructure from the ravages of climate change.[44] All of these investments would benefit the indigenous communities of Alaska while providing a dual-use capability for U.S. forces operating in the region. To show real progress on the expansion of the port of Nome—a stated strategic priority for the Arctic—Congress could ensure steady funding for the U.S. Army Corps efforts, and the U.S. government and the state of Alaska should foster public–private partnerships to expedite the economic feasibility of such a project. The United States, however, cannot solely focus on the economic sustainability of this type of port project. It has real defense and homeland security implications, and the commercial viability may not be immediately clear given the emerging nature of the Arctic market. After all, the economic and strategic wisdom of the initial purchase of Alaska from Russia, dubbed "Seward's Folly" after the U.S. secretary of state who led the negotiations, was not clear to most Americans or government officials for quite some time.[45]

- Maintaining a peaceful Arctic does not necessarily require the construction of new military bases in Alaska or throughout NATO countries, but it does require the constant maintenance of existing infrastructure, upgrades to accommodate new assets, and the proper economic infrastructure to support temporary deployments of ships and aircraft to the region. The United States will require significant investment in polar satellite coverage and other long-range communications facilities in Alaska and allied countries to sustain any future deployments while ensuring that the region remains attractive for private economic development that can benefit from similar infrastructure. Starlink and its Department of Defense equivalent, Starshield, represent a giant leap forward in the field of remote communications with the possibility for significant positive impacts on the Arctic.[46] Ensuring the reliability and security of these platforms, as well as developing alternatives, should be a priority for Arctic policymakers.

- Polar ice is melting at a rapid pace, but there will still be a significant amount of ice in the Arctic Ocean for the foreseeable future. Importantly, normal ships, including naval assets, cannot sustain contact with *any* substantial ice. This makes the need for the U.S. Coast Guard's Polar Security Cutter even more critical. Icebreakers will be key to more than just military access—they will serve as the engine of economic growth by providing much-needed sea-lane access, search-and-rescue capability, and scientific research that is vital to civilian and military knowledge of a changing planet. With the current state of the Polar Security Cutter Program in question, Congress should act rapidly to fund, man, and equip a commercially available icebreaker for the U.S. Coast Guard to operate in the interim. Research on the feasibility of this option has been ongoing for almost a decade, and it is time to execute on a leased or purchased icebreaker that can fill the gap while the Polar Security Cutter Program gets on its feet. The ability for the United States to maintain a consistent presence in the Arctic sooner, along with the critical training required to develop an icebreaker sailor for generations to come, makes this idea a relatively easy-to-execute concept with real short-term impact.

- In addition to its commitment to Alaska and overall infrastructure development, the continued expansion of access rights and partnerships with NATO Arctic nations will enhance U.S. military capabilities. The addition of Sweden and Finland to the NATO alliance presents an opportunity for NATO to revamp its High North strategy while ensuring that the Arctic does not become a zone of constant military exercises.[47] Demonstrating Arctic military capabilities in measured fashion while fostering a commitment to military support of logistically difficult and expensive Arctic research will pay dividends for the alliance and its individual members.

- While strategic competition with Russia and China may not be the primary reason to implement a sound U.S. Arctic strategy, engagements and investments should be designed to reinforce the rules-based international order. This will require a gradual, working-level reengagement with Russia on Arctic Council matters that benefit all Arctic states and their citizens. Doing so with clear-eyed, tangible non-security policy goals will provide the best hedge against Chinese disruption in the Arctic while demonstrating to Russia the benefits that they reap from the current order. This will not stop Russia's role as an unpredictable global spoiler or Chinese attempts to dominate trade and investment in the Arctic, but it is one area where distance can be reinforced between the two competitors while strengthening U.S. leadership in the region.

CAN GEOSTRATEGIC RIVALS HAVE MORE IN COMMON?

The ability of the United States to have a consistent and committed presence in the Arctic will be essential to its stated objective of "an Arctic region that is peaceful, stable, prosperous, and cooperative."[48] In this unique geographic region, despite their vast differences, Russia and the United States may have more in common than most people think. Both have territory and citizens living in the Arctic, which will always drive concerns about security and homeland defense. The current international order, developed after World War II, benefits each of them, with significant rights and jurisdiction over landmasses and water columns throughout the Arctic. Both the United States and Russia desire robust economic development in their remote territories north of the Arctic Circle as well as access to future natural resources that may be present in the Arctic.

China, however, must leverage narrow treaty rights, depend on Russia's approval, and utilize significant amounts of investment monies to achieve even the slightest foothold in the Arctic. Their support of Russia is the best option for expanded presence and access to lucrative resources. Although it may have been in their best interest to support concepts of freedom of navigation in the Arctic, such as through the Russian NSR or the Canadian Northwest Passage, they have squandered that position pretty thoroughly in the South China Sea and do not wish to support U.S.-led concepts of UNCLOS interpretation. Instead, China is likely betting on a future with a chaotic and dispersed global order in which the United States is not hegemonic, one in which they will be able to utilize the Russian Arctic for trade and commerce with Russia's tacit consent (or obligation) and still be able to use their significant investment capabilities to open Allied Arctic nation markets and resources in the Arctic.

While Washington and Moscow will not be able to use the Arctic as a panacea to their significant differences in global politics, there may be opportunities for both the United States and Russia to limit China's role in the Arctic and focus future Arctic basing and militarization on homeland defense and narrow protection of economic interests. Joint patrols between Russia and China in the near Arctic, such as the ones that occurred in August 2023 off of the Aleutian Islands, cut against this goal.[49] Washington should make it very clear to Moscow that meaningful engagement in Arctic forums of any nature are dependent on measured behaviors in the Arctic that do not encourage non-Arctic nations to build bases or deploy military assets to the region on a routine basis. At the same time, the United States should focus its joint Arctic exercise efforts on its fellow NATO Arctic nations (Norway, Canada, Sweden, Finland, and Denmark) if said exercise is to be conducted in the Arctic. This does not need to preclude NATO activities in the Arctic designed to thwart the traditional Russian nuclear threat that is the core of NATO's mission, but whenever possible, an Allied Arctic state should be the lead or the dominant core of the effort. These norms of behavior need not be ensconced in a formal agreement but should be discussed in any available forum between diplomatic and military representatives of the Arctic states. In the end, it may be a good bet that Russia does not want a sustained Chinese military presence in the Arctic.

CONCLUSION

The Arctic may eventually become just another front in the geostrategic rivalry of the twenty-first century, but it will almost certainly look different than the other regions of the world that are at the forefront of today's competition. Rather than Russia, China, and the United States seeking out new bases or forward operating locations in remote foreign countries in preparation for a global contest of influence and raw military power, they will look to partnerships and early investments, designed to gradually increase access and set the stage for a future in which the North Pole is merely a waypoint on a shipping route between global markets.

NOTES

1. The views expressed herein are solely those of the author and do not necessarily represent the views of the U.S. government, the U.S. Coast Guard, or the Brookings Institution.
2. "National Strategy for the Arctic Region," White House, October 2022, https://www.whitehouse.gov/wp-content/uploads/2022/10/National-Strategy-for-the-Arctic-Region.pdf.
3. "National Security Strategy," White House, October 12, 2022, https://www.whitehouse.gov/wp-content/uploads/2022/10/Biden-Harris-Administrations-National-Security-Strategy-10.2022.pdf.
4. Matthew Melino and Heather Conley, "The Ice Curtain: Russia's Arctic Military Presence," Center for Strategic and International Studies, March 26, 2020, https://www.csis.org/features/ice-curtain-russias-arctic-military-presence.
5. Nicole Franiok, "Russian Arctic Military Bases," American Security Project, April 22, 2020, https://www.americansecurityproject.org/russian-arctic-military-bases.
6. Sarah Rainsford, "Inside Russia's Trefoil Military Base in the Arctic," *BBC News*, May 23, 2021, https://www.bbc.com/news/av/world-europe-57206208.

7. Jacob Gronholt-Pedersen and Gwladys Fouche, "Dark Arctic," Reuters, November 16, 2022, https://www.reuters.com/graphics/ARCTIC-SECURITY/zgvobmblrpd.

8. "The Russian Discovery of Siberia," Library of Congress, 2000, https://www.loc.gov/collections/meeting-of-frontiers/articles-and-essays/exploration/russian-discovery-of-siberia.

9. Eugene Rumer, Richard Sokolsky, and Paul Stronski, "Russia in the Arctic—A Critical Examination," Carnegie Endowment for International Peace, March 29, 2021, https://carnegieendowment.org/2021/03/29/russia-in-arctic-critical-examination-pub-84181.

10. "NORAD Mission," North American Aerospace Defense Command, https://www.norad.mil/About-NORAD.

11. "NORAD Detects, Tracks, Identifies and Intercepts Russian Aircraft Entering Air Defense Identification Zone," North American Aerospace Defense Command, https://www.norad.mil/Newsroom/Press-Releases/Article/3192054/norad-detects-tracks-identifies-and-intercepts-russian-aircraft-entering-air-de.

12. Security Control of Air Traffic, 14 CFR 99, https://www.faa.gov/air_traffic/publications/atpubs/aip_html/part2_enr_section_1.12.html.

13. "The Northern Sea Route," Barentsinfo.org, https://www.barentsinfo.org/barents-region/Transport/Northern-Sea-Route.

14. Trine Jonassen, "Russian Arctic Official: 'We Will Take Military Measures to Prevent Threats to Navigation along the NSR,'" *High North News*, October 5, 2022, https://www.highnorthnews.com/en/russian-arctic-official-we-will-take-military-measures-prevent-threats-navigation-along-nsr.

15. Malte Humpert, "From Ukraine to the Arctic: Russia's Capabilities in the Region and War's Impact on the North," *High North News*, September 28, 2022, https://www.highnorthnews.com/en/ukraine-arctic-russias-capabilities-region-and-wars-impact-north.

16. Colin Wall and Njord Wegge, "The Russian Arctic Threat: Consequences of the Ukraine War," Center for Strategic and International Studies, January 25, 2023, https://www.csis.org/analysis/russian-arctic-threat-consequences-ukraine-war; "Joint Statement on Arctic Council Cooperation Following Russia's Invasion of Ukraine," U.S. Department of State, March 3, 2022, https://www.state.gov/joint-statement-on-arctic-council-cooperation-following-russias-invasion-of-ukraine.

17. Gloria Dickie, "Russian Officials Call Arctic Council Boycott 'Regrettable,'" Reuters, March 4, 2022, https://www.reuters.com/world/europe/russian-officials-call-arctic-council-boycott-regrettable-2022-03-04.

18. Dickie, "Russian Officials Call Arctic Council Boycott 'Regrettable.'"

19. "Norway Takes Over as Chair of Arctic Council," Norway Ministry of Foreign Affairs, May 11 2023, https://www.regjeringen.no/en/aktuelt/norway-takes-over-as-chair-of-the-arctic-council/id2976965/#:~:text=Today%2C%20Norway%20took%20over%20the,six%20Arctic%20Indigenous%20Peoples'%20organisations.

20. "Full Text: China's Arctic Policy," State Council of the People's Republic of China, January 26, 2018, http://english.www.gov.cn/archive/white_paper/2018/01/26/content_281476026660336.htm.

21. Rush Doshi, Alexis Dale-Huang, and Gaoqi Zhang, "Northern Expedition: China's Arctic Activities and Ambitions," Brookings Institution, April 2021, https://www.brookings.edu/research/northern-expedition-chinas-arctic-activities-and-ambitions.

22. "Full Text."

23. Jeremy Greenwood, "Is China Worried about an Arctic Choke Point?," Brookings Institution, September 22, 2021, https://www.brookings.edu/blog/order-from-chaos/2021/09/22/is-china-worried-about-an-arctic-choke-point.

24. Jeremy Greenwood and Shuxian Luo, "Could the Arctic Be a Wedge between Russia and China?," *War on the Rocks*, April 4, 2022, https://warontherocks.com/2022/04/could-the-arctic-be-a-wedge-between-russia-and-china.

25. Doshi et al., "Northern Expedition."

26. "NATO 2022 Strategic Concept," NATO, June 29, 2022, https://www.nato.int/nato_static_fl2014/assets/pdf/2022/6/pdf/290622-strategic-concept.pdf.

27. China Power Team, "What Are the Weaknesses of the China-Russia Relationship?," China Power, August 22, 2022, https://chinapower.csis.org/china-russia-relationship-weaknesses-mistrust.

28. Mikhail Korostikov, "Is Russia Really Becoming China's Vassal?," Carnegie Endowment for International Peace, June 7, 2023, https://carnegieendowment.org/politika/90135.

29. Amanda Connolly, "Canada Will Spend $40B over 20 Years to Upgrade NORAD Defences amid 'New Threats,'" *Global News*, June 20, 2022, https://globalnews.ca/news/8933288/canada-upgrading-norad-amid-new-threats.

30. "Eielson AFB Celebrates F-35 Beddown Completion," U.S. Air Force, May 19, 2022, https://www.af.mil/News/Article-Display/Article/3036523/eielson-afb-celebrates-f-35-beddown-completion.

31. "11th Airborne Division Activation Ceremony," Joint Base Elmendorf-Richardson, June 6, 2022, https://www.jber.jb.mil/News/News-Articles/NewsDisplay/Article/3057911/11th-airborne-division-activation-ceremony.

32. "National Strategy for the Arctic Region."

33. "Polar Security Cutter," U.S. Coast Guard, https://www.dcms.uscg.mil/Our-Organization/Assistant-Commandant-for-Acquisitions-CG-9/Programs/Surface-Programs/Polar-Icebreaker.

34. "Corps Hosts Virtual Public Meeting for Port of Nome Expansion Project," U.S. Army Corps of Engineers, Alaska District, May 2, 2023, https://www.poa.usace.army.mil/Media/News-Releases/Article/3382251/corps-hosts-virtual-public-meeting-for-port-of-nome-expansion-project.

35. "GAO Highlights: Coast Guard Recapitalization," U.S. Government Accountability Office, July 27, 2023, https://www.gao.gov/assets/gao-23-106948-highlights.pdf.

36. Patricia Kime, "Coast Guard Pleads for Commercial Icebreaker as Timeline for New Polar Cutter Falls Apart," Military.com, April 19, 2023, https://www.military.com/daily-news/2023/04/19/unsure-when-its-new-icebreakers-will-be-built-coast-guard-pleads-congress-commercial-stopgap.html.

37. Jasmine Scott, "U.S. Forces Prepare to Join Norway's Biennial Exercise Cold Response 2022," U.S. Navy, March 11, 2022, https://www.navy.mil/Press-Office/News-Stories/Article/2964465/us-forces-prepare-to-join-norways-biennial-exercise-cold-response-22.

38. Megan Eckstein, "U.S., U.K. Surface Warships Patrol Barents Sea for First Time since the 1980s," U.S. Naval Institute, May 4, 2020, https://news.usni.org/2020/05/04/u-s-u-k-surface-warships-patrol-barents-sea-for-first-time-since-the-1980s.

39. "U.S.-Norway Supplementary Defense Cooperation Agreement (SDCA)," U.S. Department of State, April 16, 2021, https://www.state.gov/u-s-norway-supplementary-defense-cooperation-agreement-sdca.

40. Chad Garland, "US Can Build Military Facilities in Norway under New Defense Cooperation Pact," *Stars and Stripes*, April 16, 2021, https://www.stripes.com/theaters/europe/us-can-build-military-facilities-in-norway-under-new-defense-cooperation-pact-1.670014.

41. David Vergun, "Coast Guard Commandant Wants Bigger Arctic Presence—How Cool Is That?," U.S. Department of Defense, December 4, 2018, https://www.defense.gov/News/News-Stories/Article/Article/1705544/coast-guard-commandant-wants-bigger-arctic-presence-how-cool-is-that.

42. Jeremy Greenwood, "The Polar Silk Road Will Be Cleared with Chinese Icebreakers," Brookings Institution, November 24, 2021, https://www.brookings.edu/blog/order-from-chaos/2021/11/24/the-polar-silk-road-will-be-cleared-with-chinese-icebreakers.

43. Richard Haas, "Excerpt: Foreign Policy Begins at Home," Council on Foreign Relations, February 2013, https://www.cfr.org/excerpt-foreign-policy-begins-home.

44. Erin McKittrick, "Alaska's New Climate Threat: Tsunamis Linked to Melting Permafrost," *The Guardian*, October 18, 2020, https://www.theguardian.com/environment/2020/oct/18/alaska-climate-change-tsunamis-melting-permafrost.

45. "Purchase of Alaska, 1867," U.S. Department of State, Office of the Historian, https://history.state.gov/milestones/1866-1898/alaska-purchase.

46. Mike Wall, "SpaceX Reveals 'Starshield' Satellite Project for National Security Use," Space.com, December 6, 2022, https://www.space.com/spacex-starshield-satellite-internet-military-starlink.

47. Jens Stoltenberg, "NATO Is Stepping Up in the High North to Keep Our People Safe," NATO, August 25, 2022, https://www.nato.int/cps/en/natohq/opinions_206894.htm.

48. "National Strategy for the Arctic Region."

49. Daniel Kochis, "China Is Determined to Push Its Way into the Arctic," Heritage Foundation, August 11, 2023, https://www.heritage.org/asia/commentary/china-determined-push-its-way-the-arctic.

9

European Maritime Security and Strategic Access in an Age of Great Power Competition

GEOFFREY F. GRESH[1]

In the past decade of strategic competition, China and Russia have engendered a new European maritime security dynamic through port and naval base investments that are likely to grow in prominence and complexity over time. As in other regions, the two countries seek to undermine the Western-dominated political and economic order that has existed since the end of the Cold War. They appear to be more aligned with each other than in prior historical moments and have even exercised together in the European theater through joint naval exercises. The war in Ukraine may continue to sow tension in the relationship, but even so—and despite Moscow's blunders and setbacks in Ukraine—Russia remains as an important naval spoiler and aggressor across maritime Europe; it continues to access regional maritime bases from the Baltic and Black seas to the Mediterranean (Kaliningrad in the Baltic, Crimea and Novorossiysk in the Black Sea, and Tartus in the eastern Mediterranean), as shown in figures 9.1 and 9.2, respectively.[2]

By comparison, China has created a "softer" security element with its investments in European ports and terminals. According to some estimates, China now controls approximately one-tenth of all European port capacity.[3] But these ports and terminals could become more securitized

Figure 9.1. Map of the Baltic Sea.

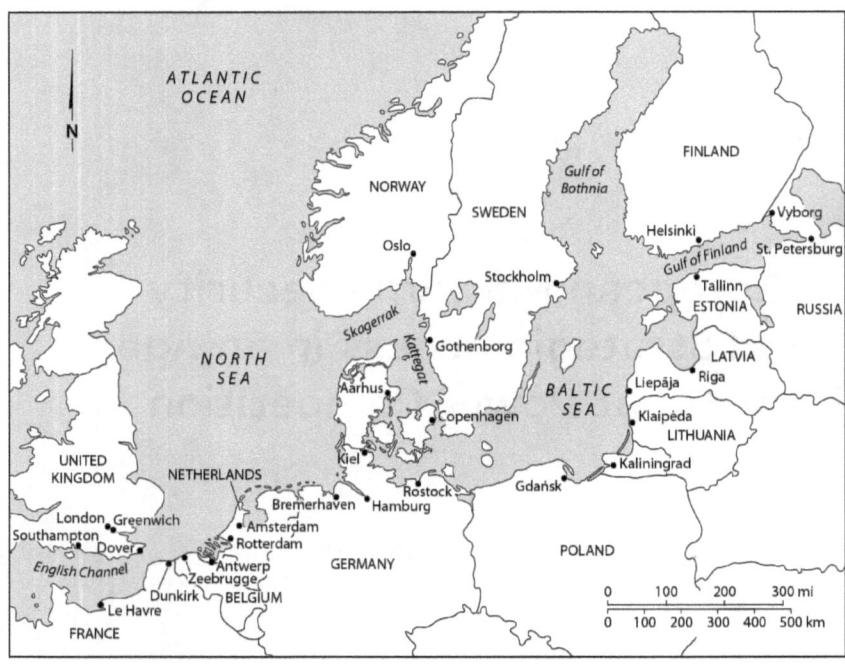

Permission by author.

Figure 9.2. Map of the Mediterranean Sea.

Permission by author.

with additional investments and reinforcements in the future. The challenge moving forward is how China will seek to leverage these ports and strategic access points. As demonstrated by the case of Djibouti, Chinese thinkers have referred to it as a "strategic strong point," framing it frequently as more of a supply and logistics facility for its navy before it was established as China's first official overseas base in 2017. It gestures toward the inherent dual-use nature of many of these port and terminal investments and how China might seek to leverage them as its security and economic interests broaden across the region.[4]

Given China's and Russia's continued ambitions, Europe will need to prioritize and manage emerging challenges for the region's long-term security and stability. Such challenges include Russian traditional naval posturing and power projection, and China's dual-use geoeconomic port investments, Russian oceanic research, and the rise of seabed warfare. This chapter begins with a brief historical perspective on Russia's relationship to maritime Europe before examining it in a present-day context as a potential naval spoiler. After examining Russia's naval posture and subsea activities, the chapter takes a closer look at China's recent port investments and the challenge they pose to Europe's maritime security. As China and Russia continue to strengthen their political and military ties, this burgeoning relationship will only complicate Europe's future ability to ensure regional maritime security and stability, making basing access evermore important for the United States and its NATO allies.

HISTORICAL VISIONS OF MARITIME PROWESS

Russia's drive to the sea and its desire to establish itself as a global sea power has been an important theme that Russian imperial and Soviet rulers frequently cite despite being consumed more often by its territorially focused history and politics. Russian tsar Peter the Great was one of the first emperors to view access to the sea as a strategic necessity for the success of the state. He helped build up Russia's first naval fleet that assisted in defeating Sweden, Russia's archrival at the time. Or, in the words of the famous Russian poet Alexander Pushkin, Russia sought "to gall our haughty neighbor" in the Great Northern War (1700–1721). In fact, Peter used captured Swedish soldiers and other conscripts to help build the Russian Empire's new imperial capital and coastal city on the Baltic, St. Petersburg, which was viewed as Russia's window to Europe. The city symbolized Peter's massive reorientation efforts to move Russian citizens out of the forests, promoting greater connectivity between Russia's riverine populations and the wider world.[5]

Following Peter the Great over several centuries, the Russian Empire (and later the Soviet Union) aspired to achieve maritime greatness as part of its core interests. Although inner Eurasia consumed much of imperial Russia's attention, it still recognized the importance of the sea for its larger development since at its height it touched three oceans and thirteen seas and had an estimated 38,000 kilometers of shoreline. Since the end of the Cold War, Russia has struggled to maintain its naval capacity across these diversified maritime regions extending from Europe to Pacific Asia and the Arctic. Many of its leaders, however, have still harkened back to the glory days of Peter the Great and others, including the Soviet naval achievements of Admiral Sergei G. Gorshkov, commander in chief of the Soviet Union's naval forces for twenty-nine years (1956–1985). Russia's desire to control its regional seas, in addition to its push for greater international prestige, has been seemingly constant. Since the Cold War, Russia has also been consistently concerned about NATO's eastward expansion and the threat it poses to Russia's regional national interests by sea, including its territorial sovereignty and ability to project power to support allies such as Syria and Egypt in the Mediterranean and beyond.[6]

RUSSIA AS NAVAL SPOILER

Russian president Vladimir Putin's invasion of Ukraine in 2022 has taken a toll on Russia's naval capabilities. Prior to 2022, however, Russia had invested in many naval platforms—mainly through its submarine program—enabling Moscow to continue its aggressive behavior across Europe and Asia. Certainly, Russia's navy confronts major financial, political, and industrial hurdles in its continuing development, but it can still act as a potent and powerful spoiler against the United States, the European Union (EU), NATO, and other European partners and allies. Moreover, Russia's increased aggression on the high seas and other "gray zone" activities, including its naval blockade of Ukrainian grain shipments in the summer of 2023, have the potential to cause an inadvertent clash or unintended outbreak of conflict at sea. Its regional naval bases and other strategic access points, including in the Baltic, Black, and Mediterranean seas, give Russia important naval maneuverability and power projection capacity. And Moscow shows no signs of slowing down; it has sought out other basing access in Libya and Sudan in addition to conducting joint exercises with China in the far eastern edges of Asia, such as in the Sea of Japan in the summer of 2023.[7]

Russia possesses what is considered one of the world's top navies, but much of its fleet comprises Soviet legacy holdouts or is largely underfunded. Based on current estimates, Russia's naval fleet has 210 surface vessels and submarines. The Russian navy also reportedly lost eleven naval vessels and boats in 2022.[8] Even amid certain Russian setbacks in Ukraine, Putin seemingly still understands the need for a maritime component in Moscow's larger strategy. Over the past decade or more, Putin has pushed Russia to focus on the Black and Baltic seas, historically considered part of Russia's traditional spheres of influence. With the takeover of Crimea in 2014, Russia established a new perch from which to carry out its larger naval and maritime ambitions. Although Ukraine has become all-consuming in 2022 and 2023, Russia still seeks to move beyond its traditional seas and garner great power status. In July 2022, Russia issued its latest maritime doctrine with largely aspirational language that is disconnected from many of its current capabilities. Nevertheless, the doctrine states that Russia endeavors to maintain "stability in the World Ocean, strengthening national influence and developing mutually beneficial partnerships in the field of maritime activities in an emerging polycentric world."[9]

Even with significant mishaps and losses in recent years, Russia continues to invest heavily in its submarine fleet, which is currently estimated at fifty-five vessels in service.[10] Although this fleet has had a mixed record—with catastrophes including the sinking of Russia's *Kursk* nuclear submarine and loss of its 118-person crew in 2000 and the nuclear submarine fire that claimed fourteen sailors in 2019—Russia's submarine fleet and other naval vessels are now more active in the Atlantic Ocean, Pacific Asia, and Arctic Ocean, much to the irritation of the United States, NATO, the EU, and others.[11] Russia's underwater capacity, historically the strongest element of its fleet, also continues to make tangible gains. In the past ten years or so, Russia has augmented its subsurface activities four to five times, according to some estimates. It has authorized thirteen new nuclear and conventional submarines since 2014, and the vessels do not appear to be experiencing the same construction delays as Russia's frigate-class warships. The submarine program remains a priority for the Kremlin despite other military cuts, evidenced by the ongoing replacement of older Delta IV nuclear-powered ballistic missile submarines with sophisticated Borei-class submarines.[12]

Russia has also engaged in nontraditional or gray zone activities below the ocean's surface by reportedly tapping into or meddling with undersea cables that the world depends on for internet and telecommunications. Many observers allege that Russia was behind the 2022 sabotage of the undersea Nord Stream pipelines, though final investigations are still forthcoming.[13] Russia has traditionally used the guise of oceanic research or search-and-rescue missions to hide illicit actions along ocean floors. Russia's main directorate of deep-sea research, or GUGI, is separate from the navy even though it has numerous nuclear submarines and surface vessels. GUGI is largely responsible for the Kremlin's seabed activities across maritime Europe and the Arctic and globally. Combined, these growing undersea capabilities will do a lot to further enhance Russia's power projection and reemergence as a more formidable maritime and nuclear power, which can, at the least, act as a spoiler.[14]

CHINESE PORT INVESTMENTS

Unlike Russia, China's emergence in Europe's maritime space is a rather recent phenomenon. China's investments in ports and terminals from Asia to Europe have similar—albeit much more peaceful—historical parallels to Europe's expansion eastward into Asia. Company-states, such as the British East India Company or the Dutch East India Company, were at the frontier of establishing footholds and treaty ports across the Indian Ocean and East Asia.[15] Today, with the support of its state-owned corporations, China has begun to develop a modern-day network of supply and logistics via its port and terminal investments that are akin to a European trading system. China's investments of the past decade have been part of its Maritime Silk Road, seemingly reflecting its view that geoeconomic and security interests are becoming increasingly intertwined; Beijing laid out a similar vision most recently with President Xi Jinping's Global Security Initiative. The challenge for Europe today, however, is that as China grows its strategic port and terminal ventures, it gains access and control over important trade and logistics nodes in addition to critical information infrastructure.

The port in Piraeus, Greece, in particular, highlights the challenges related to China's growing maritime influence and access to dual-use port facilities. With the initial goal of tapping into the EU's Trans-European Transport Network initiative, China has expanded its regional system of ports, railways, and other multimodal transportation projects across northern and southern Europe. In 2008, then president Hu Jintao solidified an estimated $5.5 billion landmark agreement that enabled the Chinese shipping group COSCO to run two of Piraeus's container terminals (Piers 2 and 3) for a period of thirty-five years. Eight years later, COSCO announced that it had acquired a 67 percent stake in Pier 1 from the company operating the port, Piraeus Port Authority S.A.[16]

Elsewhere, China and Italy reportedly were in negotiations to jointly finance the "Five Ports Alliance" as part of the larger North Adriatic Ports Association, which includes Ravenna, Venice, and Trieste in Italy; Capodistria in Slovenia; and Fiume in Croatia. The endeavor aimed at attracting a greater interest in the Adriatic region and routes to western and Central Europe as well as other European trade corridors that tie into China's Belt and Road Initiative.[17] Some reports that have scrutinized memorandums of understanding signed between China and Italy, however, assert that very little has come to fruition in the past few years.[18] In the summer of 2023, Italy's defense minister added to the complexity of diplomatic relations by asserting in an interview that Italy's membership in the Belt and Road Initiative was an "atrocious" decision that should be reconsidered. By the end of 2023, Italy's government took the formal step to end its participation in the initiative.[19]

Italy aside, Chinese firms have slowly expanded their investments in northern and southern Spanish ports since 2012. Hutchison Port Holdings, a subsidiary of the Hong Kong–based Hutchison Whampoa Limited, began at the time by investing approximately $387 million in the port of Barcelona, in addition to $184 million financing for a terminal enlargement. Since then, COSCO has been vying for Spain's other ports as well: in 2017, COSCO succeeded in purchasing a 51 percent share (worth about $228 million) in Noatum Port Holdings, which owns the main port in Valencia (where the company is headquartered) and in Bilbao (in northern Spain) as well as the major inland terminals in Madrid (Conterail) and Zaragoza (Noatum Rail Terminal Zaragoza).[20]

In the past decade, China Merchants Port Holdings similarly acquired a 49 percent stake from the French CMA CGM shipping company (Compagnie maritime d'affrètement–Compagnie générale maritime) in its subsidiary Terminal Link.[21] This deal gave China Merchants equity in thirteen terminals in eight countries, including four terminals in France, two in Morocco, one in Malta, and one in South Korea, among others; a subsequent transaction added another eight terminals to this portfolio.[22]

Chinese firms have also made inroads in northern Europe through various port and terminal investments. For example, in January 2018, COSCO successfully purchased a majority share in the Port of Bruges-Zeebrugge, Belgium's second largest, after APM (A. P. Møller) Terminals agreed to sell its 51 percent majority stake that it had owned since 2006. Zeebrugge is strategically located near the ports of Hamburg and Le Havre in Germany and France, respectively, and offers a close transit to the United Kingdom or the Baltic Sea. The port also contains a liquified natural gas terminal that handles Arctic gas shipments from the Yamal Peninsula before heading to East Asian markets.[23] In 2004, COSCO purchased a 25 percent minority stake in another Belgium port, Antwerp Gateway. The port is now 80 percent reliant on COSCO shipping and throughput. Although Belgium's foreign minister recently criticized the threat posed by China through these types of investments, the issue does not appear to have gained significant traction across other parts of Europe.[24]

China has also made parallel inroads nearby through Europe's largest port of Rotterdam, in the Netherlands, as well as through other spots along Europe's northern coastline. In 2016, a subsidiary of COSCO Shipping Corporation purchased a 35 percent stake (worth an estimated $47 million) in Rotterdam's Euromax Terminal, an automatic container terminal. It acquired its share from a subsidiary of Hutchison Port Holdings. The terminal has a capacity to handle around 3.2 million twenty-foot equivalent units of cargo every year. According to recent estimates, about a quarter of all goods offloaded at Rotterdam arrive from China.[25]

Beijing's most recent European port and terminal venture came with the announcement of COSCO's 24.9 percent investment stake at one of Hamburg's terminals. Hamburg is one of Europe's top three ports behind Rotterdam and Antwerp. As noted by one official German source, "The investment disproportionately expands China's strategic influence on German and European transport infrastructure as well as Germany's dependence on China. . . . It points to considerable risks that arise when elements of the European transport infrastructure are influenced and controlled by China."[26]

A COMPLEX MARITIME FUTURE

Due to China's and Russia's growing interests and access across maritime Europe, it will be important for the United States, the EU, and other respective partners and allies to keep seeking innovative solutions that can address a spectrum of maritime security challenges unlikely to abate in the coming decade.

To begin, NATO should consider expanding its NATO Maritime Groups and increase its number of naval exercises. In recent years, the United States has understandably been focused on developing an Indo-Pacific strategy. But it should, at the same time, continue to work with NATO to expand the overall size and composition of the Standing NATO Maritime Groups. The combination of increasing the number of ships at sea and conducting more joint exercises will help to act as a greater Russian deterrent and strengthen further interoperability. The NATO Allied Maritime Command is the key anchor for any strategy, and it has already begun to push NATO to adopt a stronger maritime posture. In the past several years, NATO has begun to think more strategically about how to manage Russia's increased naval activity. NATO has recently conducted larger and more frequent maritime exercises and patrols across NATO's area of responsibility, including Operation Active Endeavour, Sea Breeze, Dynamic Manta, and Dynamic Mongoose. Since the 2022 NATO summit in Madrid, NATO has begun to lean in more significantly on a forward security posture.[27] In November 2022, five carrier strike groups patrolled NATO's area of operations, albeit with individual mission objectives.[28] The addition of Sweden and Finland as NATO members and the alliance's expansion of its annual Freezing Winds exercise will also have important implications for future maritime security and deterrence.[29]

Indeed, one of the ongoing maritime threats posed by Russia is its ability to establish a more robust Anti-Access/Area Denial (A2/AD) "bubble" across portions of the Baltic, Black, and Mediterranean seas. This capability may carry significant repercussions for basing or other strategic access for NATO forces. Although it has relocated many of its platforms and personnel from Syria to use in the Russia-Ukraine War, Russia previously placed some of its A2/AD capabilities on display by launching missiles from its surface fleet in the Caspian Sea at targets in Syria in support of the Assad regime. This could pose a more significant threat in a potential post–Russia-Ukraine War era.[30]

As Russia and China remain strategically aligned for the foreseeable future, it will in turn place greater pressure on the United States and the NATO alliance to devise a strategy to counteract or manage this emerging dynamic. To address this ongoing challenge, the United States might consider building up a larger NATO and the U.S. Sixth Fleet basing structure inside the Mediterranean basin that can be used for naval forces in addition to enhancing its overall presence. Shutting down the Allied Maritime Command Naples in 2013 may have made sense for streamlining NATO's maritime command and control structure. However, one trade-off has been NATO's loss of a strategic regional foothold that is in closer proximity to the eastern Mediterranean Basin. Nevertheless, remaining just outside the Strait of Gibraltar in Rota, Spain, or Portugal's Azores and Madeira islands will be critical to monitor traffic entering and exiting the region.[31] China and Russia are more in sync today, and their relationship is likely to grow stronger in the near future as they advance interoperability functions through joint exercises and other power sharing measures and as they continue to reshape regional and global order. The maintenance of Russian basing across maritime Europe and other forms of strategic access for the Chinese will seemingly continue as a top priority in the coming years.

Just as NATO has embraced greater maritime domain awareness in recent years, it has also begun to think more strategically about a seabed warfare strategy. France has been at the forefront of this undertaking with the publication of its 2022 seabed warfare strategy. Following suit, the United Kingdom announced the establishment of the Centre for Seabed Mapping in its 2022 National Strategy for Maritime Security; the center aims to bolster national and regional maritime domain awareness.[32] And then in June 2023, NATO announced the establishment of a new center that will focus on Europe's subsea regions, including the protection of its undersea pipelines and fiber-optic submarine cables. This also comes on the heels of the recent and mysterious submarine cable cuts near France and the United Kingdom in the fall of 2022.[33] As noted recently by one NATO general, "Russian ships have actively mapped our critical undersea infrastructure. There are heightened concerns that Russia may target undersea cables and other critical infrastructure in an effort to disrupt Western life."[34]

Europe currently has an estimated seventeen cable systems that connect to North America, eleven to North Africa (excluding Egypt), and thirteen to Egypt and the Middle East.[35] The increase in global cyber connectivity has had a profound effect on how information is received and protected on land and at sea. The maritime sector, especially the shipping industry and major ports around the world, has started to think more critically about the necessity to secure essential cyber data streams and other critical maritime infrastructure. As China begins to establish a global submarine cable system that is more independent and acts as a possible redundancy line, as demonstrated by the multiple SEA-ME-WE (Southeast Asia–Middle East–Western Europe) submarine cable lines, it will be important for other countries to think about how information is secured, stored, and shared from one location to the next. The private sector alone is unable to tackle the breadth and scope of maritime cybersecurity for national security purposes. Therefore, the establishment of NATO's new subsea center is a step in the right direction to help in protecting this vulnerability. Other countries beyond France and the United Kingdom, however, must also engage more actively at the national level in this subsea domain.

To support these larger maritime security efforts, Frontex, the European Border and Coast Guard Agency, in conjunction with Europe's various coast guards, will be critical. Frontex was originally established in 2005 but added its coast guard component only in 2016 following Europe's migrant crisis. The EU revised its Maritime Security Strategy in 2018, updating critical components that are important for the future of Europe's coast guard operations. But coast guards are frequently underfunded or overworked, forcing them to prioritize difficult mission sets over others, while Frontex in particular has faced recent recruitment and other operational challenges in the past several years. While Europe continues to ramp up its coast guard operations overall, the U.S. Coast Guard has numerous authorities that should receive adequate or increased funding in future years to support European nations lacking capabilities or financing. Port security and maritime cybersecurity are two key areas. Since many of China's and Russia's activities are often affiliated with coastal defense or with port operations (in the case of the Chinese), coast guards are frequently the best actors to manage many of these maritime security elements.[36]

Additionally, the EU and NATO should consider the increased incorporation of more Indo-Pacific partners and allies into maritime Europe. The United States and European partners should try to host more bilateral or multilateral naval exercises with important partners or allies, such as Australia, India, Japan, New Zealand, and South Korea. In April 2022, NATO hosted a foreign ministers' meeting with several Asia-Pacific partner nations. The meeting built on prior momentum generated from the December 2020 inaugural meeting and represents an important step in the right direction.[37] And at the latest NATO summit in 2023, Japan and South Korea were on hand as more formal participants, which was seen as a positive step. NATO has similarly debated opening a small satellite office in Tokyo. Japan in particular has been more active recently in the Mediterranean due to its concerns about Ukraine and maritime trade tied to the Black Sea, contributing to the idea of establishing a more formal relationship between Japan and NATO. If and when the conflict in Ukraine subsides, Japan's minesweeping ships might similarly be best situated to begin the demining process, and the effort would be an important gesture of goodwill. With its base in Djibouti, Japan has good access to European waters to support and assist with a variety of activities.[38]

NATO and hard security aside, Europe should promote greater multinational infrastructure investment funding and intraregional coordination as a means to mitigating some of China' opaque and concerning investment patterns. According to some estimates, approximately $94 trillion will be spent globally on infrastructure by 2040.[39] With this in mind, the United States and the EU should continue to support and promote businesses that can be more involved in various (maritime) infrastructure projects. At its June 2021 summit, the G7 adopted the Build Back Better World (B3W) initiative (subsuming the multi-stakeholder Blue Dot Network, which never took off significantly).[40] While waiting to see if this reframing has achieved greater success, the United States is still in need of a better coordinating body at the National Security Council to oversee and coordinate the U.S. export credit agency EXIM Bank, the International Development Finance Corporation, the U.S. Trade Agency, the U.S. Agency for International Development, and other entities that operate in Europe and around the globe.[41] Following the 2021 G7 summit, the EU launched the $340 billion Global Gateway project to tackle similar infrastructure issues as the B3W initiative, but it is unclear how much of the funds will focus on Europe. In June 2022, the European Parliament passed a measure that created a vehicle that "restricts bids from countries that don't afford EU firms reciprocal market access in their public procurement markets." This measure adds to another framework that was adopted in 2019 for "foreign direct investment screening," but it does not appear to have been applied to China's port investments.[42] From a security infrastructure standpoint, NATO might lean more heavily on its Article 2 to partially counter China's future investments. Article 2 can be invoked to coordinate and scrutinize security infrastructure and technology projects.[43]

Europe's ongoing and future maritime security challenges in an age of great power competition for strategic access will be vast and require multiple agencies across a spectrum of actors and institutions. Between the United States, NATO, and the European Parliament, important measures and policies have already been adopted, but national governments must also continue to apply pressure toward addressing any future maritime vulnerabilities. Russia and China will indeed pose unique and different challenges to the future of maritime Europe, and these challenges will grow only more pronounced as Russia's and China's security and economic interests grow more aligned.

NOTES

1. The views expressed here are the author's alone and do not represent the National Defense University, the Department of Defense, and the U.S. government. The author would like to thank Andrew Yeo and Isaac Kardon for the opportunity to participate in the "Great Power Competition and Overseas Basing" project workshop.

2. Susannah Savage and Veronika Melkozerova, 'Russia Warns Shipping in Danger after It Quits Black Sea Grain Deal," *Politico*, July 17, 2023, https://www.politico.eu/article/russia-ukraine-war-moscow-black-sea-grain-deal-over.

3. Keith Johnson, "Why Is China Buying Up Europe's Ports? State-Owned Port Operators are the Aggressive Leading Edge of Beijing's Massive Belt and Road Project," *Foreign Policy*, February 2, 2018, https://foreignpolicy-com.nduezproxy.idm.oclc.org/2018/02/02/why-is-china-buying-up-europes-ports.

4. For additional discussion on Chinese port investments and the observed military utilization of these ports, see Isaac B. Kardon and Wendy Leutert, "Pier Competitor: China's Power Position in Global Ports," *International Security* 46, no. 4 (2022): 9–47, doi.org/10.1162/isec_a_00433; Isaac B. Kardon, "China's Global Maritime Access: Alternatives to Overseas Military Bases in the Twenty-First Century," *Security Studies* 31, no. 5 (2022): 885–916, doi.org/10.1080/09636412.2022.2137429; and Conor Kennedy, "Strategic Strong Points and Chinese Naval Strategy," *China Brief* 19, no. 6 (March 22, 2019), https://jamestown.org/program/strategic-strong-points-and-chinese-naval-strategy.

5. Peter Tsouras, "Soviet Naval Tradition," in *The Soviet Navy: Strengths and Liabilities*, ed. Bruce W. Watson and Susan M. Watson (Boulder, CO: Westview Press, 1986), 3–4; Nicholas V. Riasanovsky, *The Image of Peter the Great in Russian History and Thought* (New York: Oxford University Press, 1992), 92–93; John P. LeDonne, *The Grand Strategy of the Russian Empire, 1650–1831* (New York: Oxford University Press, 2004), 216–18.

6. See also Jeffrey Mankoff, *Russian Foreign Policy: The Return of Great Power Politics* (Lanham, MD: Rowman & Littlefield, 2012), and Sergei Chernyavskii, "The Era of Gorshkov: Triumph and Contradictions," *Journal of Strategic Studies* 28, no. 2 (2005): 283.

7. Constantine Atlamazoglou, "A Quiet US Move in the Mediterranean May Help Put More Pressure on Russia, but Not Everyone in NATO Is Happy about It," *Business Insider*, October 17, 2022, https://www.businessinsider.com/lifting-cyprus

-arms-embargo-could-pressure-russia-but-turkey-unhappy-2022-10; Patrick Kingsley and Ronen Bergman, "Russia Shrinks Forces in Syria, a Factor in Israeli Strategy There," *New York Times*, October 19, 2022, https://www.nytimes.com/2022/10/19/world/middleeast/russia-syria-israel-ukraine.html?searchResultPosition=1; Robyn Dixon, "Russia's Ally in Libya Is Battered by Defeats. But Moscow Has Wider Goals to Expand Its Influence," *Washington Post*, June 6, 2020, https://www.washingtonpost.com/world/europe/russia-libya-war-putin/2020/06/05/c3956bf4-a109-11ea-be06-af5514ee0385_story.html; Amy Mackinnon, Robbie Gramer, and Jack Detsch, "Russia's Dreams of a Red Sea Naval Base Are Scuttled—for Now," *Foreign Policy*, July 15, 2022, https://foreignpolicy.com/2022/07/15/russia-sudan-putin-east-africa-port-red-sea-naval-base-scuttled; "Russia, China End Military Exercises in Sea of Japan," Voice of America, July 23, 2023, https://www.voanews.com/a/russia-china-end-military-exercises-in-sea-of-japan/7192837.html.

8. Some estimates go as high as sixteen vessels. "Russian Federation—Navy," *Janes World Navies*, November 28, 2022, https://customer-janes-com.nduezproxy.idm.oclc.org/Janes/Display/JWNA0127-JWNA; "Russo-Ukrainian Warspotting," Warspotting.net, accessed October 21, 2022, https://ukr.warspotting.net.

9. Maritime Doctrine of the Russian Federation, July 31, 2022, translated by Anna Davis and Ryan Vest, Russia Maritime Studies Institute, U.S. Naval War College, 4, https://dnnlgwick.blob.core.windows.net/portals/0/NWCDepartments/Russia%20Maritime%20Studies%20Institute/20220731_ENG_RUS_Maritime_Doctrine_FINALtxt.pdf?sv=2017-04-17&sr=b&si=DNNFileManagerPolicy&sig=2zUFSaTUSPcOpQDBk%2FuCtVnb%2FDoy06Cbh0EI5tGpl2Y%3D.

10. "Russian Federation."

11. Jeremy Bender, "This Graphic Shows How Tiny the Russian Navy Is Compared to the Former Soviet Fleet," *Business Insider*, March 2, 2016, https://www.businessinsider.in/This-graphic-shows-how-tiny-the-Russian-Navy-is-compared-to-the-former-Soviet-fleet/articleshow/51231763.cms; Kyle Mizokami, "Tugboat Endures a Stomach-Churning Ride while Pulling a Russian Aircraft Carrier," *Popular Mechanics*, November 10, 2015, https://www.popularmechanics.com/military/navy-ships/a18141/towing-admiral-kuznetsov-video-tugboat; "What Really Happened to Russia's 'Unsinkable' Sub," *The Guardian*, August 4, 2001, https://www.theguardian.com/world/2001/aug/05/kursk.russia; Dave Majumdar, "Why the U.S. Navy Fears Russian and Chinese Submarines," *The National Interest*, May 23, 2017, https://nationalinterest.org/blog/the-buzz/why-the-usnavy-fears-russian-chinese-submarines-20800.

12. Andrew Metrick, Kathleen Weinberger, and Kathleen H. Hicks, "Undersea Warfare in Northern Europe," Center for Strategic and International Studies, July 21, 2016, 2, https://www.csis.org/analysis/undersea-warfare-northern-europe; Ihor Kabanenko, "Russian 'Hybrid War' Tactics at Sea: Targeting Underwater Communications Cables," *Eurasia Daily Monitor* 15, no. 10 (2018), https://jamestown.org/program/russian-hybrid-war-tactics-sea-targeting-underwater-communications-cables/?mc_cid=7f545b546f&mc_eid=a287832eef.

13. Joanna Plucinska, "Nord Stream Gas 'Sabotage': Who's Being Blamed and Why?," Reuters, October 6, 2022, https://www.reuters.com/world/europe/qa-nord-stream-gas-sabotage-whos-being-blamed-why-2022-09-30.

14. Samuel Bendett, Richard Connolly, Jeffrey Edmonds, Andrea Kendall-Taylor, and Michael Kofman, "Assessing Russian State Capacity to Develop and Deploy Advanced Military Technology," Center for New American Security, October 2022, https://www.cnas.org/publications/reports/assessing-russian-state-capacity-to-develop-and-deploy-advanced-military-technology; H. I. Sutton, "Russia's Growing Secret Submarine Fleet Key to Moscow's Undersea Future," *USNI News*, November 30, 2021, https://news.usni.org/2021/11/30/russia-growing-secret-submarine-fleet-key-to-moscows-undersea-future.

15. For more on the historical parallels, see J. C. Sharman, *Empires of the Weak: The Real Story of European Expansion and the Creation of the New World Order* (Princeton, NJ: Princeton University Press, 2020), and Andrew Phillips and J. C. Sharman, *Outsourcing Empire: How Company-States Made the Modern World* (Princeton, NJ: Princeton University Press, 2022).

16. In 2013, COSCO announced an additional investment of $285 million to further expand the capacity of the terminals. Xing Zhigang, "Li Charms Dock Workers in Greece," *China Daily*, June 20, 2015, https://www.chinadaily.com.cn/world/2014livisitbritaingreece/2014-06/21/content_17605748.htm; Nicola Casarini, "Is Europe to Benefit from China's Belt and Road Initiative?," Istituto Affari Internazionali Working Papers, no. 4, October 1, 2015, https://www.jstor.org/stable/resrep09729; Marina Skordeli, "New Horizons in Greek-Chinese Relations: Prospects for the Eastern Mediterranean," *Mediterranean Quarterly* 26, no. 1 (2015): 59–76, 60–62, 65–66, https://read.dukeupress.edu/mediterranean-quarterly/article-abstract/26/1/59/1918/New-Horizons-in-Greek-Chinese-Relations-Prospects; François Godement and Abigaël Vasselier, "China at the Gates: A New Power Audit of EU-China Relations," European Council on Foreign Relations, 2017, 73, https://ecfr.eu/publication/china_eu_power_audit7242; Asteris Huliaras and Sotiris Petropoulos, "Shipowners, Ports and Diplomats: The Political Economy of Greece's Relations with China," *Asia Europe Journal* 12, no. 3 (2014): 215–30, https://link.springer.com/journal/10308/volumes-and-issues/12-3; "COSCO SHIPPING—A Name Card of China in Greece on Maritime Silk Road," *China Daily*, May 8, 2017, https://www.chinadaily.com.cn/business/2017-05/08/content_29251685.htm; Andreea Brînză, "How a Greek Port Became a Chinese 'Dragon Head,'" *The Diplomat*, April 25, 2016, https://thediplomat.com/2016/04/how-a-greek-port-became-a-chinese-dragon-head; Jason Horowitz and Liz Alderman, "Chastised by E.U., a Resentful Greece Embraces China's Cash and Interests," *New York Times*, August, 26, 2017, https://www.nytimes.com/2017/08/26/world/europe/greece-china-piraeus-alexis-tsipras.html.

17. Godement and Vasselier, "China at the Gates," 49–50, appendices, "Spain," "Italy"; "The Five Port Project Creates Float All Boats Scenario for the BRI in Europe," HSBC.com, October 9, 2017, https://web.archive.org/web/20180521010438/http://www.business.hsbc.com/china-growth/the-european-five-port-project; "Italian Busi-

nesses Eye Belt and Road Initiative Potential," *China Daily*, May 17, 2017, https://www.chinadaily.com.cn/business/2017-05/17/content_29379725.htm.

18. Francesca Ghiretti, "The Belt and Road in Italy: 2 Years Later," *The Diplomat*, March 23, 2021, https://thediplomat.com/2021/03/the-belt-and-road-in-italy-2-years-later.

19. "Italy Seeking to Leave 'Atrocious' China Belt and Road Plan without Harming Ties—Minister," *The Guardian*, July 30, 2023, https://www.theguardian.com/world/2023/jul/31/italy-china-belt-and-road-initiative-atrocious-defence-minister.

20. Alberto Ghiara, "APM Terminal, First 10 Cranes Arrived in Vado Ligure," *The Medi Telegraph*, January 5, 2018, https://www.themeditelegraph.com/en/green-and-tech/technology/2018/01/05/news/apm-terminal-first-10-cranes-arrived-in-vado-ligure-1.38085913; "China Investment in Mediterranean Ports," Ports Europe, July 28, 2017, https://www.portseurope.com/china-investment-in-mediterranean-ports; Jennifer McKevitt, "Ocean Alliance Details Service Network," *Supply Chain Dive*, November 4, 2016, https://www.supplychaindive.com/news/Ocean-alliance-network-day-one/429704; Alice Woodhouse, "Cosco Shipping Buys Controlling Stake in Spanish Port for €203m," *Financial Times*, June 12, 2017, https://www.ft.com/content/26c99549-29d4-3d00-8714-e62d22e83bcf; "China's COSCO Shipping Buys $228 Million Stake in Spain's Noatum Port," Reuters, June 12, 2017, https://www.reuters.com/article/us-cosco-ship-hold-noatum-port/chinas-cosco-shipping-buys-228-million-stake-in-spains-noatum-port-idUSKBN19405I; Julia Louppova, "Chinese Expansion into Spanish Ports Market," *Port Today*, June 13, 2017, https://port.today/chinese-expansion-spanish-ports-market; Angelo Scorza, "More Greece, Spain and China in Cosco's Port Agenda," *Ship 2 Shore*, June 19, 2017, http://www.ship2shore.it/en/shipping/more-greece-spain-and-china-in-cosco-s-port-agenda_64763.htm; "Ocean Alliance: An Unmatched Service Offering," CMA CGM, accessed July 1, 2019, https://www.cma-cgm.com/local/finland/news/11/ocean-alliance-an-unmatched-service-offering; "New Shipping Alliances: What You Need to Know," iContainers, March 21, 2017, https://www.icontainers.com/us/2017/03/21/new-shipping-alliances-what-you-need-to-know; Godement and Vasselier, "China at the Gates," appendix, "Spain."

21. "CMA CGM Completes a First Transaction Relating to the Sale of Eight Port Terminals to Terminal Link for USD 815 Million in Cash," CMA CGM, March 26, 2020, https://www.cma-cgm.com/news/3047/cma-cgm-completes-a-first-transaction-relating-to-the-sale-of-eight-port-terminals-to-terminal-link-for-usd-815-million-in-cash; "CMHI and CMA CGM Complete the Terminal Link Transaction," CMA CGM-CMHI Joint Press Release, June 11, 2013, https://www.cma-cgm.com/static/News/Attachments/CMHI%20and%20CMA%20CGM%20complete%20the%20Terminal%20Link%20transaction.pdf.

22. Finbarr Bermingham, "Ports in a Storm: Chinese Investments in Europe Spark Fear of Malign Influence," *South China Morning Post*, October 30, 2022, https://www.scmp.com/news/china/diplomacy/article/3197723/ports-storm-chinese-investments-europe-spark-fear-malign-influence; Mercy A. Kuo, "The Power

of Ports: China's Maritime March," *The Diplomat*, March 8, 2017, https://thediplomat.com/2017/03/the-power-of-ports-chinas-maritime-march.

23. "COSCO SHIPPING Ports Signed a Concession Agreement with Port of Zeebrugge, Reached MOU with CMA for Strategic Partnership," COSCO Shipping Corporation, January 22, 2018, https://en.coscoshipping.com/art/2018/1/23/art_6923_72178.html; "Chinese Cosco Now Owns Entire Container Terminal in Belgian Port of Zeebrugge," NSNBC International, September 12, 2017, https://web.archive.org/web/20170912132218/https://nsnbc.me/2017/09/12/chinese-cosco-now-owns-entire-container-terminal-in-belgian-port-of-zeebrugge; Godement and Vasselier, "China at the Gates," 49–50.

24. Barbara Moens, "Belgium Triggers Chinese Backlash with Port Security Warning," *Politico*, October 25, 2022, https://www.politico.eu/article/china-fume-accusation-belgium-ports-foreign-affairs-minister-hadja-lahbib; "Belgian Professor Warns of Belgium's Dependence on China," Belga News Agency, October 5, 2022, https://www.belganewsagency.eu/belgian-professor-warns-of-belgiums-dependence-on-china; Fu Jing, "Belgium Shows Its Confidence in Belt and Road," *China Daily*, February 13, 2018, https://www.chinadaily.com.cn/a/201802/14/WS5a8221b0a3106e7dcc13c655.html; Keith Johnson, "Why Is China Buying Up Europe's Ports?," *Foreign Policy*, February 2, 2018, https://foreignpolicy.com/2018/02/02/why-is-china-buying-up-europes-ports; Julie Wang, "Cosco Pacific to Buy Stake in Terminal," *Wall Street Journal*, November 19, 2004, https://www.wsj.com/articles/SB110080426330478209.

25. "COSCO Pacific Takes 35% Stake in Terminal of Rotterdam," *China Daily*, May 13, 2016, https://www.chinadaily.com.cn/business/2016-05/13/content_25246994.htm; "COSCO Launches New Operation in the Port of Riga," Safety4Sea.com, February 8, 2018, https://safety4sea.com/cosco-launches-new-operation-in-the-port-of-riga; "China Dominates Container Transport to Port of Rotterdam," Centraal Bureau voor de Statistiek, Netherlands, September 3, 2015, https://www.cbs.nl/en-gb/news/2015/36/china-dominates-container-transport-to-port-of-rotterdam.

26. Andreas Rinke and Jan Schwartz, "German Go-Ahead for China's Cosco Stake in Hamburg Port Unleashes Protest," Reuters, October 26, 2022, https://www.reuters.com/markets/deals/german-cabinet-approves-investment-by-chinas-cosco-hamburg-port-terminal-sources-2022-10-26/#:~:text=BERLIN%2C%20Oct%2026%20(Reuters),protest%20within%20the%20governing%20coalition.

27. Stephen Erlanger, "Spotting the Fault Lines in NATO's United Front," *New York Times*, June 27, 2022, https://www.nytimes.com/2022/06/27/world/europe/nato-summit-madrid-ukraine.html; Joshua Tallis, "NATO's Maritime Vigilance: Optimizing the Standing Naval Force for the Future," *War on the Rocks*, December 15, 2022, https://warontherocks.com/2022/12/natos-maritime-vigilance-optimizing-the-standing-naval-force-for-the-future.

28. "Five Allied Carrier Strike Groups Patrol Waters in NATO's Area of Operations," NATO, November 17, 2022, https://shape.nato.int/news-archive/2022

/five-allied-carrier-strike-groups-patrol-alliance-waters#:~:text=Nov%2017%20 2022-,Five%20Allied%20Carrier%20Strike%20Groups%20patrol%20waters%20 in%20NATO's%20area,of%20their%20regularly%20scheduled%20activities.

29. Robin Häggblom, "Finnish Navy Kicks Off Freezing Winds 22 Annual Exercise," *Naval News*, November 25, 2022, https://www.navalnews.com/naval-news/2022/11/finnish-navy-kicks-off-freezing-winds-22-annual-exercise.

30. Mona Yacoubian, "Ukraine's Consequences Are Finally Spreading to Syria," *War on the Rocks*, January 10, 2023, https://warontherocks.com/2023/01/ukraines-consequences-are-finally-spreading-to-syria; Metrick et al., "Undersea Warfare in Northern Europe," 2; Ihor Kabanenko, "Russian 'Hybrid War' Tactics at Sea: Targeting Underwater Communications Cables," *Eurasia Daily Monitor* 15, no. 10 (2018), https://jamestown.org/program/russian-hy-brid-war-tactics-sea-targeting-underwater-communications-cables/?mc_cid=7f545b546f&mc_eid=a287832eef; Geoffrey Till, "Future Conditional: Naval Power Sits at Centre of Russian Strategy," *Jane's Navy International*, July 20, 2016.

31. NATO, "NATO Deactivates Allied Maritime Command Naples," Atlantic Council, March 28, 2013, https://www.atlanticcouncil.org/blogs/natosource/nato-deactivates-allied-maritime-command-naples.

32. Xavier Vavasseur, "France Unveils New Seabed Warfare Strategy," *Naval News*, February 16, 2022, https://www.navalnews.com/naval-news/2022/02/france-unveils-new-seabed-warfare-strategy; "New Maritime Security Strategy to Target Latest Physical and Cyber Threats," GOV.UK, August 15, 2022, https://www.gov.uk/government/news/new-maritime-security-strategy-to-target-latest-physical-and-cyber-threats.

33. Vilius Petkauskas, "Issues with European Subsea Cables Impact Global Internet Connectivity," *Cybernews*, October 20, 2022, https://cybernews.com/news/european-subsea-cables-cuts.

34. Lorne Cook, "NATO Moves to Protect Undersea Pipelines, Cables as Concern Mounts over Russian Sabotage Threat," Associated Press, June 16, 2023, https://apnews.com/article/nato-russia-sabotage-pipelines-cables-infrastructure-507929033b05b5651475c8738179ba5c.

35. Alan Mauldin, "Cutting Off Europe? A Look at How the Continent Connects to the World," *TeleGeography*, October 13, 2022, https://blog.telegeography.com/cutting-off-europe-a-look-at-how-the-continent-connects-to-the-world.

36. For more on Frontex, see "Who We Are," Frontex, https://www.frontex.europa.eu/about-frontex/who-we-are/tasks-mission/#:~:text=This%20Regulation%20was%20repealed%20by,(OJ%20L%20295%2C%2014.11; Aitor Hernández-Morales, Jacopo Barigazzi, and Zosia Wanat, "Frontex's Growing Pains," *Politico*, January 21, 2021; Giulia Carbonaro, "Frontex: Will the EU Border Agency Quit Greece over the Latest Migrant Boat Tragedy?," Euronews, June 29, 2023, https://www.euronews.com/2023/06/29/frontex-will-the-eu-border-agency-quit-greece-over-the-latest-migrant-boat-tragedy; Marianne Péron-Doise and Christian Wirth, "The European Union's Conceptualization of Maritime Security," Asia Maritime Transparency Initiative, Center for Strategic and International Studies,

March 4, 2022, https://amti.csis.org/the-european-unions-conceptualization-of-maritime-security; and Denis Loctier, "Europe's Coast Guards Are Preparing for the Worst-Case Scenarios to Ensure the Best Outcomes," Euronews, September 28, 2022, https://www.euronews.com/green/2022/09/27/coastex-22-preparing-the-worst-scenarios-to-ensure-the-best-outcomes.

37. "Relations with Asia-Pacific Partners," NATO, July 12, 2022, https://www.nato.int/cps/en/natohq/topics_183254.htm.

38. Matthew Brummer and Wrenn Yennie Lindgren, "Anarchy Is a Bridge: Russia and China Are Pushing NATO and Japan Together," *War on the Rocks*, July 10, 2023, https://warontherocks.com/2023/07/anarchy-is-a-bridge-russia-and-china-are-pushing-nato-and-japan-together; Stefania Benaglia, Fanny Sauvignon, and Rosanna Fanni, "Why Japan Could Be the Key to the EU's Indo-Pacific Ambitions," Center for European Policy Studies, November 21, 2022, https://www.ceps.eu/why-japan-could-be-the-key-to-the-eus-indo-pacific-ambitions/#:~:text=Together%2C%20Japan%20and%20the%20EU,transition%20to%20improved%20public%20services.

39. "World Needs $94 Trillion Spent on Infrastructure by 2040: Report," Reuters, July 25, 2017, https://www.reuters.com/article/us-global-infrastructure-report/world-needs-94-trillion-spent-on-infrastructure-by-2040-report-idUSKBN1AA1A3.

40. Matthew P. Goodman and Jonathan Hillman, "The G7's New Global Infrastructure Initiative," Center for Strategic and International Studies, July 15, 2021, https://www.csis.org/analysis/g7s-new-global-infrastructure-initiative.

41. David L. Fogel, "I Helped Defend against China's Economic Hybrid War. Here's How the US Can Respond," Hybrid Conflict Project, Atlantic Council, April 25, 2022, https://www.atlanticcouncil.org/blogs/new-atlanticist/i-helped-defend-against-chinas-economic-hybrid-war-heres-how-the-us-can-respond.

42. See also "Regulation (EU) 2019/452 of the European Parliament and of the Council of 19 March 2019 Establishing a Framework for the Screening of Foreign Direct Investments into the Union," PE/72/2018/REV/1, European Parliament, March 19, 2019; "Regulation on Distortive Foreign Subsidies," Legislative Train Schedule, European Parliament, November 20, 2022; Allison Carragher, "Hard Cash and Soft Power: When Chinese Firms Win EU Contracts," Carnegie Europe, November 2022, https://carnegieeurope.eu/2022/11/21/hard-cash-and-soft-power-when-chinese-firms-win-eu-contracts-pub-88343; and Jorge Valero and John Follain, "EU's 'Global Gateway' Infrastructure Push Offers Counter to China's 'Belt and Road,'" *Bloomberg*, November 21, 2021, https://www.bloomberg.com/news/articles/2021-11-30/eu-eyes-300-billion-euro-infrastructure-push-to-challenge-china#xj4y7vzkg.

43. Hans Binnendijk and Daniel S. Hamilton, "Face It, NATO: The North Atlantic and Indo-Pacific Are Linked," *Defense News*, June 21, 2021, https://www.defensenews.com/opinion/commentary/2022/06/21/face-it-nato-the-north-atlantic-and-indo-pacific-are-linked.

10

Strategic Competition and Basing in Central and Eastern Europe

EMILY HOLLAND[1]

EUROPEAN BASING IN HISTORICAL PERSPECTIVE

For much of the twentieth century, the European continent was the center of the global struggle for influence between East and West before receding in the face of new challenges. After the end of the Cold War, the United States slowly shifted its focus away from guaranteeing European security to focus on the Global War on Terrorism and address the rise of China in the twenty-first century.

Consequently, the United States steadily reduced the number of its troops stationed in Europe from the 1990s. Russia also withdrew a large numbers of its troops, retaining only some legacy bases in former Soviet states.

Now Russia's invasion of Ukraine has recentered Europe as a focal point of strategic competition in the modern era. Today, the loose security arrangements of the immediate post–Cold War period appear to be anomalous, with both Russia and the West enhancing their military posture and reinvesting in the region. Russia has modernized and expanded its military footprint along NATO's eastern flank. And this effort—particularly Moscow's incursions into Ukraine both in 2014 and now—has revitalized the

NATO alliance. In response to Russia's increased aggression, the United States and NATO initially set up a trip-wire defense of Europe based on rotational forward deployments. Today, with full-blown war on the continent, the United States has once again raised the number of troops deployed in Europe, including small numbers on a permanent basis.

Regardless of the outcome of the war in Ukraine, Russia will likely pose an enduring threat to peace and stability on the European continent. Given this reality, Washington faces the challenge of adjusting its basing strategy in Europe to balance its European commitments with its high-priority commitment to address emerging threats from China. The degraded European security environment is a real threat to the U.S.-led liberal order. Defending Europe and maintaining transatlantic unity are critical tasks for Washington that will likely require greater sustained troop presence in Central and Eastern Europe (CEE) as well as careful alliance management.

Of course, the contemporary global landscape differs greatly from the Cold War period. The rise of China has changed Western security priorities and weakened Russia's relative position in the international system. As a result, although the West has reaffirmed its commitment to upholding European security and NATO is experiencing a renaissance, the West is deploying significantly fewer relative resources to CEE than it did during the Cold War. Moreover, recent U.S. strategic documents, such as the National Security Strategy, highlight the American perception that while Russia is an immediate danger to Western interests, China is the only serious threat to a U.S.-led liberal world order.[2]

Historically, both the United States and Russia have been cautious and avoided placing troops in each other's historical sphere of influence. Since the Cold War, U.S. troop numbers in Europe have fallen dramatically due largely to shifts in NATO's mission and U.S. foreign policy priorities. Russia's foreign military installations in the region are mostly Soviet legacy facilities. However, Moscow has expanded its military presence near the Arctic by placing specialized brigade forces close to the borders of Finland and Norway and also in Ukraine by constructing new bases close to the border of Ukraine and in Belarus.

As the war in Ukraine continues, Russia's basing relationship with Belarus has evolved significantly. Belarus has become a de facto new military district for the Russian army and continues to act as a staging ground for Russian military operations in Ukraine. Belarus also acted as a Kremlin-nominated broker in the negotiations to end the failed coup on June 23, 2023, by the late Wagner Group leader Yevgeny Prigozhin and is currently hosting former Wagner troops after the closure of their main base in Molkino in the Krasnodar region in southern Russia.³ Despite implementing several domestic policies aimed at expanding the size of its army, including raising the top age for military service and making draft evasion more difficult,⁴ Russia has not significantly reduced the presence of its troops in other areas of the former Soviet Union.

In response to the Russia-Ukraine War, the United States has deployed additional troops to CEE and may consider stationing more permanent troops on NATO's eastern flank. However, even if it does, U.S. foreign policy will remain focused on shifting the burden of European security to NATO and European allies. Russia, meanwhile, will likely remain focused on preserving a significant military presence along its borders to protect its territory and sustain a de facto buffer zone.

THE UNITED STATES: FROM DEFENDING EUROPE TO CREATING A BALANCE

After World War II, the United States deployed hundreds of thousands of troops to western Europe both to stabilize the postwar continent and to project U.S. power. During the late 1950s, more than 400,000 U.S. troops were permanently stationed in Europe.⁵ But since then, troop levels have decreased considerably. In the early 1990s, at the end of the Cold War, the number decreased to fewer than 200,000 troops.⁶ In 1991, the Warsaw Pact ended officially on February 25, and the Soviet Union collapsed later that year, leading NATO to redefine its mission from deterring and countering Soviet aggression to upholding general European security and helping allies build their own military capabilities. These changes and the diminished perceived threat from Russia led successive U.S. presidents to reduce troop levels in Europe to fewer than 75,000 in 2018.⁷

Today, about 100,000 U.S. troops are stationed in Europe, with about half (38,000) hosted in Germany.⁸ Only a small number of these troops are permanently stationed within CEE, many of which are part of an additional 7,000 U.S. troops deployed on short rotational assignments under Atlantic Resolve, a NATO support mission.⁹ Since the end of the Cold War, the United States has signed several agreements to base U.S. troops in CEE but has created only two new foreign military facilities, one in Poland and one in Romania (see table 10.1).

Table 10.1. U.S. Military Facilities in CEE.

Country	Type of Base/Facility	Number of Troops	Formal Approval of Host Country	Contract End Date
Bulgaria	U.S.–Bulgaria joint military bases	2,500	Yes, but the bases operate under the Bulgarian flag/command	Indefinite: either party must give one year's notice to end agreement
Poland	Naval Support Facility Redzikowo	86	Yes	Initial period of twenty years, automatically renewed for five years unless either party gives two years notice
Poland	Lask Air Base (permanent home to United States Air Force detachment since 2012)	Up to 200 personnel	Yes, but the base operates under the Polish flag/command	Unknown
Romania	Naval Support Facility Deveselu	250	Yes	One party one-year written notice term

Defense Cooperation Agreement between the United States of America and Bulgaria, April 28, 2006, https://www.state.gov/wp-content/uploads/2019/02/06-612-Bulgaria-Defense-Cooperation.done_.pdf; Agreement Between the United States of America and the Government of the Republic of Poland Concerning the Deployment of Ground-Based Ballistic Missile Defense Interceptors in the Territory of the Republic of Poland, August 20, 2008, https://2009-2017.state.gov/documents/organization/180542.pdf; U.S. Department of State, "The United States and Romania: Strategic Partners for 25 Years," November 28, 2022, https://www.state.gov/the-united-states-and-romania-strategic-partners-for-25-years/; Defense Status of Forces Agreement Between the United States and Romania, December 6, 2005, https://www.state.gov/wp-content/uploads/2019/02/06-721-Romania-Defense-SOFA.pdf.

The most significant installations noted in table 10.1 are the two naval support facilities in Poland and Romania, which also host Aegis Ashore missile defense ground sites. The deployment of these defense systems to Europe caused a dispute with Moscow, which believed that they would threaten Russia's ability to target the United States with intercontinental ballistic missiles. In 2018, the Russian foreign ministry claimed that the deployment of these systems flagrantly violated the Intermediate-Range Nuclear Forces (INF) Treaty, arguing that the "launchers allow for the combat use of Tomahawk medium-range cruise missiles and other strike armaments from the ground."[10] In 2019, both the United States and Russia suspended their commitment to maintaining the INF Treaty.

Since Russia's annexation of Crimea in 2014, U.S. allies in CEE have consistently asked for more defense support and have offered to host U.S. troops. In addition to the NATO support missions outlined in table 10.2, Lithuania constructed Camp Herkus, a €7 million (approximately $8.19 million) project to entice the United States to establish a permanent military presence in Lithuania. In 2021, Lithuania's minister of national defense, Arvydas Anušauskas, stated, "We hope that this new infrastructure in Pabrade will become the second home for the U.S. force."[11] However, given U.S. national security priorities in East Asia, this is unlikely to happen.

Following the annexation, U.S. and NATO planners set up a trip-wire defense in Poland and the Baltics based on rotational deployments. At the 2016 Warsaw Summit, NATO member states decided to deploy four multinational battle groups to vulnerable areas; in 2017, groups were deployed to Estonia, Latvia, Lithuania, and Poland. After Russia's full invasion of Ukraine in

Table 10.2. NATO-Enhanced Forward Presence.

Host Country	Lead	Participating Nations	Number of Troops
Estonia (Tapa)	United Kingdom	Denmark and Iceland	1,430
Latvia (Adazi)	Canada	Albania, Czech Republic, Denmark, Iceland, Italy, Montenegro, Poland, Slovenia, and Spain	1,887
Lithuania (Rukla)	Germany	Belgium, Czech Republic, France, Iceland, Luxembourg, the Netherlands, and Norway	1,632
Poland (Orzysz)	United States	Croatia, Romania, and United Kingdom	1,033
Bulgaria (Kabile)	Italy	Albania, Greece, North Macedonia, and the United States	968
Hungary (Tata)	Hungary	Croatia, Italy, Montenegro, Turkey, and the United States	900
Romania (Cincu)	France	North Macedonia, Poland, Portugal, the Netherlands, and the United States	1,148
Slovakia (Lest)	Czech Republic	Germany, the Netherlands and Slovenia	643

"NATO's Forward Presence," June 2022, https://www.nato.int/nato_static_fl2014/assets/pdf/2022/6/pdf/2206-factsheet_efp_en.pdf; "NATO's Military Presence in the East of the Alliance," December 21, 2022, https://www.nato.int/cps/en/natohq/topics_136388.htm.

February 2022, NATO announced that it would reinforce current battle groups and establish four more in Bulgaria, Hungary, Romania, and Slovakia.[12]

This trip-wire approach, however, may no longer be sufficient in today's degraded security environment. In June 2022 at the NATO summit in Madrid, Spain, U.S. president Joe Biden announced that the United States would enhance its force posture in Europe, including by establishing a permanent Army Corps forward command post in Poland and positioning further rotational troops in Romania and the Baltics.[13] In March 2023, the U.S. Army announced the deployment of approximately 500 soldiers from the 10th Mountain Division Headquarters and 3,800 from the 1st Brigade Combat Team.[14] These troops are expected to return home in early 2024, and the Biden administration is now debating whether to replace them, continuing the enhanced presence and demonstrating support for Ukraine, or whether they should be redeployed elsewhere. The accession of Sweden and Finland to NATO will also shift the balance of forces in Europe. The participation of these states will help make NATO's vision for an integrated defense of Europe far more feasible.

These decisions indicate that the United States recognizes the need for longer-term deterrent capability in Europe regardless of when and how the Ukraine conflict ends. As a result, Washington must balance its increasing security commitments in East Asia with those in Europe. For the United States, this raises complex questions of alliance management both in Europe and in Asia with allies that may desire a greater U.S. presence in their respective regions. In Europe, U.S. efforts will likely involve sustained increases in U.S. troops in Poland, the Baltics, and in the Black Sea region as well as further integration in support of NATO's new northern flank. The war in Ukraine also has implications for the wider European region outside of NATO. The Balkans, which are a fertile breeding ground for anti-European and pro-Russian sentiment, also may require greater attention, partnerships, and engagements.

RUSSIA: FROM PROJECTING POWER TO PROTECTING THE HOMELAND

During the Cold War, the Soviet Union had an extensive network of foreign military installations—the majority of which were located in CEE in Warsaw Pact countries. In the region, Soviet military forces were based in Albania, Czechoslovakia, East Germany, Hungary, and Poland. At the end of the Cold War, Soviet forces were withdrawn from all bases outside of Soviet boundaries. Russia withdrew forces from the Baltic states in the early 1990s and closed its bases in Georgia in the 2000s.[5] It did, however, retain peacekeeping forces in the disputed territories of Abkhazia and South Ossetia and has maintained a continuous military presence in Transnistria (see table 10.3). Today, Russia has fewer than twenty foreign military bases globally, all but one of which (Tartus, Syria) are located in former Soviet states.[16] In contrast, the Soviet Union based Soviet troops at numerous installations across Africa, Southeast Asia, and Cuba.

Russia's disastrous military performance in the 2008 Russo-Georgian War became the proximate cause for a major military modernization. In

Table 10.3. Russian Military Installations in CEE.

Country	Type of Base/Facility	Number of Troops	Formal Approval of Host Country	Contract End Date
Armenia	102nd Military Base	3,300	Yes	2044
Belarus	474th Radar Station	1,450	Yes	2021
Belarus	43rd Naval Communications Center	1,450	Yes	2021
Belarus	Joint Training Center (Grodno)		Yes, but the center operates under the Belarusian flag (staging area for Ukraine)	Unknown
Georgia (Abkhazia)	7th Military Base	4,000	No (disputed)	Unknown
Georgia (South Ossetia)	4th Guards Military Base	4,000	No (disputed)	Unknown
Moldova (Transnistria)		1,500	No	2002
Ukraine/RU (disputed)	Sevastopol Naval Base (Crimea)			Unknown

Author database from working paper 2023; Margarete Klein, "Russia's Military Policy in the Post-Soviet Space: Aims, Instruments, and Perspectives," January 2019, https://www.swp-berlin.org/publications/products/research_papers/2019RP01_kle.pdf.

addition to other measures, this reform included consolidating and modernizing military infrastructure in Moscow's near abroad. The 1995 decree governing Russian policy toward the Commonwealth of Independent States (CIS) includes "maintaining reliable stability in all its meanings: political, military, economic, humanitarian, and legal" and dictates that Russia will "assist the formation of CIS states as politically and economically viable states that conduct friendly policies towards Russia."[17] Throughout the region, Moscow's legacy bases now support Russian security objectives, which focus mostly on regional threats and deterrence. Bases in the Caucasus allow Moscow to maintain the status quo, quickly deploy its troops, and uphold regional security dominance. Russia's presence in Crimea (home of the Black Sea Fleet) and along Ukraine's eastern border facilitates sustained deployments in eastern Ukraine, control of the Black Sea, and defense of a buffer zone. Its bases in Central Asia also project Russian power and allow forces to rapidly deploy along Russia's southern border in the event of a crisis. Like other great power facilities, Moscow's legacy bases aim to project status within their sphere of influence.

In recent years, Moscow's basing posture in CEE has focused on defending vulnerable areas through expanding military cooperation with Belarus and constructing new bases on its own territory around Ukraine. In 2013, Russia expressed the desire to formally build and commission an air base in Belarus that would improve its forward presence with regard to NATO. However, after Russia's annexation of Crimea in 2014, Minsk, perceiving increased bargaining power in light of Russia's dismal relations with the West, rejected Moscow's proposal. The project was then put on hold during Russia's activities in Syria, and the Russian army established a new division along its border with Belarus and reinforced air defenses in Kaliningrad. Yet years later, in May 2021, Belarusian president Alexander Lukashenko agreed to host a joint Belarusian–Russian military training unit, including combat-capable Russian forces, near Grodno. And in October 2021, reversing the earlier rejection, Lukashenko announced that Russia and Belarus have a "single army" in practice and that "a joint military base with Russia" would be created in Belarus in case of an external attack.[18]

In February 2022, Moscow deployed the largest ever number of Russian troops (approximately 30,000) and weaponry—including Iskander missiles, S-400 air defense systems, T-72B3 tanks, and rocket launch systems—to Belarus for the Union Resolve exercise.[19] Although Union Resolve 2022 officially ended on February 20, 2022, Russian forces remained in Belarus after this date and were deployed for Russia's offensive on Kyiv.²⁰ Russian bombers are also deploying from Baranovichi and Lida airfields in Belarus, and Moscow is operating fifty airborne early warning and control aircraft from these fields to coordinate its air operations in Ukraine.²¹

The Russian Wagner mercenary troops that relocated to Belarus following Prigozhin's failed coup in June 2023 are also likely to remain in Belarus for the foreseeable future. Although there are contradictory reports about the number of Wagner forces exiled to Belarus, late senior Wagner commander and chief of staff "Marx" announced that more than 10,000 "have gone or will go to Belarus."²² After their arrival in July 2023, some Wagner troops moved to the Suwalki Gap (the land corridor separating Kaliningrad and Belarus), where they were seen training Belarusian special forces only five miles from the Polish border.²³ In August 2023, defense ministers from Poland, Lithuania, Latvia, and Estonia met in Warsaw to discuss the border situation with Belarus, demanding that Belarus expel all Wagner troops from its territories immediately. Lukashenko refused, calling the demand "unreasonable and stupid" and criticizing the presence of foreign troops in Poland, Lithuania, and the other Baltic states.²⁴

The war in Ukraine has precipitated a dramatic acceleration in Russia–Belarus military cooperation and has set up a de facto lasting and indefinite military presence in Belarus despite the absence of a formal permanent Russian military base or basing agreement. Given the rapid integration of the Russian and Belarusian defense systems, it is unlikely that this cooperation will be reversed in the near future. In many respects, Belarus is now a de facto extension of Russia's Western Military District. Russia's current basing practices in Belarus are notable for their informal and flexible nature, adapting to meet Russia's wartime needs and Belarus's political agenda. This stands in stark contrast to the highly formalized process by which the United States signs agreements with partner states to support security goals.

The war and Russia's perception of a diminished security environment have also precipitated the construction of several new bases near Ukraine in the Russian regions of Belgorod, Rostov, and Voronezh. These bases are most likely to reorient Moscow's forces to surround and contain Ukraine in the coming years. Of course, Russia has also significantly expanded its military presence in annexed Crimea. Among other efforts, it has modernized twelve military facilities on the Crimean Peninsula to host a variety of permanent deployments.

Despite these expansions, in light of Russia's disastrous military performance in Ukraine and the strong probability that the conflict will continue at some level for the foreseeable future, it is unlikely that Moscow will deviate from the patterns of post-Soviet basing. And these patterns indicate that Russia's primary national security focus is protecting its homeland through maintaining a buffer zone that is supported by bases in neighboring states and in Russian regions close to Ukraine. This approach to basing, which fits with the historical Russian security perception of a vulnerable homeland, varies greatly from the power projection basing approach employed by other great powers.

FORCE POSTURE DURING WAR AND BEYOND

Estimates of Russian casualties from the war in Ukraine vary widely from around 10,000 to around 100,000.[25] Regardless of the true number, these casualties and the severe Western sanctions imposed on Moscow will have a deleterious effect on the Russian economy for decades. Prior to the war, Russia was attempting to expand its role on the global stage through limited power projection outside of its sphere of influence in Africa, Syria, and other areas. Now, with even more limited resources, militarily, Moscow will likely remain focused on defending what it perceives to be its primary sphere of influence and buffer zone: Ukraine and Belarus.[26] Politically, Moscow will likely remain focused on fracturing Western unity in NATO and the European Union. As U.S. defense planners prioritize addressing the challenge of China, maintaining a deterrent presence in the CEE will be crucial for reassuring allies and maintaining the European security architecture. However, U.S. policymakers should be cognizant that new, large deployments, as well as NATO exercises at Russia's borders, will raise alarm in a paranoid and wounded Kremlin.[27]

One key task for Western policymakers will be managing complex regional relationships, including the most critical task: upholding NATO unity. Washington must balance its long-term priority of turning over the defense of Europe to the Europeans with the near-term urgent challenge of safeguarding European security and the liberal world order. For now, Washington must continue to provide sizable military personnel and high-tech weaponry even as other alliance members promise to swiftly raise defense spending.

At the same time, the Biden administration should be cognizant that their goal of deterring China also requires paying close attention to Chinese activities in Europe. There are no Chinese military installations on the European continent, but Chinese infrastructure investments—including ports in Greece and more than $1 billion annually in the western Balkans[28]—raise the prospect of Chinese power projection in the region. China has been particularly active in courting leaders in the western Balkans, an area with both historic anti-U.S. and pro-Russian sentiment. The Biden administration should work with its European allies to strengthen Western partnerships in the western Balkans, including by supporting Bulgaria's, Croatia's, and Romania's bid for membership into the Schengen Agreement.

CONCLUSION

For the most part, since the Cold War, Washington and Moscow have avoided placing military facilities in the other's sphere of influence. However, the installations of the Aegis Ashore systems in Poland and Romania have certainly contributed to Moscow's increased threat perception and the deterioration of relations between Russia and the West over the past decade. Bolstering security in response to Russian aggression does not require a return to Cold War–era military arrangements in Europe, but it may require Washington to move away from trip-wire rotational forward deployments toward more permanent arrangements on NATO's eastern flank. Should the United States prioritize countering Russia's increased troop presence in Belarus, it might consider modestly increasing troop levels in Poland, particularly in the east near the strategically important Suwalki Gap. Options that minimize the risk of escalation include the potential deployment of another multinational brigade, with a third allied country acting as a lead nation.

Given the likelihood of extended hostilities between Russia and NATO, the role of the exposed Baltic states will be crucial. These states have long advocated for an increased NATO troop presence on their territories, and these calls have increased as a result of Russian aggression and the degraded security environment. For U.S. policymakers, there is no escaping the reality that several of its NATO allies are directly threatened by a hostile adversary, and thus it would be prudent to increase both U.S. and NATO troop presence in this area. For Washington, a primary aim of its European security policy is preparing and fostering support for a Europe-led European defense. In the Baltic region, one potential strategy to do so is supporting Sweden's suggestion to create a new Maritime Component Command in Sweden to help solidify the alliance's control of the Baltic and the Gulf of Finland.

The China challenge ensures that the United States will not expand its troop presence to the level seen during the Cold War. At the same time, Russia's aggressive action in Ukraine and major war on the European continent demonstrate that Russia is a threat not only to European peace and security but also to the global order. Deterring Russia both in Europe and in the wider international system should remain a primary priority of American foreign policy. For the foreseeable future, Washington will be forced to walk a fine line, upholding transatlantic unity on the defense of Europe while also ensuring that European states do not walk back on their promises to shoulder more of the burden.

NOTES

1. The author would like to thank Andrew Yeo and Isaac Kardon for reviewing and commenting on drafts of this chapter.
2. "Fact Sheet: The Biden-Harris Administration's National Security Strategy," White House, October 12, 2022, https://www.whitehouse.gov/briefing-room/statements-releases/2022/10/12/fact-sheet-the-biden-harris-administrations-national-security-strategy.
3. "Flying Russian Flags, More Wagner Troops Rolls into Belarus as Part of Deal That Ended Mutiny," Associated Press, July 17, 2023, https://apnews.com/article/russia-ukraine-belarus-war-putin-wagner-b6452fdd657aaa1773fad410f4b8d762.
4. Ivan Nechepurenko, "Russia, Seeking Bigger Army, Moves to Raise the Top Age for Military Service," *New York Times*, July 25, 2023, https://www.nytimes.com/live/2023/07/25/world/russia-ukraine-news/russia-military-service-age?smid=url-share.
5. Zachary Basu, "Where 100,000 U.S. Troops Are Stationed in Europe," *Axios*, March 22, 2022, https://www.axios.com/2022/03/23/where-100000-us-troops-are-stationed-europe.
6. Basu, "Where 100,000 U.S. Troops Are Stationed in Europe."
7. Basu, "Where 100,000 U.S. Troops Are Stationed in Europe." (See also the following linked article: "History of U.S. Force Posture," U.S. European Command, https://www.documentcloud.org/documents/21474071-eucom.)
8. "Fact Sheet: U.S. Defense Contributions to Europe," U.S. Department of Defense, June 29, 2022, https://www.defense.gov/News/Releases/Release/Article/3078056/fact-sheet-us-defense-contributions-to-europe; Ben Knight, "U.S. Military in Germany: What You Need to Know," *Deutsche Welle*, June 16, 2020, https://www.dw.com/en/us-military-in-germany-what-you-need-to-know/a-49998340.

9. "U.S. Army Europe and Africa Operations," U.S. Department of Defense, https://www.europeafrica.army.mil/Operations.

10. "Russia Slams US Aegis Ashore Missile Deployment as Direct Breach of INF Treaty," TASS, November 26, 2018, https://tass.com/politics/1032585.

11. Jacqueline Feldscher, "Is This the Next US Military Base in Europe?," *Defense One*, October 3, 2021, https://www.defenseone.com/policy/2021/10/next-us-military-base-europe/185808.

12. "NATO's Military Presence in the East of the Alliance," NATO, July 28, 2023, https://www.nato.int/cps/en/natohq/topics_136383.htm.

13. Jim Garamone, "Biden Announces Changes in U.S. Force Posture in Europe," U.S. Department of Defense, June 29, 2022, https://www.defense.gov/News/News-Stories/Article/Article/3078087/biden-announces-changes-in-us-force-posture-in-europe.

14. Courtney Kube, "Pentagon Officials Debate whether to Replace Extra U.S. Troops Deployed to Eastern Europe or Bring Them Home," NBC News, September 1, 2023, https://www.nbcnews.com/politics/national-security/pentagon-officials-debate-us-troops-eastern-europe-ukraine-russia-rcna102926.

15. Wendy Sloane, "Russian Army Pullout Means World War II Finally Ends in Baltics," *Christian Science Monitor*, August 31, 1994, https://www.csmonitor.com/1994/0831/31011.html.

16. Dmitry Gorenberg, "Russia's Foreign Military Basing Strategy," *PONARS Eurasia*, September 20, 2021, https://www.ponarseurasia.org/russias-foreign-military-basing-strategy.

17. President of Russia, "Указ Президента Поссискои Федерации от 14.09.1995 г. 940" [Decree of the President of the Russian Federation of September 14, 1995, No. 940], September 14, 1995, http://kremlin.ru/acts/bank/8307.

18. "Belarus Can Turn into Joint Military Base with Russia in Case of Aggression—Lukashenko," TASS, October 2, 2021, https://tass.com/world/1345023.

19. Paul McLeary and Alexander Ward, "Russian Military Build-Up Continues, despite Moscow's Promises of a Drawdown," *Politico*, February 19, 2022, https://www.politico.com/news/2022/02/19/russian-military-build-up-continues-despite-moscows-promises-of-a-drawdown-00010372.

20. András Racz, "Becoming a Military District: Deepening Military Cooperation between Russia and Belarus," European Union Institute for Security Studies, March 14, 2022, https://www.iss.europa.eu/content/becoming-military-district#_introduction.

21. Tom Ripley, "Ukraine Conflict: Belarus-Based A-50 AEW&C Aircraft Lead Russian Air Offensive on Ukraine," *Jane's Defence Weekly*, February 28, 2022, https://www.janes.com/defence-news/news-detail/ukraine-conflict-belarus-based-a-50-aewc-aircraft-lead-russian-air-offensive-on-ukraine.

22. Guy Falconbridge and Felix Light, "Wagner Mercenaries Train Belarus Special Forces Near Polish Border," Reuters, July 20, 2023, https://www.reuters.com/world/europe/belarus-forces-holding-exercises-with-wagner-fighters-border-with-poland-2023-07-20.

23. Falconbridge and Light, "Wagner Mercenaries Train Belarus Special Forces Near Polish Border."

24. Claudia Chiappa, "Lukashenko Scoffs at Demands for Wagner Troops' Expulsion from Belarus," *Politico*, August 31, 2023, https://www.politico.eu/article/alexander-lukashenko-pushback-wagner-troops-expulsion-belarus.

25. Olivier Knox, "Russia Has Lost Up to 80,000 Troops in Ukraine. Or 75,000. Or Is It 60,000?," *Washington Post*, August 9, 2022, https://www.washingtonpost.com/politics/2022/08/09/russia-has-lost-up-80000-troops-ukraine-or-75000-or-is-it-60000; Neil MacFarquhar, "Counting Russia's War Dead, with Tips, Clips and a Giant Spreadsheet," *New York Times*, December 18, 2022, https://www.nytimes.com/2022/12/18/world/europe/russia-death-toll-war.html.

26. Bryan Frederick, Matthew Povlock, Stephen Watts, Miranda Priebe, and Edward Geist, "Assessing Russian Reactions to U.S. and NATO Posture Enhancements," RAND Corporation, 2017, https://www.rand.org/pubs/research_reports/RR1879.html.

27. Dmitry Trenin, "Russia-NATO: Controlling Confrontation," *Politiques Étrangères*, no. 4 (2016): 87–97, https://www.cairn-int.info/article-E_PE_164_0087--russia-nato-controlling-confrontation.htm.

28. Bojan Stojkovski, Ivana Jeremic, Samir Kajosevic, Ivana Nikolic, Ivan Angelovski, Fatjona Mejdini, and Ivan Pekmez, "China in the Balkans: Controversy and Cost," *Balkan Insight*, December 15, 2021, https://balkaninsight.com/2021/12/15/china-in-the-balkans-controversy-and-cost.

11

Competing for Consent

Public Support and the Foundations of U.S. Overseas Basing in Europe

MICHAEL ALLEN
MICHAEL E. FLYNN
CARLA MARTÍNEZ MACHAIN[1]

The United States has had unparalleled military access to Europe since the dissolution of the Soviet Union. Events like the war in Kosovo, the expansion of NATO, humanitarian interventions, and the war in Afghanistan reshaped and redefined the role of the United States and NATO in Europe. Contrary to some observers' expectations that the United States would withdraw from Europe and that NATO would cease to exist following the end of the Cold War, both the United States and NATO remain active, and ties between the United States and NATO member states are deeper than ever.[2] The Russian invasion of Ukraine in 2022 has reminded the world that wars of territorial conquest are still possible in Europe, reinvigorating NATO's core collective defense functions and increasing the demand for a U.S. military presence in Europe.

Despite the *absolute* strength of its position, the *relative* dominance of the United States in overseas military bases shows signs of decline. Although U.S. service members have remained a common sight in cities and towns in European countries like Germany, Poland, England, and many others, the United States has been downsizing its military presence for the past thirty years as its mission has shifted from countering the Soviet Union to maintaining regional stability. Some downsizing has occurred in response to domestic pressures to decrease military spending and U.S. interventionism abroad.[3]

Additionally, since the end of World War II, U.S. allies have been growing increasingly assertive when determining the terms of U.S. basing and deployments in their territories. Some European host states have pushed the United States to curb negative externalities historically associated with basing, such as crime.[4] In other cases, host governments have asked the U.S. military to leave entirely.[5] Even without the United States being forced out, any opposition in European host countries can make it more costly for the United States to maintain its military presence there. Leaders affected politically by populations' dissatisfaction will likely pass those costs on to the United States and attach more conditions to basing agreements.

Presently, U.S. dominance in overseas basing is also increasingly subject to challenges by rival states like Russia and China. Not only will more democratic host countries consider the political costs of hosting U.S. military forces that are unpopular with their populations, but they will increasingly have the outside option of granting access to the militaries of other major powers. The People's Republic of China's rise offers an alternative model to the U.S.-led order. Russia's invasion of Ukraine attempts to create a hard line against the further expansion of western European and U.S. influence in eastern Europe and Central Asia. We argue that the United States has entered an era in which it needs to win the support of domestic audiences to maintain its overseas security arrangements—particularly in regions close to rival major powers that seek to project their own influence in those regions.

While the United States is unlikely to lose basing access in its closest military allies, such as NATO member states, it also maintains security cooperation arrangements, deployments, and access rights in many other countries. Although basing arrangements with the former may be more secure, the status of basing and deployments in the latter is far more uncertain. Since the future of power projection may focus less on traditional, large-scale military installations and more on smaller, lily-pad sites, joint training exercises, and access agreements, cooperation with partners that go beyond traditional allies will be essential.[6] The very flexibility that this kind of "light footprint" provides also means that the costs of asking the United States to remove its presence in the face of domestic opposition are also potentially lower in cases where domestic constituencies may be exposed to the ills of basing and deployments without being invested in the positives.

As China increases its overseas basing network, the places where the United States has long held a monopoly of influence and access may become subject to greater contestation between rival major powers. Even though elites may be more wary of the potential threats a rising China poses, the people's preferences are still likely to shape policy outcomes in democratic societies. The European states we discuss in this chapter are among the staunchest of U.S. allies, but even in these cases, we may see, if not direct challenges to U.S. basing, efforts to curb U.S. influence and access rights. If the United States desires to maintain its current global presence, it will increasingly have to turn its attention to promoting its values, missions, and world vision to host-state civilians. More substantial buy-in by host populations concerning the benefits of the U.S. presence and the limitations of alternative security networks will facilitate broader operational freedom than the nearest competitors of the United States.

Although elites and not the general public make foreign policy decisions, research has shown that public opinion can matter for basing policy and, more broadly, for a state's foreign policy.[7] Although mobilization requires overcoming collective action problems, once groups can mobilize (especially if key groups like industrial workers or the urban middle class can be recruited), they may even lead to regime change.[8] Since interest groups care more about particular issues than the rest of the population and are willing to exert more effort to change policy on those issues, mobilizing a large majority of the population is not required to pressure the government into policy change.[9] A country does not need to be fully democratic for public opinion to influence the leader's decision calculus when accepting a U.S. military presence in its territory. Existing work shows that nondemocratic states with anti-American populations will accept U.S. military aid only when it can be kept hidden from their populations. A U.S. military installation does not meet that criteria, as its presence is easily evident to a population.[10]

Using surveys conducted in the United Kingdom, Germany, Italy, Belgium, the Netherlands, Portugal, Spain, Turkey, and Poland, we find evidence that, in general, the United States enjoys substantial popular support among many European audiences. Still, that support is contingent on its engagement with those audiences. The future of the U.S. military presence in Europe and its continued leadership in security affairs are not based purely on external challenges from rival states but also on the ability of the United States to show that it is responsive to the demands of host-state populations.

Our first set of surveys is from before the invasion of Ukraine in 2022. However, we followed up with a 2023 survey in Poland to help understand how the war in Ukraine affects public support in crucial U.S. allies. If the trends of our previous surveys follow what we have found in Poland, then we expect that support for the U.S. presence has increased noticeably due to the immediate nature of Russia's invasion of Ukraine.

RESEARCH METHODS: SURVEYS AND INTERVIEWS

In 2018, 2019, and 2020, we conducted surveys in fourteen countries with a significant U.S. military presence.[11] Here, we focus on the nine European countries in our sample—Germany, England, Italy, Belgium, the Netherlands, Portugal, Spain, Poland, and Turkey. We use "European" to refer to this group of respondents throughout this chapter.[12] In 2023, we ran an additional survey in Poland. This new Poland survey allows us to gain more insight into how the ongoing war in Ukraine has shifted public opinion since 2020. It also allows us to determine how predictive the prewar results would be of levels of support for the United States and NATO during the war. In other words, the pre- and postwar surveys allow us to answer the question of whether a security threat weakens or strengthens support for the U.S. military presence. This is particularly relevant in the case of a frontline ally, such as Poland.

In the initial rounds, we surveyed approximately 1,000 people per country annually, giving us a sample of about 27,000 European respondents across the nine countries listed above.[13] In our 2023 survey of Poland, we obtained a sample of approximately 2,250 Polish adults. Additionally, in July 2019, we traveled to England and Germany to conduct qualitative interviews with elite actors, including local government officials, journalists, U.S. military and diplomatic personnel, and activists. Given the U.S. presence in each of these countries, our first line of questions was on how host-state civilians viewed the U.S. military presence in their country, the U.S. government, and the U.S. people generally. American service members are the frontline contact for many host-state civilians—a resident of a country with a significant U.S. military presence is far more likely to have contact with a U.S. service member

Figure 11.1. Respondent Views of U.S. Actors in European Host States, 2018–2020.

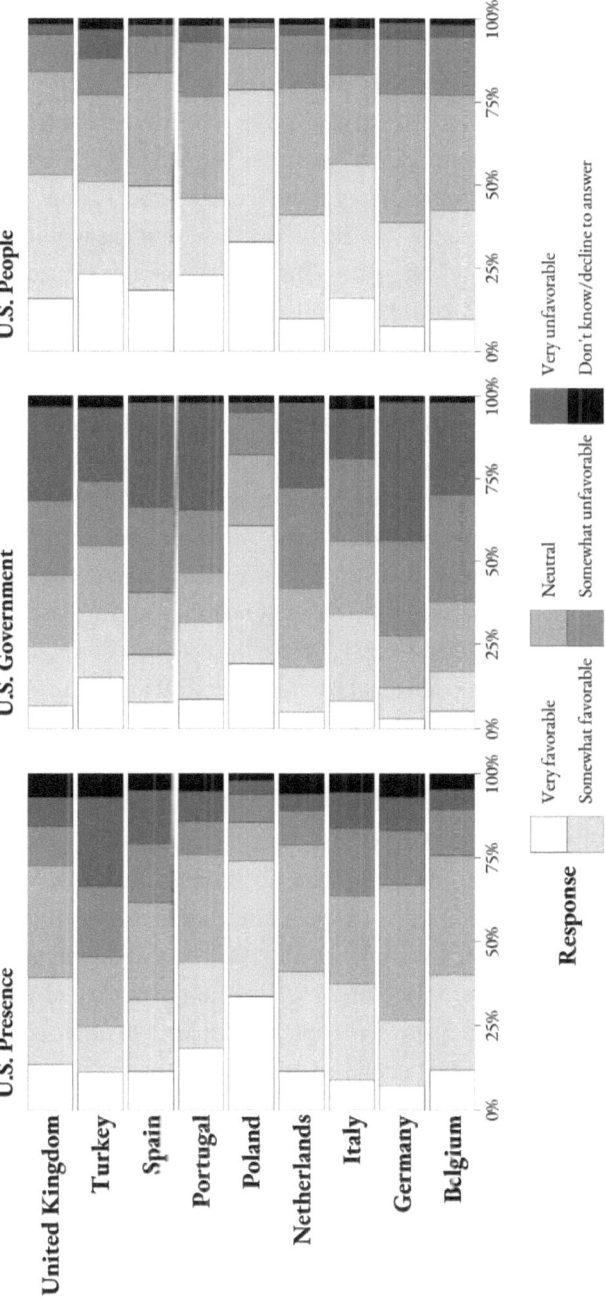

Authors' survey, 2018–2020.

than with an official diplomat. As such, service members often function as de facto diplomats of the United States. The survey allows us to see if views of the U.S. presence correspond to the views of the government and the people.

Figure 11.1 shows respondents' views of these three groups in each country included in the 2018–2020 survey. There is substantial variation across countries concerning respondents' attitudes toward the U.S. military presence in their country. In some states, like Germany and Turkey, public views of the U.S. military presence are fairly low. In these cases, the number of respondents expressing a "very favorable" or "somewhat favorable" view of the U.S. presence in each country is only about 25 percent when combining these categories. In the case of Turkey, this low level of support is mirrored by a more substantive proportion of the public expressing a negative view of the U.S. presence. In contrast, Germany has a much larger "neutral" response category and fewer unfavorable responses. Even before the Ukraine war, Poland stood out as the most supportive country of the U.S. presence, with almost 75 percent of respondents saying they have a "very favorable" or "somewhat favorable" view of the U.S. military presence in Poland, with very few expressing unfavorable views. Overall, support for the United States is mainly favorable across all surveyed European countries.

Despite the variation across individual countries, European respondents express fairly positive views of the U.S. people and the U.S. military presence in their country. Fifty percent of all respondents express "very favorable" or "somewhat favorable" views of the U.S. people. Alternatively, respondent views of the U.S. government are more negative than the other two groups. Only 28 percent of respondents hold favorable views of the U.S. government. There also appears to be a correlation between views on the different U.S. actors. For example, countries where respondents are more supportive of the U.S. military presence in their territory also tend to be more supportive of the U.S. government as compared to other countries. We have found in our work that economic benefits from the military presence and contact with U.S. service members can potentially build support for the U.S. military presence.[14] Notably, personal contact is related to more positive views of the U.S. military, even after considering the effect of economic benefits. This finding follows the logic of contact theory, suggesting that the more interactions people have with an outsider group like foreign-deployed military personnel, the more likely they are to drop their biases about that group and assess them positively. We argue that they are thus also more likely to support their country's foreign presence.[15]

CONTRASTING VIEWS OF THE UNITED STATES AND CHINA

Viewing perceptions of the United States in isolation shows support for the U.S. military presence in Europe. Yet we need to know how this support compares to the levels of support enjoyed by competitors to have context for those findings. Our survey results regarding China help provide some of that context.

In our surveys, we were also interested in how host-state civilians viewed China. As a rising major power with global influence, China represents the major challenger to U.S. global leadership. While our surveyed countries do not have security relationships with China, it is feasible that China could seek such partnerships in the future or, at the very least, act as a foil to curb U.S. security arrangements. The example of NATO ally Greece ceding control of its largest commercial port, Piraeus, to a Chinese shipping corporation is perhaps a telling example.[16]

We could not directly ask how people saw the Chinese military presence in their country, as these are nonexistent in any comparable sense. However, people in European countries have seen increased Chinese economic and cultural influence both locally and globally. We thus asked in our surveys and fieldwork interviews about how people viewed China overall and how they viewed Chinese influence within their country.

Figures 11.2 and 11.3 provide the breakdown of the views of China and its influence on the different European countries. Figure 11.2 shows respondents' views of the Chinese government and Chinese people. As is the case when asked about the United States (figure 11.1), European respondents generally hold more favorable views of the Chinese people than of the Chinese government. Across all nine countries, we see similar patterns compared to views of the United States, with 44 percent of all respondents holding "very favorable" or "somewhat favorable" views of the Chinese people. If we also include the "neutral" category, we see large majorities expressing neutral to positive views. Alternatively, views of the Chinese government are far more negative. Across all nine countries, only 16 percent of respondents expressed a "very favorable" or "somewhat favorable" view of the Chinese government. Turkey is a notable outlier, with approximately 34 percent of respondents expressing a "very favorable" or "somewhat favorable" view of it. It is of note that Turkey also holds the most unfavorable views of the U.S. military in the survey, thus suggesting that the positive views of China may be related to dissatisfaction with the U.S.-led order and Turkey's role in it.

Figure 11.2. Respondent Views of Chinese Actors in Nine European Host States, 2018–2020.

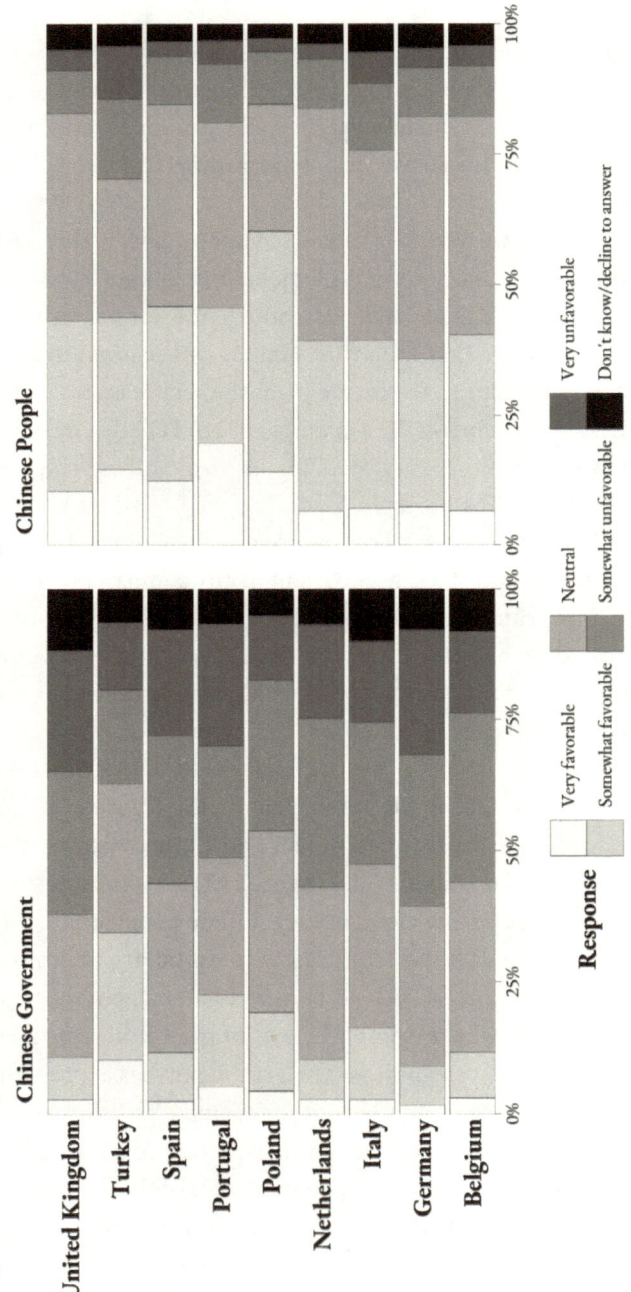

Authors' survey, 2018–2020.

Figure 11.3. Respondent Views of Chinese Influence in Host Countries, 2018–2020.

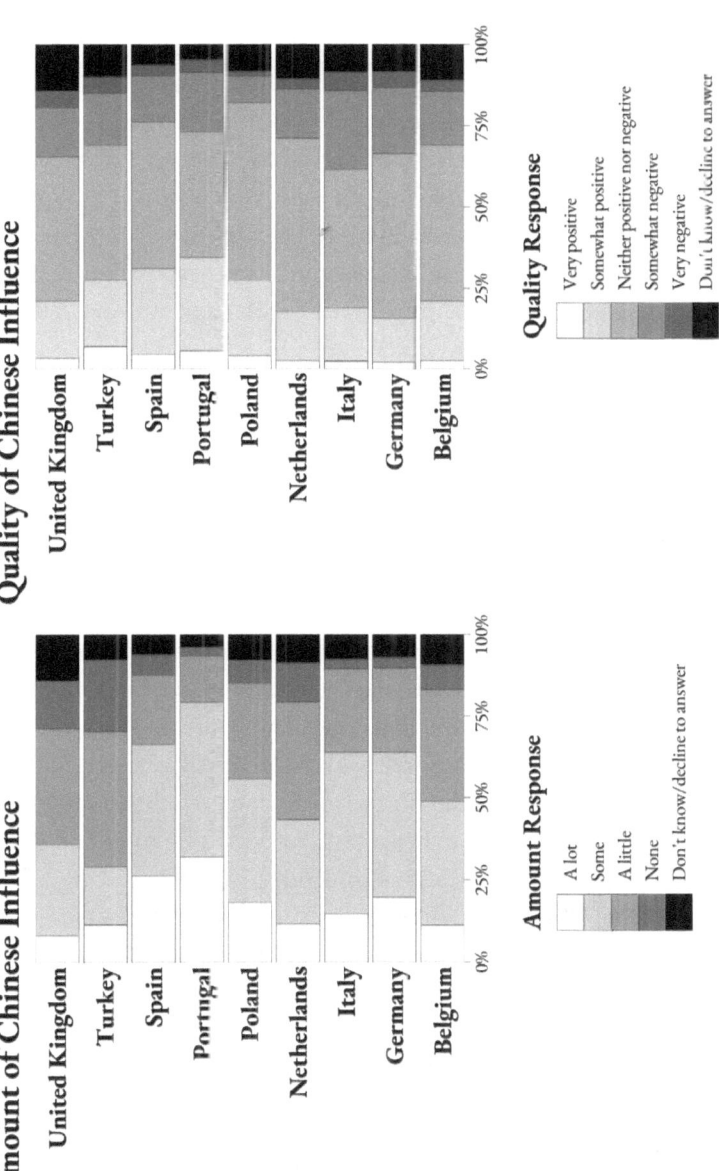

Authors' survey, 2018–2020.

Figure 11.3 shows respondent views on the amount and the quality of Chinese influence in their country. Across all nine countries, 54 percent of respondents think that China has "a lot" or "some" influence on the host state, with 17 percent responding that China has "a lot" of influence. Notably, European publics do not generally view this influence as positive. Although there are large swaths of people across all countries viewing China's influence as "neither positive nor negative," only about 24 percent of respondents across all countries view Chinese influence as "very positive" or "somewhat positive," with only 4 percent viewing it as "very positive." Similar proportions of the public view Chinese influence as "very negative" or "somewhat negative." These numbers are approximately equivalent to views of the quality of U.S. influence (not shown here).

When we interviewed a sitting member of Parliament (MP) in the British House of Commons, we asked about Chinese influence in Great Britain.[17] She said that the public was generally unaware of the regional or global security implications of China's power projection; instead, they just thought that China was a good place to get cheap electronics, like Huawei cell phones, and that they did not cause any problems within the country (as expressed by a Parish Council member in Lakenheath, England, "Can't say [China] comes up a lot. You hear more about potholes and parking on pavement").[18] The MP commented that the elite political view of China was vastly different and much more concerned and cautious than the average person's view. A second MP, one with a Scottish constituency and a member of the Defence Committee at the time of the interview, echoed some of these ideas. He noted that the public has a positive view of China and does not care about the security implications of using Chinese hardware and software. If anything, China represents a good business opportunity for them.[19]

In Germany, we received a similar response from a peace activist who, while acknowledging that there was not a standard German view of China "as a whole," told us that the German population was very supportive of China's economic progress and that some even view it with "a little bit of cheer," recognizing their achievement and progress. He also noted that most policy debates regarding China were "mainly among the more educated part of [German] society." Although he did not take an explicitly pro-China stance, he noted the importance of China as an economic partner for Germany ("All the big German companies are producing with China") and the potential for profit to be made with China.[20]

The Labour MP in Britain also offered her perspective on the decision process for countries considering a choice between U.S. and Chinese security networks. She noted that while elites may hold different views from the public in the United Kingdom, elites in other countries, including other European ones, may see China as a better deal for economic development and security. According to the MP, China will offer to build infrastructure projects, like ports or airports, without preconditions.[21] In contrast, the United States has explicit caveats for human rights and anti-corruption standards that a government must meet to do business with the United States. If all else were equal, the costs of doing business with the United States would be higher and a worse deal. Of course, she argued that security concerns regarding China made the "all else" not equal.

Regarding security, the German activist did not see China as a threat, or at least not more of a threat than the United States posed. He noted the need to accept a multipolar world with "three or four" major powers. He told us that it was not the idea of China being a great power that was threatening but rather the lack of rules for great power interaction in the international system. He noted that with a rising China and Russia, there was a need to develop "rules of behavior" between the great powers to avoid conflict.[22]

Our data thus highlight two crucial points. First, politicians and elites may overestimate how favorably the general public views the Chinese government and its influence. European publics had mixed to negative views of the Chinese government—45 percent of adults surveyed expressed a *negative* view of it, and 20 percent of respondents said Chinese influence in their country was negative. These figures represent European views before the Russian invasion of Ukraine. China's support for Russia's war effort has, of course, created tensions with the EU. In April 2023, ahead of a diplomatic visit to China by EU Commission president Ursula von der Leyen and French president Emmanuel Macron, the EU's foreign policy chief, Josep Borrell, condemned China for "siding with the aggressor" in the Ukraine conflict.[23]

However, not all Europeans view China negatively after the Russian invasion of Ukraine. In Poland's case, we find evidence that public views of the Chinese government have become substantially *more positive* in 2023 after the invasion of Ukraine. Although China's actions have largely supported Russia, its public-facing language has tried to position it as a neutral party in the conflict. The increase in public support within Poland for the Chinese government may reflect the effect of this language. As noted previously, this may also be reflected in the schism between elites, who are aware of China's support for Russia during the war, and the general public, who may be more likely to be influenced by China's public statements of neutrality. We do not have a comparable survey of elite actors and their assessments of public views of China, so caution is in order.[24]

The second point highlighted by our data is that while Americans are generally well-liked in Europe (50 percent of all respondents express "very favorable" or "somewhat favorable" views of the U.S. people), the countries that have an overwhelmingly positive view of the U.S. military, like Poland, are outliers. Instead, Europeans' most common response when asked about their views of the U.S. military in their country is "neutral." This result paints a picture of a Europe that may be genuinely susceptible to influence campaigns by both great powers. The next few years will thus be crucial in determining the outcome of this competition and the future of U.S. access in Europe.

Of course, as noted by the German activist, the competition for influence in Europe is not just between the United States and China. Europe also has to deal with a more proximate major power—Russia. Russia's role as a more active major power with power projection capability is at the forefront of U.S. relations with Europe. The fact that U.S.–China competition is in part framed by both major powers' actions toward the Russian invasion of Ukraine is telling of Russia's role as a major power player in the competition for influence. The following section explores European views of Russia and its influence.

POLAND AND RUSSIA'S INVASION OF UKRAINE: A FRONTLINE ALLY CASE

We conducted our fieldwork interviews in the summer of 2019, several years after the Russian annexation of Crimea in 2014 and before the 2022 invasion of Ukraine. At the time, views toward Russia seemed to lean conciliatory in their tone. A Wiesbaden city official noted that German people could separate their views of the Russian people from those of Russian president Vladimir Putin, much like they did for the American population and then U.S. president Donald Trump.[25]

The German peace activist expressed hope (though, as he said, this was mostly a "dream" of his for how to shut down U.S. military bases in Ger-

Figure 11.4. Respondent Views of Polish–Russian Relations, 2023.

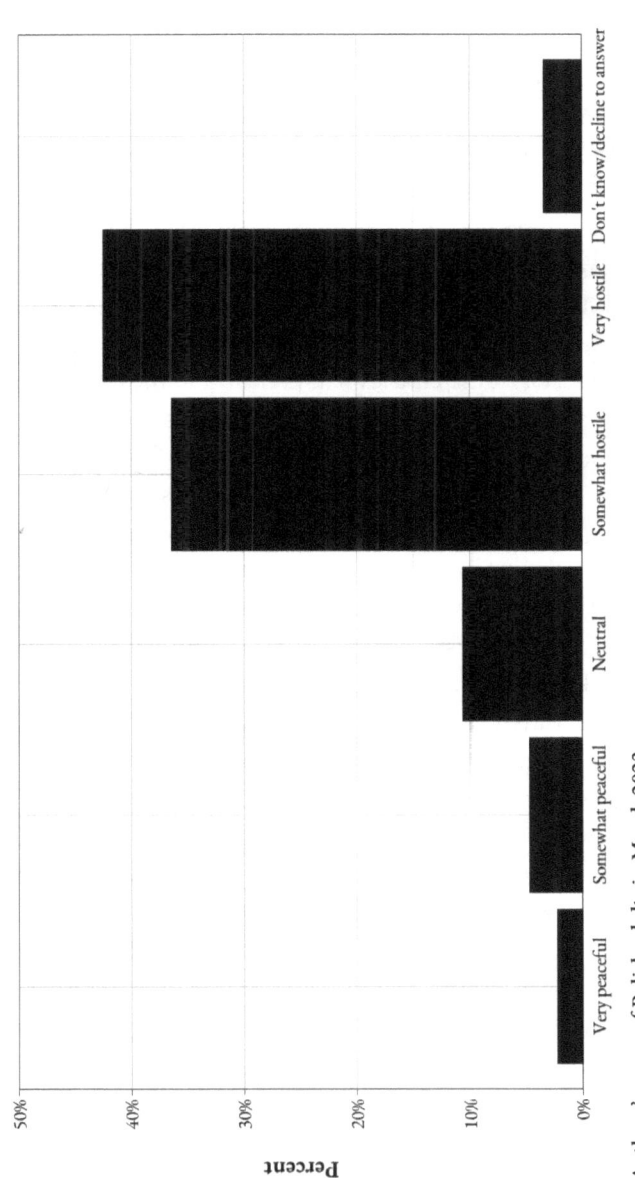

Authors' survey of Polish adults in March 2023.

many) for European "common security" with Russia such that there would no longer be a need for a U.S. military presence in Germany. Yet, despite a desire for engagement with Russia, he did not view this as being at odds with the NATO alliance. He noted that the German people are "very much peace-oriented and pacifistic" and desired "peaceful relations with Russia" along with NATO enlargement.[26] In hindsight, it is easy to see that Russia's opposition to NATO enlargement and increased influence would stand in the way of achieving these goals.

The Russian invasion of Ukraine in early 2022 galvanized European views on the role of the United States and NATO on the continent. Sweden and Finland, two countries that maintained neutrality and nonalignment throughout the Cold War and into the present, decided in 2023 that it was time to join NATO. At the elite level, it is clear that the demand for the U.S. presence is at a post–Cold War high, as the threat to European security and territorial integrity is more serious than it has been for decades.

In early 2023, we followed our first round of surveys with a targeted survey in Poland. Given the targeted focus, we surveyed 2,250 respondents to draw more robust conclusions compared to the 1,000 per year we had done previously. Poland offered an interesting case for further understanding the role of competing security pressures in Europe.

Figure 11.4 shows Polish adult respondents' views of Poland's relations with Russia in March 2023. A large majority—79 percent—view relations with Russia as "somewhat hostile" or "very hostile." Alternatively, only about 11 percent of respondents view relations with Russia as "neutral," and about 7 percent view relations as "very peaceful" or "somewhat peaceful." While we did not have separate questions asking respondents about their views of the Russian government and Russian people, it stands to reason that patterns we observe in the cases of the United States and China may hold here as well. Polish respondents likely associate hostile relations between Poland and Russia with Putin's government specifically.

Poland has historically had a complicated relationship with Russia. Despite Poland's being a former Warsaw Pact ally and hosting thousands of Soviet troops in its territory during the Cold War, Russia has also violated Poland's sovereignty.[27] Poland's choice to align with NATO has further deepened the rift with Russia.

In addition, Poland maintains a border with Russia. The Kaliningrad Oblast is an exclave of Russia with a substantial military presence and Russia's only port in the Baltic Sea. Given Russia's proximity, its invasion of

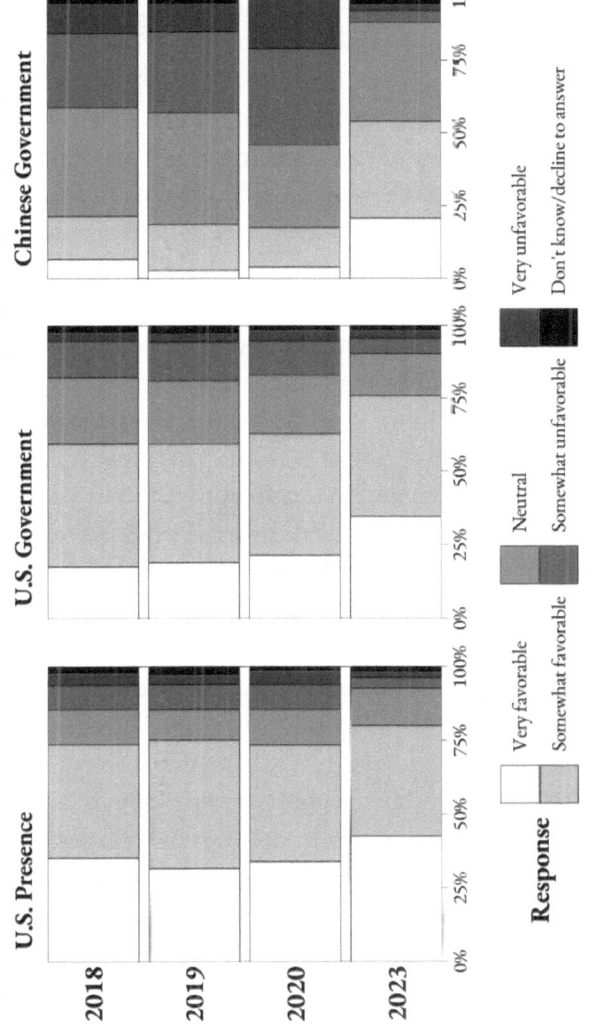

Figure 11.5. Polish Adults' Views of U.S. and Chinese Actors, 2018, 2019, 2020, 2023.

Authors' survey of Polish adults in 2018, 2019, 2020, 2023.

Ukraine centered security concerns in Poland. As figure 11.5 shows, Polish support for the U.S. presence is noticeably higher than before Russia's invasion. Russia's annexation of Crimea in 2014 reminded Polish citizens that Russia was expansionist in its territorial aims. Still, the full invasion of its "special military operation" in Ukraine was a much starker signal about Russian aims in eastern Europe.

This response has also had a spillover result: Polish people have far more favorable views of the U.S. government than they did a few years prior. The views of the U.S. government were stable in the 2018–2020 survey rounds. However, the positive views of the government jumped noticeably higher and passed the 75 percent mark in 2023. This increase in positive views matches the decreases in the three remaining categories: neutral, somewhat unfavorable, and very unfavorable views shrink relative to 2020.

As was evident in our 2018–2020 surveys, Poland was one of the strongest supporters of the U.S. presence in the country. Historically and geographically, onlookers should not be surprised by such support. Polish volunteers fought in the American Revolution, U.S. volunteers fought against the Soviet army in the 1919 Polish-Soviet War, and Woodrow Wilson supported Polish independence. The Soviet occupation of Poland in 1939 and control of its government and foreign policy during the Cold War did not endear Russia to Polish citizens or elites. At the end of the Cold War, Poland turned westward for economic and security integration and became a full NATO member in 1999.[28]

When reviewing the data, we also noticed a secondary phenomenon that we did not expect: views of the Chinese government became more favorable in Poland in the same survey round. While we noted above that European elites had been skeptical of how supportive the public is of Chinese economic influence, at the time of our initial round of surveys, the majority of Poles had unfavorable views of China. This previous majority no longer holds in 2023. Instead, most Poles have a favorable view of China. Approximately 54 percent of those surveyed expressed a "very positive" or "somewhat positive" view of the Chinese government. Further, as shown in figure 11.6, Polish adults' views of Chinese influence have remained roughly consistent with their 2018–2020 values, with some possibility of a slight decline. Few Poles see Chinese influence in Poland as decidedly positive, but their views of the Chinese government appear to be improving over time.

This change in views of the Chinese government follows a change in Polish foreign policy. In 2021, China and Poland began hosting high-level meetings,

Figure 11.6. Respondent Views of Chinese Influence in Poland, 2023.

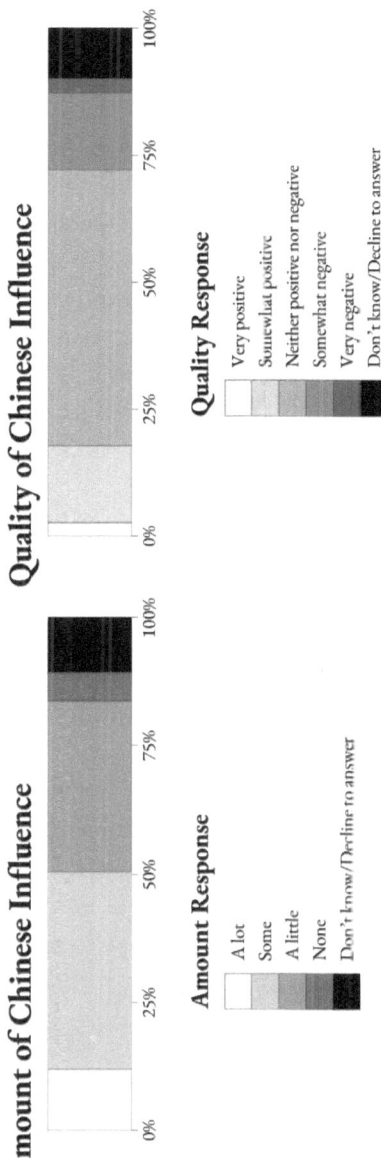

Authors' survey of Polish adults in 2023.

culminating in President Duda's participation in the 2022 Winter Olympics in Beijing.[29] Previous research suggests an interrelationship between elite opinion and public opinion, and, in this case, there is some preliminary evidence that elite behavior is leading public views on foreign policy.[30]

A second possibility for this shift is Russia's invasion of Ukraine. China has publicly positioned itself as a more neutral actor in the conflict, actively trying to end it. This stance is only surface level, as its actions and proposals have largely favored Russia's position in the conflict.[31] Regardless of the actual substance of its proposal, China's public-facing approach to the conflict may be winning it support in Poland, as any proposal to end the conflict decreases the likelihood that Poland gets drawn into the fight or that accidental or wayward attacks fall on Polish territory. Chinese public relations attempts at being a peace bringer in the region may be working whether its neutrality is sincere or not. It is of note that our survey ended on March 8, 2023, a few weeks after the United States warned China against formally providing military aid to Russia.[32]

Related to its attempts at mediation, China may also be offering a second alternative to a strong Russian presence in eastern Europe. While Poland strongly supports the U.S. presence, if Polish civilians are forced to choose between Russia and China in their geopolitical neighborhood, China offers an economic and diplomatic alternative to Russia's territorial expansionism.

Russia has lost the public relations game within much of Europe. While there is support for Russia in Belarus, Serbia, and Hungary, Russia's invasion has caused foreign policy elites and mass publics to see only the insecurity offered by Russia's security network. China, alternatively, is generally viewed much more positively throughout Europe. China's gains have been along economic and diplomatic fronts. While military hard power is the immediate concern of Europe with Russia, neglecting the soft power dimension of influence misses how great power competition can rapidly shift.

THE FUTURE OF COMPETITIVE CONSENT IN EUROPE

While the United States has previously sought partnerships with nondemocratic countries for basing in Europe, such as in Franco's Spain, these choices are less palatable to U.S. elites and the public now than they were during the Cold War. In addition, the autocracies in Europe have almost entirely been replaced by democratic governments. The United States is increasingly entering a world where it must persuade the populations of other countries of its mission in a setting in which host-state publics have access to democratized media (through the internet and social media) and democratic institutions for decision making. These combined processes mean that a country's security and foreign policy are more subject to citizens' views than at any point in history. By extension, not only does the United States need to convince its citizens of U.S. global objectives, but it must also convince the citizens of other countries that they want—or can at least tolerate—a U.S. presence where they live.

In the places we surveyed, support for the U.S. presence in Europe remained positive, but it was not without its detractors. When we interviewed a journalist in London, he mentioned how people no longer have access to go inside installations where the United States operates, and they wonder what the United States could be hiding from British citizens.[33] Support in Turkey is far weaker compared to other European countries and, to some extent, reflects the conflict that Turkey has had with other NATO members over the accession of Finland and Sweden. But with the addition of Finland (and the pending addition of Sweden) to NATO secured, the U.S. presence in Europe will likely expand in the coming years. What its presence in these new member states looks like and how the new host publics receive it remains to be seen.

Importantly, our recent survey in Poland shows that external actors can heavily influence support for the United States. The Russian invasion of Ukraine has dramatically increased the demand for U.S. security cooperation. New countries—Finland and Sweden—began to seek NATO membership, and the United States sent its first permanent deployment to Poland due to the invasion, which has stalled or reversed the decline of support for the U.S. peacetime presence. That support across our preinvasion European sample has likely also increased due to the war.

Past work shows that there are many steps the United States can take to build support for its mission overseas.[34] Yet nothing promotes the need for security among NATO allies like the insecurity of a NATO neighbor brought on by a traditional interstate war. Russian tanks invading a European country have become one of the strongest promotional tools for the U.S. presence in Europe. While the conflict continues, support for the U.S. presence in Europe will likely match the Balkans crisis or even the Cold War period. The nature of the outcome of the war in Ukraine may also influence this newfound support for U.S. troops overseas. A Russian victory in Ukraine would continue to show the danger of future Russian aggression, while a decisive

Ukrainian victory could lead to new requests by Ukraine to join NATO. A negotiated settlement would likely be unstable, making a U.S. presence an appealing long-term solution for any country that shares a border with Russia.

However, regardless of its outcome, the high salience of the Ukraine conflict is temporary, and the United States cannot rely on its competitors to continue making missteps. As noted earlier, while Russia's image among Europeans may be damaged for quite a long time, our surveys suggest that many European publics' views on China may be improving. Although many remain wary of Chinese influence, views of the Chinese government appear to be becoming more positive. With ample cash reserves and a large domestic market capable of consuming European exports, China may be able to capitalize on its improving image. While it seems unlikely that this will pose a direct challenge to the United States in the near term, stronger relations between China and the closest allies of the United States may nevertheless enable China to make it harder for the United States to achieve its desired policy goals.

China's decision making in the upcoming years can either limit or increase the operational space for the United States. If minor powers view China as an active supporter of Russian behavior in Europe and draw parallels between Chinese aggression toward Taiwan and Russia's in Ukraine, the United States will be able to broaden its possible partnerships, the scope of its current deployments, and its influence globally. Alternatively, if China maintains a semblance of neutrality in geopolitical disputes while expanding its economic soft power in contested areas, then the United States has a genuine competitor for military access. Great power competition is (at least) a two-player strategic game, and actions by both the United States and China will shape the future of deployments.

Peacetime deployments risk losing support as conflicts with rivals become distant memories. NATO support wavered in the early post–Cold War era, as NATO's utility was not clear to European nations. As Chinese economic soft power grows in Asia, Africa, and Europe, U.S. forces overseas will face similar questioning. Whether the United States can maintain broad coalitions among and within democratic nations will be the challenge of the next thirty years as the Chinese military and economic ascent continues. If China seeks out democratic partners in its security coalition, the public diplomacy of the U.S. military in the present will set the course for where China will succeed or fail.

NOTES

1. This material is based on work supported by, or in part by, the Minerva Research Initiative, U.S. Army Research Laboratory, and the U.S. Army Research Office under grant W911NF-18-1-0087. Our 2023 survey in Poland was supported by the Jones Family Faculty Award for Eastern European Studies at Kansas State University. Opinions and interpretations are those of the authors.

2. John J. Mearsheimer, "Back to the Future: Instability in Europe after the Cold War," *International Security* 15, no. 1 (Summer 1990): 5–56, https://doi.org/10.2307/2538981.

3. Kathleen Hicks, "Getting to Less: The Truth about Defense Spending," *Foreign Affairs*, February 10, 2020, https://www.foreignaffairs.com/united-states/getting-less.

4. For example, see Daniel J. Nelson, *Defenders or Intruders?: The Dilemmas of U.S. Forces in Germany* (Abingdon, NY: Routledge, 1987), and Claudia Junghyun Kim, *Base Towns: Local Contestation of the U.S. Military in Korea and Japan* (New York: Oxford University Press, 2023).

5. Alexander Cooley, *Base Politics: Democratic Change and the US Military Overseas* (Ithaca, NY: Cornell University Press, 2012).

6. Renanah M. Joyce and Becca Wasser, "All about Access: Solving America's Force Posture Puzzle," *Washington Quarterly* 44, no. 3 (2021): 45–67, https://doi.org/10.1080/0163660X.2021.1970335.

7. Kent E. Calder, *Embattled Garrisons: Comparative Base Politics and American Globalism* (Princeton, NJ: Princeton University Press, 2010); Michael A. Allen, Michael E. Flynn, Carla Martínez Machain, and Andrew Stravers, *Beyond the Wire: US Military Deployments and Host Country Public Opinion* (New York: Oxford University Press, 2022).

8. Sirianne Dahlum, Carl Henrik Knutsen, and Tore Wig, "Who Revolts? Empirically Revisiting the Social Origins of Democracy," *Journal of Politics* 81, no. 4 (2019): 1494–99, https://www.journals.uchicago.edu/doi/abs/10.1086/704699?af=R&mobileUi=0&.

9. Maria J. Stephan and Erica Chenoweth, *Why Civil Resistance Works: The Strategic Logic of Nonviolent Conflict* (New York: Columbia University Press, 2011), 7–44.

10. Roseanne W. McManus and Mark David Nieman, "Identifying the Level of Major Power Support Signaled for Protégés: A Latent Measure Approach," *Journal of Peace Research* 56, no. 3 (May 2019): 364–78, https://www.jstor.org/stable/48596198.

11. Michael A. Allen, Michael E. Flynn, Carla Martínez Machain, and Andrew Stravers, "Outside the Wire: U.S. Military Deployments and Public Opinion in Host States," *American Political Science Review* 114, no. 2 (May 2020): 326–41, https://dx.doi.org/10.1017/S0003055419000868.

12. We include Turkey as one of our European countries of focus due its role in NATO; its geographic location, which is partially in Europe; and its continued bid to join the European Union (EU).

13. Allen et al., *Beyond the Wire*.

14. Allen et al., *Beyond the Wire*.

15. G. W. Allport, *The Nature of Prejudice* (Boston: Addison-Wesley, 1954).

16. Sophie Meunier, "A Tale of Two Ports: The Epic Story of Chinese Direct Investment in the Greek Port of Piraeus," Council for European Studies, 2015, https://mnccenter.org/sites/default/files/publication_files/Meunier%20A%20Tale%20of%20Two%20Ports%20CritCom.pdf.

17. Author interview with British Labour member of Parliament in London #1, July 17, 2019.

18. Author interview with Parish Council member in Lakenheath, England, July 18, 2019.

19. Author interview with British Labour member of Parliament in London #2, July 17, 2019.

20. Author interview with German peace activist in Berlin, July 23, 2019.

21. Author interview with British Labour member of Parliament in London #1, July 17, 2019.

22. Author interview with German peace activist in Berlin, July 23, 2019.

23. Raf Casert and Samuel Petrequin, "EU Lashes Out at China for Support of Russia in Ukraine War," Associated Press, April 4, 2023, https://apnews.com/article/eu-china-blinken-russia-ukraine-61c81520b6a97e0a90c97a2402cda5b3.

24. Although the 2023 Poland survey data were gathered after the war began, it is possible that the dramatic increase in favorable views toward the Chinese government may represent sampling variability. However, we think that this is unlikely to be the case, as the sample size from the 2023 surveys ($N = 2{,}254$) should be large enough to produce a standard error of ≤ 0.01.

25. Author interview with Wiesbaden city official in Wiesbaden, Germany, July 25, 2019.

26. Author interview with German peace activist in Berlin, July 23, 2019.

27. In the eighteenth century and lasting until 1918, Prussia, Austria, and Russia divided and occupied Poland's territory. See Patrice M. Dabrowski, *Poland: The First Thousand Years* (Ithaca, NY: Cornell University Press, 2014).

28. Michael A. Allen, Michael E. Flynn, and Carla Martínez Machain, "Great Powers in My Backyard: Frontline Ally Support for the U.S. Military" (working paper, 2023).

29. Lunting Wu and Kamil Mastusie Wicz, "China-Poland Relations amid the Ukraine War," *The Diplomat*, October 13, 2022, https://thediplomat.com/2022/10/china-poland-relations-amid-the-ukraine-war.

30. Jennifer Cunningham and Michael K. Moore, "Elite and Mass Foreign Policy Opinions: Who Is Leading This Parade?," *Social Science Quarterly* 78, no. 3 (September 1997): 641–56, https://www.jstor.org/stable/42863558.

31. Michael Allen, "Russia Wants Military Aid from China—Here's Why This Deal Could Help China, Too," *The Conversation*, March 8, 2023, https://theconversation.com/russia-wants-military-aid-from-china-heres-why-this-deal-could-help-china-too-201284.

32. Lynn Berry, "US Warns China Is Considering Arming Russia in Ukraine War: 'That Would Cause a Serious Problem,'" *The Independent*, February 20, 2023, https://www.independent.co.uk/news/world/europe/antony-blinken-china-arms-russia-war-b2285558.html.

33. Author interview with British journalist in London, July 15, 2019.

34. Allen et al., *Beyond the Wire*.

12

The Future of Geostrategic Competition and Overseas Bases

Lessons for U.S. Strategic Planners

MICHAEL E. O'HANLON
MELANIE W. SISSON
ANDREW YEO

At present, the Ukraine war is poised to enter its third year. Competition between the United States and China continues to accelerate as the United States takes steps to increase the technology gap and outcompete China. History, of course, does not proceed in a linear fashion, and predictions of a new Cold War between the United States and China, leading to greater bifurcation between democracies and autocracies, are not forgone conclusions. Nevertheless, geostrategic competition has not abated, reflected in the shifting military postures of the U.S., Chinese, and Russian militaries.

This volume examined current trends in U.S., Chinese, and, to a lesser extent, Russian overseas military bases in the context of geostrategic competition. Great power competition is indeed real and carries an impact on global politics. However, rivalry and competition have not been uniform across all regions. As the contributors to this volume have shown, whether, how, and to what extent Washington, Beijing, and Moscow will compete (or cooperate) with one another will differ across geographic regions. Defense strategist

Stephen Biddle captured this sentiment when discussing U.S.–China competition and competing spheres of influence, arguing that there would be a "more differentiated pattern of power and influence in the region," where a single hegemon may not be able to "go anywhere they want and do whatever they want."[1] Likewise, basing opportunities and constraints are likely to vary across geographic locales. Hence, even though geostrategic competition is defined in global terms, it makes more sense to analyze geostrategic competition and disaggregate priorities and risks related to Chinese, Russian, and U.S. overseas basing across different regions.

In this concluding chapter, we address the future of geostrategic competition with a focus on U.S force posture. More specifically, by building on insights from the preceding chapters, we offer a forward-looking assessment on force posture amid U.S.–China rivalry and Russia's war in Ukraine and their longer-term impact. Particular attention is given to Europe, the Middle East, and the Indo-Pacific regions, where geostrategic rivalries remain most acute and U.S. force posture is most heavily invested. The main focus is on U.S. policy options; however, since our study carries a comparative and competitive element throughout the volume, it is also useful to consider how Russia and China might see their options in these regions.

THE DYNAMIC NATURE OF OVERSEAS BASING AND FORCE POSTURE

Before assessing future basing scenarios in Europe, the Middle East, and the Indo-Pacific, we briefly address the dynamic nature of U.S. force posture since the Cold War. Overseas military basing is a direct reflection of how policymakers understand the role of the United States in the world. The locations, types, and quantities of its forces permanently stationed or rotated abroad are inseparable from how the United States defines its interests and determines what is required functionally and financially to promote and defend them. Usually, this is conceptualized as being able to successfully deter some states from behaving in ways that are contrary to U.S. preferences and reassure others that the United States is committed to fulfilling obligations it has made to their security. Where the U.S. military is and is not, in what proportions, and with which capabilities is therefore a constant preoccupation for policymakers and analysts not only within the United States but indeed worldwide.

During the Cold War, basing needs were defined by the ebb and flow of the U.S. rivalry with the Soviet Union, designed to deter an invasion of Europe and to insulate other regions against communist encroachment. In the post–Cold War period, initial retrenchment of U.S. presence was followed by a redistribution meant to meet the needs of the offense-oriented Global War on Terrorism. Today, the intense interest in basing is a product of the localized destruction and extended anxiety produced by Russia's 2022 invasion of Ukraine and of the growth in China's understanding of and ability to promote its own role in the world. Both trends warrant a renewed debate about where U.S. forces need to be to contain Russian aggression, to deter Beijing from challenging vital U.S. and allied interests, and to reassure allies and partners in multiple regions.

As policymakers consider these demands, they will also need to acknowledge important differences between the context in which the United States military operates today and those of periods prior. During the Cold War, facing a country with overtly expansionist territorial goals and a large standing military, there was no substitute for basing. To deter and reassure effectively, the U.S. military simply had to be "over there" in quantity and all the time. During the War on Terrorism, the U.S. military was in pursuit of small, disaggregated, and mobile actors. The nature of the war's missions and a high operational tempo convinced some that it was necessary to expand the U.S. basing footprint by adding small en route and support facilities in the Middle East and Africa and to reduce basing infrastructure or at least force posture in Europe and Asia.[2] Neither of those models is necessarily well-suited to the missions and conditions of military operation today.

EUROPE, THE UKRAINE WAR, AND SHIFTS IN NATO AND U.S. FORCE POSTURE

Despite Russia's invasion of Ukraine in February 2022, U.S. presence combined with NATO's capabilities and resolve helped Ukrainians survive what could have been a much worse outcome in the early days of the war. The movement of additional U.S. troops into the region in the immediate aftermath of the invasion also helped boost Ukrainian morale and deter Vladimir Putin from taking more ground. Russia's military capabilities also proved to be far less formidable than feared and then were further degraded in the course of combat. Far from being divided or weakened by Putin's gamble, NATO coalesced and, with the accession of Finland and Sweden, gained the strength of two sophisticated and highly professionalized militaries.

While the demands of assuring NATO's easternmost members and of fully integrating Finland and Sweden into NATO operations make a reduction of prewar U.S. presence unwise, neither do they necessitate any expansion of the U.S. basing footprint. Nonetheless, and even with Russia on its heels in Ukraine and Putin in some political peril at home, it may be prudent or simply politically expedient for NATO to shore up its eastern flank in the months and years to come. If such a judgment is made, particular consideration should be given to Estonia and Latvia, where many native Russian speakers live, and those areas in Poland where NATO is shepherding supplies into Ukraine.[3]

To be sure, NATO should reassess its capabilities and posture in other parts of Europe, too. The United States can work with European allies to advance NATO interoperability, preposition materiel, and retrofit old and build new infrastructure to enhance allied mobility. The Black Sea region, explored in chapter 9, also merits further attention with particular focus on Romania, Bulgaria, and Turkey.[4] With the accession of Sweden and Finland to NATO, the alliance will need to address the Nordic subregion as well. But while sensitive and important, these other regions do not involve Russian-speaking peoples and are less relevant to the ongoing Ukraine crisis. The Baltics, as well as Poland, are arguably the heart of the matter. NATO has already been adjusting, of course. In the early months of 2022, the United States added roughly 20,000 troops to the 80,000 who were previously in Europe, with virtually all of the increase in Germany and pointing eastward.[5]

The United States already has a strong presence in Poland. At this juncture, if enhancements are to be made, the central priority should be to make what has been a continuous rotational presence since 2017[6] more permanent and to enlarge it somewhat as well in keeping with various ideas that have been developed in recent years.[7] This is largely a matter of building infrastructure suitable for a long stay, with Poland likely footing much or most of the bill as it has offered to do.

Similarly, if alliance management or U.S. risk aversion proves compelling, then adding a division headquarters to oversee the activities of the brigade combat team already in Poland, as well as smaller elements in the east near the Suwalki Gap, makes sense in keeping with the recommendations found in a December 2018 Atlantic Council task force report.[8] In such a scenario, the U.S. military should follow through on its plan to place stocks of prepositioned equipment for an armored brigade in Poland as well. The U.S. Army also needs more transportation assets, such as tank transporters, to help move additional forces into the Baltics in a crisis. The United States should also buttress its numbers of engineering units to repair damaged infrastructure as well as air and missile defense units to reduce damage to such infrastructure during periods of conflict. European countries as well will need to continue to improve some elements of their infrastructure to transport equipment rapidly from western to eastern Europe in times of crisis; this effort could require modest increases in NATO infrastructure funds.[9]

If changes to basing combat capability in the Baltics are to be made, then something in the range of 10,000 American troops makes sense—made up of a brigade combat team (with some 4,000 soldiers plus support), an army combat aviation brigade, and/or two or three squadrons of U.S. Air Force tactical aircraft. These types of units are the basic building blocks of U.S. combat power.[10] NATO would need to include not just combat platforms with these units but also robust networks of advanced sensors and ample stocks of precision munitions and possibly rapidly deployable smart mines. Together, these capabilities constitute the kinds of "kill chains" that strategist Christian Brose rightly emphasizes as the correct central focus for modern U.S. defense planning.[11] Washington should also attempt to persuade other NATO nations to make increases in combat capability in the Baltic region comparable to its own increases. Other changes, such as expedited procedures for NATO to gain priority access to Central Europe's rail network in a crisis, should also be pursued promptly.

The good news is that these changes do not require major additional expenses and therefore need not fundamentally disrupt the Pentagon's understandable desire to focus its future modernization efforts in the Indo-Pacific. Once facilities are built, keeping U.S. forces abroad rather than at home typically adds about 10 percent to their annual cost.[12] For 15,000 U.S. military personnel, that would equate to the rough vicinity of $1 billion per year.[13] Local partners can handle many of the expenses of building those new facilities, though it would be prudent to assume some U.S. contributions as well, even above those funded through the current European Deterrence Initiative. In rough numbers, that may imply another $1 billion per year this decade.

If the U.S. Army and the U.S. Air Force permanently station small numbers of units abroad in Poland and the Baltics rather than maintaining a new forward posture with frequent rotations of numerous units, they can likely sustain this burden without enlarging their force structures. The army's past preference to rotate units into Poland (and South Korea) is understandable. This approach gives more soldiers experience at preparing for deployment as well as a chance to serve abroad. However, such deployments also create a strain on the force structure given that at least three units are needed to sustain a single continuous deployment (due to the need for training, preparation, and then recovery). At this juncture, NATO's long-standing policy of not basing combat units in eastern member states—as a nod to Russian security sensitivities—is no longer relevant in light of Russia's attack on Ukraine. Moreover, the very modest stationing of combat units proposed here for the Baltics and Poland cannot pose a meaningful threat of cross-border aggression against Russia.

FORCE POSTURE IN THE MIDDLE EAST

The U.S. presence in the Middle East now looks roughly right sized. However, arguments that favor further reductions from the 30,000[14] or so U.S. troops and other personnel in the region also persist. For example, there may be ways to thin out U.S. presence and troop numbers in Kuwait and perhaps also in Bahrain and Qatar. The Kuwait presence remains in part a vestige of the large U.S. operation in Iraq over the past twenty years and may still be bigger than need be. The Bahrain presence is centered on the Fifth Fleet headquarters, and often U.S. military headquarters are larger than truly required. Qatar is home to al-Udeid air base. While it still remains very important for surveillance flights, the end of the Afghanistan mission means that al-Udeid's function as a regional hub for logistics and operations has ended. Hence, reassessing the size and scale of the U.S. presence may make sense.

Nevertheless, thinking more broadly, the United States should not wish to embolden Iran, worry key security partners, or create vacuums that Russia and China might try to exploit in the region. Barring any major geostrategic shifts in the region, the current (albeit reduced) U.S. presence should therefore still be sustained. After the hasty U.S. withdrawal from Afghanistan in 2021, further decisions to lessen U.S. presence and activity in the broader region, however desirable they might have initially seemed to the Biden administration (like the Trump and Obama administrations before it), now risk sending a message of unhealthy American disengagement. More recently, Hamas's brazen attack on Israel in October 2023 and the potential for further regional instability in the aftermath also warrant sustaining U.S. presence in the region for now.

Washington must still keep an eye on Russian and Chinese opportunities and interests in the region, which have grown in recent years. Russia has moved forces into Syria and Belarus (and, of course, Ukraine) over the past decade and also displayed an interest in establishing various other kinds of military or paramilitary presence from Libya to Sudan to the Central African Republic to Mali and beyond. China has solidified its position in Djibouti and shown interest in gaining access in the UAE as well as other regional countries as outlined in chapters 4 and 6, respectively.

China's limited military inroads to the region result largely from its robust interest in protecting vital energy flows. Dependence on the oil and gas of the region has perplexed leaders in Beijing for decades. Instead of mitigating this dependence, however, China has simply doubled down. It has invested in the political stability of oil-producing countries in the region, building infrastructure to augment trade and provide facilities that can support its relatively modest (current) mission set, in particular to protect the vulnerable sea-lanes connecting the Persian Gulf to East Asia.[15]

NAVIGATING A TURBULENT INDO-PACIFIC

As argued in chapter 3, the United States (but also China and Russia) must adapt to new realities in East Asia that change how U.S. forces will need to operate and for what purposes. American bases in the western Pacific initially set the trajectory of Japan's post–World War II development and since then have ensured ongoing U.S. access and demonstrated the extent of U.S. investment in regional stability. Its alliance and basing structures were proof positive that the United States could (and indeed would during the Vietnam War) bring to bear immediate war-fighting capabilities and transport reinforcements if needed. This construct was sensible and successful for decades; it enabled the United States to reassure allies and partners, to respond quickly to North Korean agitations and to constrain its leaders' worst impulses, and to underwrite pursuit of a peaceful resolution to the Taiwan question.

China's success in modernizing its own military has negated two of the foundational, interrelated premises on which this Cold War era force posture design long relied. The first is confidence in the defensibility of U.S.

bases.[16] The second is confidence that the United States can prevail in any conflict with any regional adversary. The very intentional and focused preparation by the People's Liberation Army (PLA) for a local, technologized war in its near seas, most particularly over Taiwan, has succeeded in making U.S. bases vulnerable to such an extent that hardening them is now an expensive undertaking with an uncertain outcome.[17] For this reason—and for reasons related to China's military advances—sober analysis has concluded that it is not possible to predict who would win a U.S.–China war, only to calculate how much both sides stand to lose.[18]

Integrated deterrence, the central conceptual feature of the 2022 National Defense Strategy, is tacit acknowledgment that military basing cannot achieve today what it has achieved previously. Reminders of the extent of U.S. war-fighting capability are no longer sufficient to defend U.S. interests in East Asia, including deterrence in service of the status quo over Taiwan. Instead, these objectives now and into the future will require the U.S. military to operate in ways that remind China which regional behaviors the United States can tolerate and which it will not—like lax enforcement or nonenforcement of illegal fishing, the building and militarization of artificial islands, and harassment of airplanes and ships in transit consistent with international law—together with strategies for promising and imposing punishments to enforce those limits.

This, of course, means that policymakers will need to make two prior determinations: which behaviors the United States will not tolerate and whether it is prepared to have its military operate as a constabulary force in order to demonstrate as much. If it is, then either the U.S. Navy will need to learn to operate more like the U.S. Coast Guard or the U.S. Coast Guard will need to expand in size and reach.[19] In either case, permanent basing will be of less use than maintaining a robust network of global sensing and detection capabilities. Purposeful distribution of access and prepositioning agreements that support a regularized and steady cadence of transits and of engagements with interested regional actors may also support strategic needs that were once addressed by permanent U.S. bases.[20] Here, additional basing access, such as the four bases granted by the Philippines in 2023, may support intelligence, surveillance, and reconnaissance deployments to combat PLA gray-zone tactics.

Although China's recent security agreements with Pacific Island nations have been interpreted by some as evidence of Beijing's global military ambitions, the reality is that the PLA's combat reach does not yet extend meaningfully beyond its near seas. Thus far, the purpose of China's more distant access arrangements appears consistent with an immediate interest in ensuring safe passage for the shipment of materials and the transportation and safety of the people needed to sustain its sizable development and infrastructure initiatives in Africa. This is reflected in China's active role in UN peacekeeping and anti-piracy operations.[21] Nevertheless, caution is still warranted given how forward leaning China has been in developing security relationships and military access in even far-reaching places such as Africa. As argued in chapter 4, China's high degree of economic dependence on resources, such as critical minerals and energy, has made the region a military-security priority.

Meanwhile, as highlighted in chapter 2, China's growing presence in Oceania should be unsurprising, as it is entirely in keeping with Beijing's long-standing and well-understood desire to deny, where possible, U.S. presence and otherwise to complicate U.S. operations in the Indo-Pacific. There is little that China can do in the near term, however, to catch up with, to compensate for, or to substantially degrade the advantages conferred on the United States by its large and long-standing bases in globally strategic locations and by its smaller outposts and access points worldwide. These legacies of prior geopolitical periods uniquely endow the United States not only with in-place assets and infrastructure but also with decades of experience managing relationships that are routinely subject to pressures at both domestic and international levels. The imperative for the United States today is not to be baited—or, worse, frightened—into unnecessary expansion of its presence in Europe or into a basing competition with China. It is, instead, to balance a rightful confidence in its ability to project military power worldwide with a genuine interest in the non-crisis interests and needs of the countries that U.S. military power serves and on which it relies.

CONCLUSION

In the post–Cold War period, the United States has remained the only major power capable of maintaining a truly global network of overseas military bases and force presence. In recent years, however, China and, to a lesser extent, Russia have expanded their own strategic reach beyond their near abroad. Beijing and Moscow are still years behind Washington in terms of establishing a network of overseas bases (or basing access) and will unlikely be able to replicate the type of basing infrastructure or level of access obtained by the United States given host-nation sensitivities to sovereignty norms.[22] In an era of geostrategic competition, however, China and Russia may search for alternative means and strategies to expand their military presences across different regions. This includes China's strategy of developing dual civilian–military use ports that could function as a de facto network of bases for the PLA Navy (PLAN). Beijing's efforts to strengthen non-Western regional and global institutions, such as the Shanghai Cooperation Organization and BRICS, or Moscow's diplomatic outreach to authoritarian regimes in need of Russian energy and political support, such as Syria and Cuba, could also pave the way for greater military access should these countries remain dissatisfied with the U.S.-backed liberal international order.

For now, the Indo-Pacific, Europe, and the Middle East continue to remain the primary focus of U.S. military concerns. However, some movement has already taken place within these regions in light of geostrategic competition. For example, more attention has been placed in the Indian Ocean region and the South Pacific than in the past in response to China's expanded geopolitical interests. Regarding U.S.–China competition, threats may currently be concentrated in the Indo-Pacific rather than globally. However, it may still be prudent to consider keeping an eye on Chinese presence in the Middle East, sub-Saharan Africa, and the Indian Ocean region.

In western Europe, U.S. force presence has been in decline since the 1990s. However, Russia's invasion of Ukraine has offered a clear rationale for reinforcing NATO bases (and U.S. presence) in areas such as the Baltic Sea and Black Sea regions, which have not traditionally been a stronghold of U.S. forces.

As others in this volume have suggested, the United States need not play whack-a-mole and beat back every military base or strategic foothold gained by China and Russia. However, when reviewing its global force posture, Washington will need to determine which regions (or subregions) remain critical to U.S. long-term interests and allocate its resources and budget accordingly. By approaching force posture from an "integrated deterrence" perspective and drawing on support from its allies, the United States may be able to overcome potential gaps in basing needs in case of budget windfalls. It is entirely possible that by 2050, the United States may no longer be the sole great power carrying an extensive network of overseas bases. Yet the United States can still maintain its competitive edge by periodically reconfiguring its force presence and cultivating ties with existing and new partners that offer basing access. Support from U.S. allies has been critical in sustaining the vast network of U.S. overseas bases, a fact that gives the United States an edge over its great power competitors.

In keeping with the spirit and broader themes of this book, Washington can expect Moscow and Beijing to continue looking for overseas opportunities. Sometimes, they will succeed in gaining access in specific places. Tactically, Russian or Chinese basing in this broader region can complicate U.S. operational security as well as security relationships with specific countries. Strategically, however, the United States should proceed with an attitude of quiet confidence in the breadth and extent of its network of 500-plus foreign bases. The world is becoming more complicated to be sure as Russian revanchism and China's rise complicate U.S. national security strategy even in places far from Russia or China. But the U.S. network of allies, partners, bases, and access points remains remarkable by any comparative or historical perspective. That is a good thing, and a capability to be treasured and preserved.[23] It creates asymmetric strategic and military advantages and options for Washington that serve its interests well in times of peace, crisis, and potential war.

NOTES

1. Michael Schuman, "China Could Soon Be the Dominant Military Power in Asia," *The Atlantic*, May 4, 2023, https://www.theatlantic.com/international/archive/2023/05/china-military-size-power-asia-pacific/673933.

2. "U.S. Military Overseas Basing: New Developments and Oversight Issues for Congress," Congressional Research Service, January 26, 2006, https://www.everycrsreport.com/reports/RL33148.html; "U.S. National Security Strategy," White House, 2002, 29.

3. See Vladimir Putin, "Article by Vladimir Putin 'On the Historical Unity of Russians and Ukrainians,'" Kremlin, Moscow, July 12, 2021, http://en.kremlin.ru/events/president/news/66181; Robert Coalson, "Putin Pledges to Protect All Ethnic Russians Anywhere. So, Where Are They?," Radio Free Europe/Radio Liberty, April 10, 2014, https://www.rferl.org/a/russia-ethnic-russ.fication-baltics-kazakhstan-soviet/25328281.html; Fiona Hill and Clifford G. Gaddy, *Mr. Putin: Operative in the Kremlin*, new and expanded ed. (Washington, D.C.: Brookings Institution Press, 2015), 369–76; Kathryn E. Stoner, *Russia Resurrected: Its Power and Purpose in a New Global Order* (Oxford: Oxford University Press, 2021); and Angela E. Stent, *The Limits of Partnership: U.S.-Russian Relations in the 21st Century* (Princeton, NJ: Princeton University Press, 2015).

4. On this region, see Steven Kenney, "Alternative Futures for the Black Sea Region," Middle East Institute, March 2021, https://www.mei.edu/sites/default/files/2021-03/0302%20Alternative%20Futures%20-%20FINAL%20.pdf.

5. "Fact Sheet—U.S. Defense Contributions to Europe," U.S. Department of Defense, June 29, 2022, https://www.defense.gov/News/Releases/Release/Article/3078056/fact-sheet-us-defense-contributions-to-europe/#:~:text=Since%20February%202022%2C%20DoD%20deployed,100%2C000%20service%20members%20across%20Europe.

6. "Increasing the US Military Presence in Poland," Ministry of National Defense, Republic of Poland, https://www.gov.pl/web/national-defence/increasing-the-us-military-presence-in-poland.

7. See Mark T. Esper, *A Sacred Oath: Memoirs of a Secretary of Defense during Extraordinary Times* (New York: HarperCollins, 2022), 420–30.

8. General Philip Breedlove and Ambassador Alexander Vershbow, "Permanent Deterrence: Enhancements to the US Military Presence in North Central Europe," Atlantic Council, December 2018, https://www.atlanticcouncil.org/in-depth-research-reports/issue-brief/permanent-deterrence-enhancements-to-the-us-military-presence-in-north-central-europe.

9. Daniel Michaels, "Ukraine War Spurs NATO to Improve Transport of Military Equipment," *Wall Street Journal*, January 5, 2023, https://www.wsj.com/articles/ukraine-war-spurs-nato-to-improve-transport-of-military-equipment-11672871478?mod=mhp.

10. Michael E. O'Hanlon and Christopher Skaluba, "A Report from NATO's Front Lines," Brookings Institution, June 13, 2019, https://www.brookings.edu/blog/order-from-chaos/2019/06/13/a-report-from-natos-front-lines.

11. Christian Brose, *The Kill Chain: Defending America in the Future of High-Tech Warfare* (New York: Hachette Book Group, 2020).

12. Michael J. Lostumbo et al., *Overseas Basing of U.S. Military Forces: An Assessment of Relative Costs and Strategic Benefits* (Santa Monica, CA: RAND Corporation, 2013), https://www.rand.org/pubs/research_reports/RR201.html.

13. "The U.S. Military's Force Structure: A Primer," Congressional Budget Office, July 2016, https://www.cbo.gov/publication/51535; Michael E. O'Hanlon, *Defense 101: Understanding the Military of Today and Tomorrow* (Ithaca, NY: Cornell University Press, 2021), 70–80.

14. C. Todd Lopez, "Defense Official Says U.S. Remains Committed to Middle East," *Department of Defense News*, June 5, 2023, https://www.defense.gov/News/News-Stories/Article/Article/3417495/defense-official-says-us-remains-committed-to-middle-east.

15. Isaac Kardon and Wendy Leutert, "Pier Competitor: China's Power Position in Global Ports," *International Security* 46, no. 4 (Spring 2022): 9–47.

16. David E. Sanger and Julian E. Barnes, "U.S. Hunts Chinese Malware That Could Disrupt American Military Operations," *New York Times*, July 29, 2023, https://www.nytimes.com/2023/07/29/us/politics/china-malware-us-military-bases-taiwan.html?smid=nytcore-ios-share&referringSource=articleShare.

17. James Holmes, "Are U.S. Bases in Asia Vulnerable to Chinese Missiles? Very," *The National Interest*, April 27, 2021, https://nationalinterest.org/blog/reboot/are-us-bases-asia-vulnerable-chinese-missiles-very-183734; Eric Heginbo-

tham et al., *The U.S.-China Military Scorecard: Forces, Geography, and the Evolving Balance of Power, 1996–2017* (Santa Monica, CA: RAND Corporation, 2015), https://www.rand.org/pubs/research_reports/RR392.html.

18. Michael E. O'Hanlon, "Can China Take Taiwan? Why No One Really Knows," Brookings Institution, August 2022. https://www.brookings.edu/articles/can-china-take-taiwan-why-no-one-really-knows.

19. Kirsty Needham, "Exclusive: US Coast Guard Seeks Bigger Role to Search, Board Vessels in Pacific," Reuters, July 26, 2023.

20. Melanie Sisson and Dan Patt, "A Deterrence Response Monitoring Capability for the U.S. Department of Defense," Brookings Institution, June 2023, https://www.brookings.edu/articles/a-deterrence-response-monitoring-capability-for-the-us-department-of-defense.

21. "China's Engagement in Djibouti," Congressional Research Service, September 4, 2019, https://sgp.fas.org/crs/row/IF11304.pdf.

22. Sebastian Schmidt, *Armed Guests: Territorial Sovereignty and Foreign Military Basing* (New York: Oxford University Press, 2021); Andrew Yeo and Stacie Pettyjohn, "Bases of Empire? The Logic of Overseas U.S. Military Base Expansion, 1870–2016," *Comparative Strategy* 40, no. 1 (2021): 18–35.

23. Much of the thinking of the late 2010s and early 2020s about getting the United States largely out of the Middle East ignored this point and went too far.

INDEX

A2/AD. *See* Anti-Access/Area Denial
Abkhazia, 163
access, 30, 72; in Arctic Circle, 121–22; in Middle East, 73–74; port, 6, 43, 94, 137, 139
Aegis Ashore missile defense, 160, 167
aerial ports, 74–75
Aerienne 188, 87
Afghanistan, 54, 73; Aria Water Plant, 77; Operation Enduring Freedom in, 111; transportation assets in, 76; U.S. relation to, 5, 11, 68, 71, 103, 104, 113, 116, 200
Afghan National Army, 115
Africa, 92; humanitarian assistance in, 94–95; infrastructure in, 203; port access in, 94. *See also* sub-Saharan Africa
African American soldiers, 108
African Growth and Opportunity Act, 79
African Union, 85, 94
Agenda 2063, 79

Air Defense Identification Zone, 122–23
Akayev, Askar, 113
Alaska, 127, 128–29
Aleutian Islands, 40, 131
Allied Maritime Command Naples, 145, 146
allies, of U.S., 1–2, 9, 55, 67, 79, 204–5; in Europe, 173–74, 198; as host nations, 172; investment in, 73; in IOR, 59 multilateral naval exercises with, 147; shared bases with, 71. *See also* NATO
American Revolution, 186
Andaman Island, 57
Andersen Air Force Base, 22
Andijon massacre, 113
Angola, 94
Antarctic waters, 21
Anti-Access/Area Denial (A2/AD), 145
Antwerp Gateway, 144
Anušauskas, Arvydas, 161
A. P. Møller Terminals, 144

Aquino, Cori, 108
Arabian peninsula, 54
Arab Spring, 109
Arctic Circle, 5; China relation to, 124–26; infrastructure in, 128–29; NATO relation to, 127–28, 131–32; natural resources in, 11–12, 121–22, 131; Russia relation to, 122–23, 124
Arctic Council, 9, 124, 130
Arctic Ocean, 122, 124–25, 141
Aria Water Plant, 77
Armenia, 5
Assad regime, in Syria, 145
Association of Southeast Asian Nations, 28
Atlantic Council, 198
Atlantic Ocean, 92, 141; PLAN in, 11
Atlantic Resolve, 159
AUKUS. *See* Australia–U.K.–U.S. framework
Australasia, 19–20, 30
Australia, 19, 54; China relation to, 10; Darwin, 40; Great Britain relation to, 21; IOR and, 53, 58; PNG relation to, 28; Solomon Islands relation to, 26–27; U.S. relation to, 30, 36
Australia–U.K.–U.S. framework (AUKUS), 58–59, 62
authoritarian regimes, 108, 109; in Central Asia, 104, 112–14; Russia relation to, 204
autonomous weapons, 44
autonomy, 110; of host nations, 106

B3W. *See* Build Back Better World
Bab-el-Mandeb Strait, 54, 89, 90–91
Bahrain, 200
Baikonur, Kazakhstan, 110–11
Bakiyev, 113–14
Balkans, 2, 167
Balkan Wars, 109
Baltic Sea, 5, *138*, 204; A2/AD in, 145; port investments in, 12; Russia relation to, 137, 141

Baltic States, 161, 162, 163, 167, 198–99; NATO relation to, 200
Barcelona, Spain, 143
Barents Sea, 127–28
base politics, 3, 14n13; in Central Asia, 103–4
basing agreements, 105, 109–10; brokering for, 106; public opinion and, 172; quid pro quo for, 107, 113–14
Bay of Bengal, 51
Beijing. *See* China
Belarus, 5; Russia relation to, 2, 158–59, 164, 201; Wagner Group in, 165
Belgium, 144
Belt and Road Initiative, of China, 48n27; in Central Asia, 114; North Adriatic Ports Association and, 143; sub-Saharan Africa relation to, 85
Biddle, Stephen, 195–96
Biden, Joe, 27, 115, 162; China relation to, 45; Pacific Island Country Summit of, 28–29
Biden administration, 36, 40–41, 200; Arctic Circle relation to, 121, 128; China relation to, 45–46, 167; Marcos relation to, 43
bipolarity, 14n13
Black Sea, 5, 198, 204; A2/AD in, 145; Japan relation to, 147–48; port investments in, 12; Russia relation to, 137, 141, 164
blockade, 140; China relation to, 24–25; in South China Sea, 29
Blue Dot Network, 148
Blue Pacific grouping, 28
Borei-class submarines, 141
Borrell, Josep, 181
BRICS, 204
British East India Company, 142
British House of Commons, 180
British Indian Ocean Territories, 53
brokering, for basing agreements, 106
Brose, Christian, 199

Build Back Better World (B3W), 148
Bulgaria, 198
Bush administration, 112

C-17A transport aircraft, 74–75
C-130J transport aircraft, 74–75
Camp Herkus, 161
Camp Lemonnier, 86, 87, 90
Canada, 122–23
Canberra. *See* Australia
Cape of Good Hope, 73
Carter administration, 108
Caspian Sea, A2/AD in, 145
CCP. *See* Chinese Communist Party
CEE. *See* Central and Eastern Europe
Central African Republic, 201
Central and Eastern Europe (CEE), 158; NATO in, 161, *161*, 162; Russia relation to, 163, *163*, 164; U.S. relation to, 159, *160*, 161
Central Asia, 11, 116–17, 165; authoritarian regimes in, 104, 112–14; base politics in, 103–4; China relation to, 48n27, 114–15; counterordering efforts in, *116*; Global War on Terrorism in, 111; NATO in, *112*; sovereignty in, 110
Centre for Seabed Mapping, of U.K., 146
Chagos Archipelago, 53, 63n3
Changi Naval Base, in Singapore, 55
Chile, 108
China. *See specific topics*
China-Iceland Arctic Science Observatory, 125
China Merchants Port Holdings, 143
Chinese Communist Party (CCP), 38, 39
Chinese–Russian collusion, 40, 44
choke points: in IOR, *52*, 53; for trade, 54
CIS. *See* Commonwealth of Independent States
civilians, in host nations, 173

climate change, 27, 34n35, 68; Arctic Circle relation to, 11–12, 121–22; Oceania relation to, 22–23; Pacific Islands relation to, 29; Pacific Ocean relation to, 26
CMA CGM shipping company, 143
cobalt, 24
Cold War, 105, 122, 158, 195, 197; NATO relation to, 171, 190; Poland during, 186; rivalries in, 37; Soviet Union in, 162–63
Collective Security Treaty Organization, 106, 111, 112, 113
colonization, of sub-Saharan Africa, 83
Color Revolutions, 109, 112–13
commercial interests, 7–8, 38
Commonwealth of Independent States (CIS), 164
Compacts of Association, 22
competition. *See specific topics*
Contracting Parties to the Spitsbergen Treaty, 125
cooperation, 195; in Arctic Circle, 130–31; in Central Asia, 117; for maritime security, 62; in sub-Saharan Africa, 95, 96
cooperative security locations, 8
COSCO, 143–44, 151n16
counterordering efforts, in Central Asia, *116*
counter-piracy operations, 56, 60; of China, 24; Djibouti relation to, 85–86; in Gulf of Guinea, 95
counterterrorism activities, 90, 95; in sub-Saharan Africa, 96
crime, 172
Crimea, 114, 141, 161, 164, 165, 186
crises, 44; economic, 107
cruise missiles, of China, 39
Cuba, 10, 104–5, 204

Darwin, Australia, 40
decolonization, 105

deep-sea mining: in Arctic Ocean, 124–25; in Oceania, 22
Delta IV nuclear-powered ballistic missile submarines, 141
democracy, 188–89
Democratic Republic of Congo, 85
Department of Defense, U.S. (DOD), 35, 36, 68, 70–71; China relation to, 86, 87–88
Department of State, U.S., 78
development assistance, in basing agreements, 107
Diego Garcia, 53, 55, 59, 63n3, 63n6, 78–79
Direct Commercial Sales, for host nations, 77–78
disaster relief, 56
disinformation campaigns, 106
distributed lethality, 49n28
Djibouti, 61; China relation to, 2, 24, 85–87, 91, 95, 139; PLA in, 56; SLOCs relation to, 86, 91; U.S. relation to, 78–79, 90–91, 96
"Djibouti model," 61–62
DOD. See Department of Defense, U.S.
Doshi, Rush, 126
dual-use facilities, 12, 126, 204
Dutch East India Company, 142
Duterte, Rodrigo, 43

East Africa, 91; SLOCs and, 11
East Asia, 35, 40, 201; treaty ports in, 142; U.S.–China rivalry in, 41; U.S. relation to, 37, 38, 44, 46
East China Sea, 20, 90; Chinese–Russian collusion in, 44; PLAN in, 23–24; territorial disputes in, 84
Easter Island, 19
economic crises, 107
economic interests, 6; in Arctic Circle, 131; of China, 59–60, 69–70, 93, 139
Egypt, 140
Eielson Air Force Base, 127

elites, 105–6, 173; China relation to, 10, 26, 180–82, 186, 188
Equatorial Guinea, 92
Eritrea, 89, 92
Espiritu Santo, Vanuatu, 27
Estonia, 198
EU. See European Union
Eurasian Economic Union, 114
Euromax Terminal, in Rotterdam, 144
Europe, 54, 196; China relation to, 188; maritime security in, 137, 144–45, 148–49; port investments in, 12, 167; public opinion in, 12–13, 177, 182, 189; Russia relation to, 67; U.S. allies in, 173–74, 198; U.S. Army in, 199–200; U.S. relation to, 37, 68, 157–58, 162, 166, 168, 171–72, 203, 204
European Deterrence Initiative, 199
European Union (EU), 113, 140; China relation to, 181; Global Gateway project of, 148; Maritime Security Strategy of, 147; Russia relation to, 166; Trans-European Transport Network initiative of, 142–43
Evenes Military Air Station, 128
Ever Given blockage, 54
exclusive economic zone, of France, 21–22
Exercise Cold Response, 127–28

F-35A wing, 127
far seas protection, 60–61
"Far Seas" strategy, of China, 24
FDI. See foreign direct investment
Federated States of Micronesia, 26, 29
Fiji, 21, 28
Finland, 122, 125; NATO relation to, 130, 145, 162, 184, 189, 198; Russia relation to, 158
Fires Command, 68
Five Ports Alliance, 143
FMS. See U.S. Foreign Military Sales

Force Design 2030, of U.S. Marine Corps, 42
foreign direct investment (FDI): of China, 84, 148; of Russia, 88; of U.S., 89
foreign policy: of China, 61; public opinion relation to, 173; of Russia, 128; of U.S., 128–29, 158, 159, 168
Forum on China–Africa Cooperation, 85, 94
France, 43; Djibouti relation to, 87; exclusive economic zone of, 21–22; India relation to, 29; IOR and, 53, 58; Mali relation to, 90; sub-Saharan Africa relation to, 105, 107; Tajikistan relation to, 111
Franc Zone, 107
"Freedom Agenda," 112
Freely Associated States, 22, 28–29
Freezing Winds, 145
Frontex, 147
Fukushima, Japan, 38

G7 summit, 148
Galwan, 58
Gates, Robert, 114
Gaza, 61
geography: of Indian Ocean, 10; of IOR, 63
Georgia, 5, 112, 163
Germany, 111; Hamburg, 144; public opinion in, 176, 180, 182, 184; U.S. relation to, 68, 159
global cyber connectivity, 146–47
Global Fragility Act, 78
Global Gateway project, of EU, 148
global hierarchy, 106
globalization, 56
Global Posture Review, of DOD, 36, 68
Global Security Initiative, of China, 142
Global South, 34n35; China relation to, 84

Global War on Terrorism, 109, 157, 197; in Central Asia, 111
goods substitution, 104, 109
Gorshkov, Sergei G., 140
gray zone activities, 142
Great Britain, 6; China relation to, 180–81; Oceania relation to, 21. *See also* United Kingdom
Great Northern War, 139
great powers. *See specific topics*
Greece, 105; Piraeus, 142–43, 177
Greenland, 126
ground transportation, infrastructure for, 75
Guam, 20, 30; U.S. relation to, 22, 36, 37, 40–41, 45
Guantanamo Bay, Cuba, 104–5
GUGI, 142
Gulf of Aden, 85, 86
Gulf of Guinea, 95
Gulf of Oman, 54

Haifa, China relation to, 24
Hamas, 201
Hamburg, Germany, 144
Hawaii, 19, 20, 22
High North strategy, of NATO, 130
Hobson, J. A., 6
Honiara. *See* Solomon Islands
Horn of Africa, 51, 54, 61, 87
host nations, 3, 69, 75; access with, 73; civilians in, 173; Direct Commercial Sales for, 77–78; ordering mechanisms of, 107; political liberalism and, 108–9; public opinion in, 174, 176, 178, 179; respondent views in, 175; sovereignty of, 104–5, 106, 203–4; U.S. allies as, 172
Host Nation Support, 106
humanitarian assistance, 56; in Africa, 94–95; Djibouti relation to, 86
human rights, 61; in host nations, 108

Hutchison Port Holdings, 143, 144
Hutchison Whampoa Limited, 143
hydrocarbons, 61

I2U2. *See* India–Israel–U.S.–UAE
Iceland, 107, 108; China relation to, 125–26
illegal fishing, 202; in Oceania, 22; in South China Sea, 42
imperialism, in Pacific Islands, 21
Incirlik, 105–6
India: Djibouti relation to, 87; France relation to, 29; IOR and, 53, 57–58; U.S. relation to, 93
India–Israel–U.S.–UAE (I2U2), 62
Indian Ocean, 5, 74, 204; access in, 73; China relation to, 11, 43, 48n27; geography of, 10; logistics networks in, 79; rimland position in, 51, 63n1; supply lines in, 62; treaty ports in, 142; U.S. relation to, 9, 40, 42
Indian Ocean region (IOR), 51; China in, 56–57, 60–62, 64n8; choke points in, 52, 53; geography of, 63; India and, 53, 57–58; SLOCs in, 57, 93–94, 96; U.K. and, 58–59; U.S. in, 55, 59
Indian Ocean Rim Association, 70
indigenous communities, 129
Indonesian archipelago, 54
Indo-Pacific Maritime Domain Awareness initiative, 29
Indo-Pacific region, 13, 40–41, 54, 62, 196; China in, 13n1, 42, 203; U.S. in, 8, 10, 45, 199, 204
Indo-Pacific Strategy, of DOD, 36
industrial development, 77; Agenda 2063 and, 79; in "whole-of-government" approach, 72
INF. *See* Intermediate-Range Nuclear Forces Treaty
infrastructure, 69, 148; for aerial ports, 75; in Africa, 203; in Arctic Circle, 128–29; for global cyber connectivity, 146–47; for industrial development, 77; in Middle East, 201; military, 163, 164; in Pacific Islands, 29; in Poland, 198–99; in "whole-of-government" approach, 72
Ingimundarson, Valur, 108
inland transportation, 74
integrated deterrence, 45–46, 50n46, 202
intercontinental ballistic missile, 127, 160
Intermediate-Range Nuclear Forces Treaty (INF), 160
internal institutional silos, 79
International Court of Justice, 63n3
International Institute for Strategic Studies, 122
international law, 9
International Monetary Fund, 107
international orders, 103–4, 109, 117; sovereignty and, 104
international relations theory, 14n13
international security, 1
interoperability, 77–78
investment, in U.S. allies, 73
IOR. *See* Indian Ocean region
Iran, 54, 108, 200; China relation to, 87, 98n30; DOD relation to, 68; Russia relation to, 70; U.S. relation to, 56
Iraq, 5, 54, 200; transportation assets in, 76; U.S. relation to, 68, 112
Israel, 201
Italy, 105; China relation to, 143

Japan, 45, 127; China relation to, 10, 20; Djibouti relation to, 61, 87; East Asia relation to, 35; Kiribati relation to, 27; NATO relation to, 147–48; Pacific Islands relation to, 21; Russia relation to, 40, 44; Ryukyu Islands, 42; U.K. relation to, 29; U.S. relation to, 36, 37, 38, 43, 44, 45, 201
Jinping, Xi, 39, 142

Jintao, Hu, 39, 143
joint naval exercises: China–Russia, 137; U.S.–NATO, 145
Joint Region Marianas, 22

Kaliningrad Oblast, 184
Kamchatka Peninsula, 40
Karimov, Islam, 113
Kasputin Yar, Kazakhstan, 110–11
Kazakhstan, 110–11
Keflavik airport, 107
Kenya, 90; U.S. relation to, 96
Khanabad, 111
kill chains, 199
Kiribati, 27–28
Kirkpatrick, Jean, 108
Kola Peninsula, 122
Korchunov, Nikolai, 123, 124
Korean Peninsula, 6, 36–37, 46; Soviet Union and, 35; U.S. relation to, 38, 40
Korean War, 35
Kuril Islands, 40, 44
Kursk (submarine), 141
Kuwait, 200
Kuwait International Airport, 71
Kyrgyzstan, 110, 112; Manas Transit Center in, 103, 113–14; U.S. relation to, 111

Lake, David, 106
Latin America, 39
Latvia, 198
Leyen, Ursula von der, 181
liberal ordering, 110; in Central Asia, 112
Libya, 86–87, 141; Russian base at, 201
Lithuania, 161
logistics networks, 11, 70, 73; Agenda 2063 and, 79; host nations relation to, 77–78; in "whole-of-government" approach, 72
Lombrum Naval Base, 28
London. *See* Great Britain

Lukashenko, Alexander, 164, 165
Luzon Strait, 24

Macron, Emmanuel, 181
Madagascar, 88; Russia relation to, 70
Malacca Dilemma, 23, 54
Malay Peninsula, 54
Maldives, 40
Mali, 90, 201
Malolo massacre, 21
Manas Transit Center, Kyrgyzstan, 103, 113–14
manganese, 24
manufacturing economy, 77
Manus Island, PNG, 26, 28, 30
Marcos, Ferdinand, Jr., 38, 107, 108; Biden relation to, 43
the Marianas, 20
Maritime Component Command, in Sweden, 167–68
maritime security, 12; cooperation for, 62; in Europe, 137, 144–45, 148–49
Maritime Security Strategy, of EU, 147
Maritime Silk Road, 142
Marxist-Leninist regimes, 108
material handling equipment, 76–77
Mauritius, 59, 63n3
McKenzie, Kenneth, 115
Mediterranean Sea, 54, 138, 140; A2/AD in, 145; China relation to, 24; Japan relation to, 147–48; port investments in, 12
mega facilities, 42
Melanesia, 19–20; France relation to, 21–22; U.S. relation to, 30
Micronesia 19–20, 26, 29, 30
Middle East, 13, 51, 196; access in, 73–74; Arab Spring in, 109; China relation to, 39, 48n27, 98n30; infrastructure in, 201; logistics networks in, 79; North African countries in, 97n2; shared bases in, 71; SLOCs in, 94, 96; U.S. relation

to, 2, 5, 37, 55–56, 200, 204. *See specific countries*
military infrastructure, 163, 164
military training: from China, 85; from U.S., 78
mineral rights, 69
Ministry of Defense, of China, 38, 86
Moscow. *See* Russia
Mozambique, 70
Al-Mubarak Air Base, 71
Multi-Domain Task Force, 68
multilateral naval exercises, 147
multinational infrastructure investment, 148
mutual defense commitments, 4

Namibia, 94
National Defense Strategy, U.S., 36, 50n46, 79, 202
National Party Congress of the Twentieth Central Committee of the Chinese Communist Party, 64n7
National Security Council, 148
National Security Law, of China, 86–87
National Security Strategy, U.S. (NSS), 1, 36, 42, 67–68, 79, 121; Arctic Circle in, 128; China and, 158
National Strategy for Maritime Security, of U.K., 146
National Strategy for the Arctic Region, U.S., 121, 128
NATO, 5, 78, 105–6, 109, 199; Allied Maritime Command Naples of, 145, 146; Arctic Circle relation to, 127–28, 131–32; in CEE, 161, *161*, 162; in Central Asia, *112*; Cold War relation to, 171, 190; Finland relation to, 130, 145, 162, 184, 189, 198; High North strategy of, 130; Japan relation to, 147–48; Russia relation to, 12, 122, 140, 157–58, 166, 167, 200; Soviet Union relation to, 159; Turkey relation to, 189, 192n12;

Ukraine relation to, 197–98, 204; U.S. relation to, 15n19
NATO Maritime Groups, 145
natural resources, in Arctic Circle, 11–12, 121–22, 131
Naval Base Camilo Osias, 43
Naval Computing and Telecommunications Station Guam, 22
Naval Doctrine, of Russia, 7
Naval Information Forces, 22
Naval Mobile Construction Battalion 5, of U.S., 28
Navy, Russian, 139–41
near-seas defense strategy, of China, 23–24
Netherlands, Rotterdam, 144
net security provider, India as, 57
New Zealand, 19, 21
Nicobar Island, 57
Niger, 90, 96
Nigeria, 92
Noatum Port Holdings, 143
Nome, Alaska, 127, 129
NORAD. *See* North American Aerospace Defense
Nord Stream pipelines, 12, 142
North Adriatic Ports Association, 143
North African countries, 97n2
North American Aerospace Defense (NORAD), 122, 127
Northeast Asia, 10, 41; U.S. relation to, 44
Northern Sea Route (NSR), 123, *123*, 131
North Korea, 44, 46, 68, 201; nuclear arsenal of, 38, 45
Northwest Passage, *123*, 131
Norway, 124, 127–28; China relation to, 126; Russia relation to, 158
NSR. *See* Northern Sea Route
NSS. *See* National Security Strategy, U.S.

nuclear arsenal: of North Korea, 38, 45; of Soviet Union, 122

Obama, Barack, 36, 40
Oceania, 30; China relation to, 10, 26, 28, 203; UNCLOS relation to, 23; U.S. relation to, 6, 22; in World War II, 21
Office of the U.S. Trade Representative, 79
Okinawa, Japan, 40
Operation Damayan, 38
Operation Enduring Freedom, 111
Operation Tomodachi, 38
ordering mechanisms, of host nations, 107
Otunbayeva, Roza, 114
overseas bases. *See specific topics*

Pacific Deterrence Initiative, of DOD, 36
Pacific Island Country Summit, 28–29
Pacific Islands, 5, 6, 10; China relation to, 26, 30–31, 43, 202–3; U.S.–China rivalry in, 20–21; U.S. relation to, 28–29, 40
Pacific Islands Forum, 27, 28–29
Pacific Ocean, 2, 19, 124, 141; climate change relation to, 26; rare earth metals in, 24
Pakistan, 34n35; China relation to, 69
Papua New Guinea (PNG), 19; Manus Island, 26, 28, 30
Paracel Island, 39
Paramushir, 44
peaceful rise, of China, 38
peacekeeping, 56; Djibouti relation to, 86; in sub-Saharan Africa, 90
Pearl Harbor, 20, 21
Pelosi, Nancy, 44
People's Liberation Army (PLA), 2, 38, 56; CCP relation to, 39; in South Pacific, 35

People's Republic of China (PRC). *See specific topics*
"period of strategic opportunity," 56, 64n7
Persian Gulf, 51, 54, 201
persistent access, in Oceania, 30
Peter, the Great, 139–40
the Philippines, 19, 48n24, 202; Subic Bay, 32n16; U.S. relation to, 36, 37–38, 40, 43, 44, 107
Philippine Sea, 24–25
Pincus, Rebecca, 123
Piraeus, Greece, 142–43, 177
Pitcairn Island, 21
PLA. *See* People's Liberation Army
PLAN Air Force, 30
PLA Navy (PLAN), 6, 23–24, 204; in Arctic Ocean, 125; in Atlantic Ocean, 11; in IOR, 57; in Vanuatu, 27
Platt Amendment, 104–5
PNG. *See* Papua New Guinea
Poland, 159 160, 161, 167; public opinion in, 174, 176, 181–82, *183*, 184, *185*, 186, *187*, 188, 192n24; Russia relation to, 189; U.S. Army in, 162, 199–200; U.S. relation to, 198–99
polar satellite coverage, 129
Polar Security Cutter, 127, 129–30
"Polar Silk Road," 121
Polish-Soviet War, 186
political liberalism, 104; host nations and, 108–9
Polynesia, 19–20; France relation to, 21–22
port access: in Africa, 94; for China, 6, 43, 137, 139
Port Blair, 57
port investments: of China, 139, 142–44; in Europe, 12, 167. *See also* foreign direct investment
Port of Bruges-Zeebrugge, 144

PRC. *See* People's Republic of China
Prigozhin, Yevgeny, 89, 158–59
private corporations, 75; in Arctic Circle, 129
private military contractors, 8
Prosper Africa Initiative, 89
provision, 104, 105
public opinion, 105–6; basing agreements and, 172; on China, 177, *178*, *179*, 180–82, 190; in Europe, 12–13, 182, 188, 189; foreign policy relation to, 173; in host nations, 174, 176, *178*, *179*; in Poland, 174, 176, 181–82, *183*, 184, *185*, 186, *187*, 188, 192n24; on Russia, 182, *183*, 184; Ukraine relation to, 174, 189–90; on U.S., 188–89
Puget Sound, 20
Pushkin, Alexander, 139
Putin, Vladimir, 6, 111, 115, 140, 141, 197–98; public opinion on, 182

Qatar, 72–73, 200
Quadrilateral Cooperation and Coordination Mechanism, 115
Quadrilateral Security Dialogue (Quad), 28, 43, 58; Indo-Pacific Maritime Domain Awareness initiative of, 29; maritime security cooperation with, 62
quasi bases, 8
quid pro quo, for basing agreements, 107, 113–14

rail systems, 76
RAMSI. *See Regional Assistance Mission* to Solomon Islands
rare earth metals, 24, 64n8
Red Sea, 54; China relation to, 24; Russia relation to, 69; SLOCs in, 89, 92
regime type, 3; of host nations, 105
Regional Assistance Mission to Solomon Islands (RAMSI), 26

Remote Sensing Satellite North Polar Ground Station, 125
respondent views, in host nations, *175*
right-wing dictatorships, 108
rimland position, in Indian Ocean, 51, 63n1
rivalries, 132, 195; Cold War, 37; U.S.-China, 20–21, 39, 41, 196; U.S.-Soviet Union, 197
Rocket Force, of China, 30
Romania, 159, 160, 162, 167, 198
Rotterdam, Netherlands, 144
rules-based international order, 9, 124, 130
Russia. *See specific topics*
Russia-Africa Economic and Humanitarian Forum (2019), 88
Russian 201st Motorized Division, 110
Russia-Ukraine War, 5, 12–13
Russo-Georgian War, 163, 164
Rygge Military Air Station, 128
Ryukyu Islands, Japan, 42

sanctions, 126, 166
Saudi Arabia, 87
say-do gap, 36
Schengen Agreement, 167
Scheppele, Kim Lane, 109
Schmidt, Sebastian, 104
Schultz, Karl, 128
SCO. *See* Shanghai Cooperation Organization
seabed warfare, 139, 146
sea-lane protection, 60
sea lines of communication (SLOCs), 6–7, 43; China relation to, 39, 61; Djibouti relation to, 86, 91; East Africa and, 11; in IOR, 57, 93–94, 96; in Red Sea, 89, 92; sub-Saharan Africa and, 83; U.S. relation to, 38
Sea of Japan, 40, 44, 141
second island cloud, 25, *25*
security assistance, in basing agreements, 107

security communities, 104, 105, 109
Sembawang, Singapore, 21
Senkaku/Diaoyu islands, 20
Shanghai Cooperation Organization (SCO), 109, 113, 204
shared bases, in Middle East, 71
Shoigu, Sergei, 7, 44
Siberia, 122
Singapore, 21, 55; U.S. relation to, 40
Sino-Russian relations, 92–93
60K Tunner aircraft cargo loader, 76–77
SLOCs. *See* sea lines of communication
social control, of China, 61
socialism, 108
social protests, 106
soft power, 10; of China, 190; of Russia, 70
Sogavare, Manasseh, 26–27
Sola Military Air Station, 128
Solomon Islands, 26–27, 28
Somalia, 90; U.S. relation to, 96
Somaliland, 89, 92
sound island chain, 25
South Asia: China relation to, 48n27; U.S. relation to, 42–43
South China Sea, 10, 63n1, 90, 124, 131; blockade in, 29; China relation to, 20, 37, 48n24, 49n28; PLAN in, 23–24; territorial disputes in, 84; U.S.–China rivalry in, 39; U.S. Coast Guard in, 42
Southeast Asia, 40–41; China relation to, 48n27; U.S. relation to, 42–43
South Korea, 10, 108, 147; U.S. Army in, 68; U.S. relation to, 36, 38, 43, 44, 45
South Ossetia, 163
South Pacific, 35, 42, 204
sovereignty, 6, 110, 140; of host nations, 104–5, 106, 203–4; of Poland, 184
Soviet Union, 2, 108, 127, 140, 186, 197; in Cold War, 162–63; Japan relation to, 35; NATO relation to, 159; nuclear arsenal of, 122

Spain, 105, 108, 143, 188; Barcelona, 143
Spratly Island, 39
Spykman, Nicholas, 63n1
Sri Lanka, 69
Starlink, 129
Starshield, 129
status-of-forces agreements, 4
Stevenson, Jonathan, 45, 48n24
St. Petersburg, Russia, 139–40
Strait of Gibraltar, 146
Strait of Hormuz, 54, 88, 93
Strait of Malacca, 57
Subic Bay, the Philippines, 32n16
submarine fleet, of Russia, 141–42
sub-Saharan Africa, 5, 11, 74, 97n2; access in 73; China relation to, 39, 84–85, 88, 91, 93–94; cooperation in, 95, 96; France relation to, 105, 107; logistics networks in, 79; Russia relation to, 88–89, 92–93; SLOCs and, 83; U.S. relation to, 9, 89–90; Wagner Group in, 88, 89, 95–96
Sudan, 69, 83–89, 141, 201
Suez Canal, 73
supply lines, 54–55; in Indian Ocean, 62
surveillance, 61, 109
Suwalki Gap, 165, 167, 198
Svalbard Islands, 125
Sweden, 122, China relation to, 125, 126; Maritime Component Command in, 167–68; NATO relation to, 130, 145, 162, 184, 189, 198; Russia relation to, 139–40
Syria, 8, 70, 140, 145, 201, 204

Taiwan, 27, 28, 46, 84; China relation to, 2, 10, 23–25, 49n28, 201–2; U.S. relation to, 43–44
Taiwan Strait, 20, 36–37, 46, 90; blockade in, 29; U.S.–China rivalry in, 39; U.S. relation to, 38
Tajik Civil War, 110

Tajikistan, 110, 111, 114–15
Taliban, 115
Tanzania, 85
Tartus, 7–8, 137
Terminal Link, 143
territorial disputes, 84
terrorism, 90. *See also* Global War on Terrorism
Tomahawk medium-range cruise missiles, 160
Townsend, Stephen, 92
tractor and trailer trucking systems, 76
trade, 7; choke points for, 54; in IOR, 56; in sub-Saharan Africa, 84
Trans-European Transport Network initiative, of EU, 142–43
Transnistria, 163
Transpolar Sea Route, *123*
transportation: inland, 74; logistics networks for, 73; of U.S. Army, 199
transportation assets, 75–76
treaty ports, 142
Trump, Donald, 36, 40, 106, 182
Turkey, 105–6, 176, 177, 198; NATO relation to, 189, 192n12
Turkmenistan, 110
Tuvalu, 28
25K Halverson aircraft cargo loader, 76–77
Typhoon Hayan, 38

UAE. *See* United Arab Emirates
al-Udeid air base, 200
U.K. *See* United Kingdom
Ukraine, 112, 166, 171, 186, 195, 197; Belarus relation to, 164–65; China relation to, 181–82; NATO relation to, 197–98, 204; public opinion relation to, 174, 184, 189–90; Russia relation to, 2, 5–6, 12, 89, 93, 123, 124, 137, 140, 157–58, 196; U.S. relation to, 15n19, 68, 162

UN Charter, 9, 124
UN Convention on the Law of the Sea (UNCLOS), 9, 20, 23, 124, 125, 131
Union Resolve exercise, 164–65
United Arab Emirates (UAE), 62, 201; China relation to, 98n30
United Kingdom (U.K.), 63n3; Centre for Seabed Mapping of, 146; IOR and, 58–59; Japan relation to, 29
United States (U.S.). *See specific topics*
United States–Africa Leaders Summit, 79, 89
United States Agency for International Development (USAID), 70
UN Security Council, RAMSI of, 26
U.S. *See* United States
U.S. 5th Expeditionary Air Mobility Squadron, 71
U.S. 10th Mountain Division Headquarters, 162
U.S. 10th Sustainment Brigade, 77
U.S. 11th Airborne Division, 127
U.S. 386th Air Expeditionary Wing, 71
U.S. Africa Command Joint Task Force for the Horn of Africa, 87
U.S. Agency for International Development, 28
USAID. *See* United States Agency for International Development
U.S. Air Force, 45, 74, 76–77, 90, 199–200
U.S. Army, 68, 162, 199–200
U.S. Coast Guard, 22, 29, 42, 202; Polar Security Cutter of, 127, 129–30
U.S. Exploring Expedition, 21
U.S. Foreign Military Sales (FMS), 77
U.S.–India–France trilateral framework, 43
U.S. International Development Finance Corporation, 69
U.S.–Japan–South Korea trilateral cooperation, 45

U.S. Marine Corps, 22, 42
U.S. National Strategy for the Arctic Region, 127
U.S. Navy, 55, 202
U.S.-Norway Supplementary Defense Cooperation Agreement, 128
U.S.-Philippine Enhanced Defense Cooperation Agreement, 37–38
Uyghur population, 111
Uzbekistan, 110, 111, 113, 115

Vanuatu, 27
Venezuela, 10
violent extremist organizations, 68; in sub-Saharan Africa, 90
Vladivostok, 40

Wagner Group, 11, 158–59; in Belarus, 165; in sub-Saharan Africa, 88, 89, 95–96
Wake Island, 22
Warsaw Pact, 159, 184
Warsaw Summit, 161
Washington. *See* United States
water, industrial development for, 77
weapon sales, in basing agreements, 107
wedging, for basing agreements, 106
West Africa, 91
"whole-of-government" approach, 72
World Bank, 107
World War II, 21

Xiaoping, Deng, 64n7

Yamal Peninsula, 144
Yellow River Research Station, 125
Yellow Sea, PLAN in, 23–24
Yemen, 86–87
Yi, Wang, 26
YJ-12B anti-ship cruise missiles, 39
YJ-62 anti-ship cruise missiles, 39

ABOUT THE AUTHORS

MICHAEL ALLEN is a professor in the School of Public Service at Boise State University. His coauthored book *Beyond the Wire: U.S. Military Deployments and Host Country Public Opinion* (2022) examines how the United States creates and hurts support for its global security network in other countries. His research generally focuses on the positive and negative externalities of U.S. foreign policy, with a particular focus on overseas military deployments.

ALEXANDER COOLEY is the Claire Tow Professor of Political Science and vice provost for research, libraries, and academic centers at Barnard College, Columbia University. From 2015 to 2021, he served as the thirteenth director of Columbia University's Harriman Institute. He is the author and/or editor of eight academic books, including *Dictators without Borders: Power and Money in Central Asia* (2017), coauthored with John Heathershaw, and *Exit from Hegemony: The Unravelling of the American Global Order* (2020), coauthored with Daniel Nexon.

MICHAEL E. FLYNN is a professor of political science at Kansas State University. He received his PhD in political science from Binghamton University in 2013. His research focuses on the social, political, and economic consequences of overseas military deployments. His recent coauthored book, *Beyond the Wire: U.S. Military Deployments and Host Country Public Opinion* (2022), examines the domestic sources of support for and opposition to U.S. military deployments in host countries around the world.

JEREMY GREENWOOD is a career U.S. Coast Guard officer and a former federal executive fellow in Foreign Policy at the Brookings Institution. Having served in a wide variety of operational and policy jobs both ashore and at sea for more than twenty years, he has published extensively on matters of Arctic governance as well as maritime safety and security issues around the world. He has worked at the State Department's Bureau of Oceans and International Environmental and Scientific Affairs (representing the United States at the Arctic Council), the Arctic Coast Guard Forum, and the International Maritime Organization. As a judge advocate in the U.S. Coast Guard and a cutterman with nearly ten years of sea service across the globe, he brings a unique insight to law-of-the-sea matters and U.S. Arctic policy.

GEOFFREY F. GRESH is a professor of international relations at the College of International Security Affairs, National Defense University, Washington, D.C. His latest book is *To Rule Eurasia's Waves: The New Great Power Competition at Sea* (2020), including a Chinese-language version published in 2022. He is also the author of *Gulf Security and the U.S. Military: Regime Survival and the Politics of Basing* (2015), editor of *Eurasia's Maritime Rise and Global Security: From the Indian Ocean to Pacific Asia and the Arctic* (2018), and coeditor of *U.S. Foreign Policy in the Middle East: From American Missionaries to the Islamic State* (2019). Since 2020, he has been the series editor for Palgrave Studies in Maritime Politics and Security.

EMILY HOLLAND is an assistant professor in the Russia Maritime Studies Institute at the U.S. Naval War College. Previously, she was an assistant professor at the U.S. Naval Academy, a postdoctoral fellow at the Davis Center for Russian and Eurasian Studies at Harvard University, and a visiting fellow at the German Institute for Economic Research (Berlin) and the European Council on Foreign Relations (Berlin). Her research has appeared in the *Journal of International Affairs*, *Newsweek*, and *Lawfare*, among other publications.

About the Authors

BRUCE JONES is a senior fellow in the Strobe Talbott Center for Security, Strategy, and Technology and the Center for Asia Policy Studies at the Brookings Institution, where he works on grand strategy and global issues. He is the author of several books, essays, and reports on the changing dynamics of international order. His most recent book is *To Rule the Waves: How Control of the World's Oceans Shapes the Fate of the Superpowers* (2021), which charts the role of naval power, maritime commerce, and ocean sciences in the role of great power competition.

ISAAC KARDON is senior fellow for China studies at the Carnegie Endowment for International Peace. He studies Chinese foreign policy with a focus on maritime power. His book *China's Law of the Sea: The New Rules of Maritime Order* (2023) analyzes China's influence on the "rules" of the law of the sea. His research on China's foreign ports and basing appears in the *New York Times*, *International Security*, *Security Studies*, *Foreign Affairs*, and the *Naval War College Review*; it was also delivered as congressional testimony.

CARLA MARTÍNEZ MACHAIN is a professor of political science at the University at Buffalo. Her research (funded by the Department of Defense's Minerva Initiative and the Army Research Office, among others) focuses on foreign policy analysis, especially military policy and international conflict. Her new coauthored book is titled *Beyond the Wire: U.S. Military Deployments and Host Country Public Opinion* (2022).

DAWN C. MURPHY is an associate professor of national security strategy at the U.S. National War College. Her research analyzes China's interests and behavior as a rising power toward the existing international order in the Middle East and Africa. She is the author of the book *China's Rise in the Global South: The Middle East, Africa, and Beijing's Alternative World Order* (2022).

MICHAEL E. O'HANLON is a senior fellow and director of research in Foreign Policy at the Brookings Institution, where he specializes in U.S. defense strategy, the use of military force, and American national security policy. He directs the Strobe Talbott Center for Security, Strategy, and Technology and is the inaugural holder of the Philip H. Knight Chair in Defense and Strategy. He codirects the Africa Security Initiative as well. He is the author of more than twenty books on defense, geopolitics, and foreign policy, including his latest books: *The Art of War in an Age of Peace* (2021) and *Military History for the Modern Strategist* (2023).

MELANIE W. SISSON is a fellow in the Foreign Policy program's Strobe Talbott Center for Security, Strategy, and Technology at the Brookings Institution, where she researches the use of the armed forces in international politics, U.S. national security strategy, and military applications of emerging technologies. Her current work focuses on U.S. Department of Defense integration of artificial intelligence and machine learning capabilities into war-fighting and enterprise operations.

JASON B. WOLFF is a colonel in the U.S. Air Force and a former federal executive fellow in Foreign Policy at the Brookings Institution and serves as an air force logistics readiness officer. His expertise is with joint and allied humanitarian operations and coalition deterrence operations specializing in the use of military force. He has deployed in support of Operations Enduring Freedom, Iraqi Freedom, Freedom's Sentinel, Inherent Resolve, and Resolute Support. His staff assignments include tours at the Air Force Logistics Management Agency, The Joint Staff, and U.S. Forces Japan.

ANDREW YEO is a senior fellow and the SK-Korea Foundation Chair in Korea Studies at the Brookings Institution's Center for Asia Policy Studies. He is also a professor of politics at The Catholic University of America in Washington, D.C., and the author or editor of five books, including *Asia's Regional Architecture: Alliances and Institutions in the Pacific Century* (2019) and *Activists, Alliances, and Anti-U.S. Base Protests* (2011). His research interests include Asian regional architecture, U.S. grand strategy and force posture, narratives and discourse in U.S. foreign policy, South Korean foreign policy, and North Korea.

www.ingramcontent.com/pod-product-compliance
Lightning Source LLC
Chambersburg PA
CBHW032213230426
43672CB00011B/2544